The History of the Stasi

THE HISTORY OF THE STASI
East Germany's Secret Police, 1945–1990

Jens Gieseke

Translated by
David Burnett

berghahn
NEW YORK • OXFORD
www.berghahnbooks.com

Published in 2014 by
Berghahn Books
www.berghahnbooks.com

Published by Berghahn Books with the German Federal Commissioner for the
Stasi Records, in cooperation with the Centre for Contemporary History, Potsdam

Original title:
Die Stasi, 1945–1990
By Jens Gieseke
© 2001 by Deutsche Verlags-Anstalt,
a division of Verlagsgruppe Random House GmbH, Munich, Germany

© 2014, 2015 Verlagsgruppe Random House GmbH
First paperback edition published in 2015

Library of Congress Cataloging-in-Publication Data

Gieseke, Jens.
[Mielke-Konzern. English]
  The history of the Stasi : East Germany's secret police, 1945–1990 / Jens Gieseke ;
translated by David Burnett.
     pages cm
Originally published under title: Mielke-Konzern. Stuttgart : Deutsche Verlags-
Anstalt, 2001.
  Includes bibliographical references and index.
  ISBN 978-1-78238-254-6 (hbk) — ISBN 978-1-78533-024-7 (pbk) —
  ISBN 978-1-78238-255-3 (ebook)
  1. Germany (East). Ministerium für Staatssicherheit—History. 2. Internal
security—Germany (East)—History. 3. Secret service—Germany (East)—
History. I. Title.
  HV8210.5.A2G53513 2014
  363.28'30943109045—dc23
                                                                        2013017988

British Library Cataloguing in Publication Data

A catalogue record for this book is available from the British Library

ISBN: 978-1-78238-254-6 hardback
ISBN: 978-1-78533-024-7 paperback
ISBN: 978-1-78238-255-3 ebook

I repeat once again: we must know everything! Nothing can get past us. And some directors are not yet doing this. They don't even notice it, comrades, some of those among us. They don't even really understand it yet. That, precisely, is the dialectic of class warfare and of the work of the Chekists.

—Erich Mielke, Berlin-Lichtenberg, 1981

I would do one thing: I would not give the others the opportunity to leave all the responsibility to us. State Security, State Security! You wouldn't believe the kind of trifles we had to deal with! If something wasn't working on the supply side, if it was raining through the roof of a hospital, for instance, year after year, that's when they called on us. And we tried to help out. Even though we weren't responsible. We couldn't just stand there and watch if the others took care of nothing. We were the maids of all work, just as now we're the whipping boys.

—Erich Mielke, Berlin-Moabit, 1992

CONTENTS

Abbreviations

ABV	Abschnittsbevollmächtigter (beat patrol officer of the People's Police)
AfNS	Amt für nationale Sicherheit (Office for National Security)
AGM	Arbeitsgruppe des Ministers (Minister's Working Group)
AGM/S	Arbeitsgruppe des Ministers/Stöcker [oder Sonderfragen] (Minister's Working Group/Stöcker [or Sonderfragen, i.e., Special Issues])
ANC	African National Congress
APN	Außenpolitischer Nachrichtendienst (Foreign Political Intelligence Service)
BKK	Bereich Kommerzielle Koordinierung (Area of Commercial Coordination, KoKo)
BND	Bundesnachrichtendienst (Federal Intelligence Service)
CDU	Christlich-Demokratische Union (Christian Democratic Union)
CPSU	Communist Party of the Soviet Union
CSCE	Conference on Security and Cooperation in Europe
CSU	Christlich-Soziale Union (Christian Social Union)
DA	Demokratischer Aufbruch (Democratic Awakening)
DGB	Deutscher Gewerkschaftsbund (Confederation of German Trade Unions)
DGSE	Direction Générale de Sécurité Extérieure (General Directorate for External Security)
DKP	Deutsche Kommunistische Partei (German Communist Party)
DSU	Deutsche Soziale Union (German Social Union)

DVdI	Deutsche Verwaltung des Innern (German Administration of the Interior)
FDGB	Freier Deutscher Gewerkschaftsbund (Free German Trade Union Federation)
FDJ	Freie Deutsche Jugend (Free German Youth)
FDP	Freie Demokratische Partei (Free Democratic Party)
FIM	Führungs-IM (controller IM)
GDR	German Democratic Republic
GI	Geheimer Informator (secret informer)
GM	Geheimer Mitarbeiter (secret collaborator)
GMS	Gesellschaftlicher Mitarbeiter für Sicherheit (social collaborator for security)
GPU	Gosudarstvennoye Politicheskoye Upravlenie (State Political Directorate, the Soviet secret police)
HA	Hauptabteilung (main department)
HIM	Hauptamtlicher Inoffizieller Mitarbeiter (full-time unofficial collaborator)
HVA	Hauptverwaltung Aufklärung (Main Administration for Reconnaissance)
IM	Inoffizieller Mitarbeiter (unofficial collaborator)
IMB	Inoffizieller Mitarbeiter mit Feindberührung (unofficial collaborator with enemy contact)
IME	Experten-IM (expert IM)
IMK	Inoffizieller Mitarbeiter für Konspiration (unofficial collaborator for conspiracy)
IMS	Inoffizieller Mitarbeiter zur Sicherung des Verantwortungsbereiches (unofficial collaborator for securing an area of responsibility)
JHS	Juristische Hochschule (College of Law, MfS university)
K-5	Branch 5 of the criminal police, the political police
KgU	Kampfgruppe gegen Unmenschlichkeit (Combat Group Against Inhumanity)
KPD	Kommunistische Partei Deutschlands (Communist Party of Germany)
KuSch	Kader und Schulung (Cadre and Training)
LAR	Legal abgedeckte Residentur (legally covered residency)

LDPD	Liberal-demokratische Partei Deutschlands (Liberal Democratic Party of Germany)
MAD	Militärischer Abschirmdienst (Military Counterintelligence Service)
MdI	Ministerium des Innern (Ministry of the Interior)
MfS	Ministerium für Staatssicherheit (Ministry for State Security)
MK	Umkhonto we Sizwe
NKVD	Narodnyi Komissariat Vnutrennikh Del (People's Commissariat of Internal Affairs)
NSDAP	Nationalsozialistische Deutsche Arbeiterpartei (National Socialist German Workers' Party = Nazi Party)
NVA	Nationale Volksarmee (National People's Army)
OibE	Offizier im besonderen Einsatz (officer on special assignment)
OPK	Operative Personenkontrolle (operational person control)
OV	Operativer Vorgang (operational case)
PID	Politisch-ideologische Diversion (political-ideological diversion)
POZW	Partner des operativen Zusammenwirkens (partners of operational cooperation)
PUT	Politische Untergrundtätigkeit (political underground activities)
RAF	Rote Armee Fraktion (Red Army Faction)
RIAS	Rundfunk im amerikanischen Sektor (Radio in the American Sector)
RSFSR	Russian Socialist Federative Soviet Republic
SA	Sturmabteilung(en) (Nazi storm troopers, a.k.a. "Brownshirts")
SBZ	Sowjetische Besatzungszone (Soviet Occupation Zone)
SD	Sicherheitsdienst (Nazi Security Service)
SDP	Sozialdemokratische Partei der DDR (Social Democratic Party of the GDR)
SED	Sozialistische Einheitspartei Deutschlands (Socialist Unity Party of Germany)
SGDN	Secrétariat Générale de la Défense Nationale (Secretariat General of National Defense)

SIRA   System der Informationsrecherche der Aufklärung
(System of Reconnassiance Information Research)

SMAD   Sowjetische Militäradministration in Deutschland (Soviet
Military Administration in Germany)

SMA   Sowjetische Militäradministration (Soviet Military
Administration)

SPD   Sozialdemokratische Partei Deutschlands (Social
Democratic Party of Germany)

StGB   Strafgesetzbuch (Criminal Code)

SWAPO   Southwest African People's Organization

SWT   Sektor Wissenschaft und Technik (Science and Technology
Sector)

Cheka   Chrezvychaynaya Komissiya (Extraordinary Commission)

UFJ   Untersuchungsausschuß Freiheitlicher Juristen
(Investigating Committee of Free Jurists)

VEB   Volkseigener Betrieb (People's Own Enterprise, a state-
owned company in the GDR)

VVN   Vereinigung der Verfolgten des Naziregimes (Association
of Persecutees of the Nazi Regime)

ZAIG   Zentrale Auswertungs- und Informationsgruppe (Central
Evaluation and Information Group)

ZAPU   Zimbabwe African People's Union

ZI   Zelleninformator (cell informer)

ZK   Zentralkomitee (Central Committee)

ZKG   Zentrale Koordinierungsgruppe Flucht und Übersiedlung
(Central Coordination Group for Flight and Emigration)

ZKK   Zentrale Kontrollmission/Zentrale Kommission für
staatliche Kontrolle (Central Control Commission/
Central Commission for State Control)

Introduction

Ten Years and Forty-five Days

Shortly before midnight on 13 March 1990, Federal Chancellor Helmut Kohl of the conservative Christian Democratic Union (CDU) disembarked from the Federal Border Guard helicopter in the garden of his official residence to relax and have a drink in the chancellor's bungalow. He was joined by his wife, by Bernd Neumann, the chairman of the CDU in Bremen, who was working at the time as an election-campaign advisor in the German Democratic Republic (GDR), and by Michael Roik, Kohl's office manager at CDU party headquarters. The chancellor had just returned from an election campaign appearance in the GDR. It was only five days until the first free elections to the East German parliament, the Volkskammer, and not even the pollsters could give a reliable prediction as to how they would turn out. The first polls showed the center-left Social Democratic Party (SPD) clearly in the lead, but the Alliance for Germany coalition, supported by the Western CDU, seemed to be gaining ground.

Suddenly the chancellor received word from East Berlin that, according to the East German attorney general's office, one of CDU's main hopefuls, Wolfgang Schnur, was actually a longtime IM, or unofficial collaborator, of the East German Ministry for State Security (MfS). Schnur was chairman and the leading candidate of the Democratic Awakening (Demokratischer Aufbruch) party, which together with the East German CDU and the German Social Union (DSU) formed the Alliance for Germany coalition, forged by Kohl and CDU headquarters in Bonn. Kohl alerted the CDU's general secretary:

I immediately called Volker Rühe, who was already in bed, and asked him to come over right away. Then we called Eberhard Diepgen in Berlin and woke him up too, to tell him that Neumann would be landing on the first plane at Tegel [airport]. Both men together were to contact Schnur immediately in order to question him and clear things up.[1]

The two emissaries acted fast. Schnur had checked into St. Hedwig's Hospital in Berlin just a few days earlier, allegedly on account of physical exhaustion caused by the strain of campaigning. Before the news could reach the press, Schnur attested to his MfS involvement and announced from his sickbed to Neumann and Diepgen that he was resigning from all his offices. The two CDU politicians rushed to Cottbus, where Kohl had just made the second to last of his six big campaign appearances. The news went straight to the press.

The political career of Schnur was over—a man who had shown a commitment to change like no other in the preceding months, attempting to bring the motley opposition force of Democratic Awakening in line with the chancellor's policy. Like many organizations of the citizens' movement, Democratic Awakening had been founded in October 1989 by a rather chance mixture of seasoned dissidents. Its leading figures were theologians like Rainer Eppelmann, Ehrhart Neubert, Edelbert Richter, and Friedrich Schorlemmer, as well as neurologist Sonja Schröter. As a synod member of the Protestant Church and the lawyer of countless conscientious objectors and dissidents, Schnur, too, came from this scene. The pro-CDU policy of Chairman Schnur had led to fierce conflicts within the party in December 1989 and January 1990, causing the left wing of the movement to leave the party and join other organizations such as Alliance 90 (Bündnis 90) or the SPD. Others such as the physicist Angela Merkel, the future federal chancellor, joined the party during these weeks.

Schnur and his "turncoats of the Revolution"[2] found an open door at CDU headquarters in Bonn, helping its campaign planners out of a fix. The SPD had somewhat unexpectedly acquired a partner in the East, in October 1989, with the founding of the Social Democratic Party of the GDR (SDP), and began to reminisce about the ancestral heartland of the workers' movement in Thuringia and Saxony. Its top candidate was the colorful Ibrahim Manfred Böhme, who was also later revealed to have been a longtime informer for the Stasi. Unlike the newly founded SDP, the East German CDU had for decades been a compliant bloc party whose chairman, Gerald Götting, was in every way equal to SED leaders in terms of his smugness and ignorance. Only in November 1989 did the bloc party seek to become independent of the "vanguard party" of the GDR. The CSU, the CDU's Bavarian sister party, had already found a partner in the DSU, a new conservative party founded in December 1989 by hitherto low-profile figures.

The Christian Democrats in Bonn made a virtue out of necessity. In early February they had summoned the chairmen of the Eastern CDU, Democratic Awakening, and the DSU to West Berlin, where they forged the electoral coalition Alliance for Germany, taking advantage of the West German chancellor's great popularity in East Germany. Whereas the Eastern CDU, unloved in Bonn, contributed a considerable amount of staff and organizational resources, Schnur and his party colleagues stood for the alliance's civil-rights legacy. The DSU distinguished itself by its strident anti-socialist tone. Though the alliance was primarily conceived as an election-campaign platform for the federal chancellor, who obviously enjoyed enormous popularity in the GDR, Schnur had his sights set on the office of East German minister-president, should the alliance emerge victorious in the elections.

The exposure of Schnur in the homestretch of the campaign came at the worst possible time for the Kohl alliance, and yet it was not quite as surprising as the chancellor made it out to be later in his memoirs. As early as 29 January, the Hessian State Office for the Protection of the Constitution had informed the state's minister of the interior, Gottfried Milde (CDU), about a list of twenty-three prominent Stasi informers, among them Wolfgang Schnur and general secretary of the CDU, Martin Kirchner. The names were supplied by a high-ranking MfS officer who had defected to the West. The Federal Office for the Protection of the Constitution in Cologne, West Germany's domestic intelligence agency, was also involved in questioning the Stasi officer. Both Offices for the Protection of the Constitution confirmed the names on the list after Hessian CDU general secretary Franz-Josef Jung lodged an inquiry. Whether people in the government offices and party headquarters believed the news is unclear. They had reason enough to suspect targeted disinformation campaigns designed to damage the reputations of the new political hopefuls, not to mention the fact that there was little interest in burdening the already uncertain election outcome even more by publicly discussing such things.

Civil-rights activists at the Central Round Table—the discussion forum of reform-willing government forces and opposition groups in the GDR—had received anonymous letters to the same effect in early January. The letters named the correct MfS unit and one of Schnur's code names. They, too, were not out to make the case public, given the lack of substantial evidence. Schnur pressed charges against persons unknown, claiming he had been defamed. The allegations gained substance, however, when in Schnur's hometown of Rostock the investigative groups of the local citizens' committee, the state prosecutor, and the archivists appointed to the case came across extensive written documents under the code names "Dr. Ralf Schirmer" and "Torsten." A total of thirty-one well-filled filing folders revealed without a doubt that attorney Schnur had been an unofficial collaborator of State Security under these code names since 1964 and had received numerous honoraria and awards for his work. A handwriting analysis ordered by the attorney general's office in East Berlin left no doubt about the matter.

From 5 to 8 March 1990, the Rostock citizens' committee confronted Schnur with its findings and informed the party executive of Democratic Awakening, as well as the federal chancellor. Schnur denied having been a Stasi collaborator and severely reproached the alleged smear campaign of the citizens' committee. Numerous Alliance politicians such as its general secretary, Volker Rühe (West German CDU), and Oswald Wutzke (Democratic Awakening) joined the chorus of condemnation. Meanwhile Schnur retreated to his sickbed.

On Monday, 12 March, a former Stasi case officer of Schnur's reported in *Spiegel* magazine about his agent's work as an IM. Visited at his hospital bed by longtime friend and companion Rainer Eppelmann, Schnur continued to deny having any connection with the Ministry for State Security. Two days later, the web of lies unraveled. Kohl recalled:

> That same day the second-to-last mass rally had already begun in Cottbus, where I was scheduled to speak. The speaker before me was Pastor Oswald Wutzke. I remember him passionately defending Schnur as the victim of malicious slander when, from afar, I saw Diepgen and Neumann—who had just arrived from Berlin—approaching through the crowd. . . . Others in the Bonn CDU had also broken a lance for the DA [Democratic Awakening] chairman, which made it rather difficult to openly admit Schnur's involvement with the Stasi. Of course, we had to do it fast, to cut our losses with a view to the impending elections on Sunday.[3]

On 15 March the central committee of Democratic Awakening expelled Schnur from the party and elected Rainer Eppelmann as its chairman. Politicians from all parties expressed their consternation. The SPD's leading candidate, Ibrahim Böhme, mindfully pointed out that Schnur had "helped many people in the last fifteen years, advising and defending them."[4]

If Democratic Awakening had stood any chance of winning the election before these revelations, they had certainly lost it afterwards. On the evening of 18 March 1990, they garnered a mere 0.9 percent of the vote. The CDU, by contrast, was the happy winner at the polls, with 40.9 percent. The SPD took a distant second place, with 21.8 percent. Kohl's plans had worked, even without Schnur.

What came as an awkward incident in the final days of the election frenzy in fact turned out to be the harbinger of a new era. For the very first time, newly accessible files put under public control had led to the exposure of prominent unofficial collaborators.

Using anonymous letters and information provided by the defector in January, former full-time employees of the Stasi were harnessing their inside knowledge to deflect public attention away from themselves and their apparatus, in an attempt to shift the spotlight to the unofficial collaborators. Others were trying to take revenge on erstwhile informers, who had severed ties with the Stasi and were now making headway in politics.[5] Indeed, it was precisely Schnur's new political commitment that presumably provoked MfS officers to expose him in the first place. This tactic was not only lucrative, allowing some of them to cash in on rewards for providing information to the media and Western secret services, but also acted as a smokescreen.[6]

The Rostock revelations provided a second turn of events. It was the first time that news of entanglement in the web of East Germany's State Security had come not from the secret world of intelligence services and defectors, but from the hands of a citizens' committee—that is to say, an institution which, by its own lights, stood for publicity and transparency. With that, the first step had been taken on the special East German path for coming to terms with the legacy of the Communist secret police. The step was as painful as it was instructive. On top of the personal disappointment suffered by Schnur's companions and clients, it is clear in hindsight that irreparable damage was done to the opposition movement.

True, there had always been some suspicions against the ambitious attorney. Bärbel Bohley made no secret of her mistrustfulness, and in the fall of 1989 had refused to work with Democratic Awakening. *Spiegel* correspondent Ulrich Schwarz once confronted Rainer Eppelmann with similar concerns in a private conversation, but Eppelmann defended Schnur. Schnur had actively defended his legal clients and sometimes fervently prayed with them. He had even cried with one of his clients in 1988, when singer-songwriter Stephan Krawczyk broke into tears in pretrial detention upon being informed by Schnur that his wife, Freya Klier, had also been arrested in connection with the Liebknecht-Luxemburg demonstration. Yet none of this prevented Schnur from meeting with his case officer almost every night while all of this was going on, revealing secret messages and betraying the contents of confidential talks with his clients. He had taken part in countless clandestine meetings of dissidents in the 1980s. Only later did his former companions discover that in this and a number of other cases they were dealing with a person who was leading a strange kind of double life. As Eppelmann later wrote:

> Wolfgang Schnur, like many of his fellow IMs, was a conflicted individual. He identified almost completely with his job, to the point of self-abandonment. This destroyed his family. And he was a man with an enormous craving for recognition, validation, and public prestige, who strove to have power over others. He enjoyed consorting with state functionaries and liked when they took his work seriously. Reporting gave him the feeling of exercising power over people.[7]

The thought was certainly not reassuring that this man had come close to becoming head of state of the GDR or at least one of its ministers. It soon became apparent that orderly, public access to the files would be a better way to handle the situation rather than leaving things at the mercy of those who harbored secrets from the past and were now trying to use them for their own purposes. It was no coincidence that the demand soon surfaced for all representatives in the newly elected Volkskammer to be vetted for possible collaboration with the Ministry for State Security. The Volkskammer itself, just a few weeks later, created a legislative framework for opening the files.

The exposure of Schnur was followed by that of many others—some cases just as clear-cut and well documented, others still waiting to be resolved on account of the destruction of files or contradictory evidence. Some IMs approached their friends and colleagues before or after being exposed. Many others did not. Some claimed they had nothing at all to do with the Stasi, whereas others saw themselves as victims. Some saw nothing objectionable about their breach of confidence; others considered themselves middlemen in a dialogue between state and society.

To be sure, it was never only about unmasking MfS employees and their informers. Those who were persecuted or kept under surveillance later had the opportunity to read their files and learn about the measures taken against them. They could see which supposed friend had betrayed them and which individuals secretly suspected of working with "the Firm" had actually refused to collaborate.

The decision of civil-rights activists, the Volkskammer, and later the Bundestag to open the files of the Ministry for State Security was ultimately intended to clear the way for a critical, scholarly assessment of the role and activities of this institution and to inform the public about this. It enabled the workings of the Ministry for State Security to be reconstructed on the basis of its own, largely unfiltered archives. Of course in the winter of 1989–90 the Stasi succeeded in destroying or making off with much of the material (according to more recent estimates, about one-quarter of its files, especially regarding the most recent cases and foreign espionage). But with 111 miles of files from end to end, researchers have an exceptional find at their disposal—even leaving aside the canteen bills and empty forms that make up part of it.

The Stasi as History

This volume was only possible thanks to the decision, unique throughout the world in kind and degree, to open up these secret files. It is based on the research of many dozens of political scientists and historians, interested laypeople and the formerly persecuted who have taken it upon themselves in the intervening decades to work through mountains of paperwork in order to shed some light on this tangle of intrigues. Using this work, I assess some central issues that have emerged in recent scholarly debates about the history of the Ministry for State Security of the German Democratic Republic.

Perhaps the most important result of opening the files is the proof that State Security acted beyond the rule of law and in flagrant disregard of human dignity and civil rights. This proof has been furnished using original evidence from the inner workings of the secret apparatus and is widely acknowledged—even if a handful of old generals and colonels has banded together now and then to vociferously claim the contrary. This is the starting point of this volume. The aim is to better understand the role and function of the MfS as part of the state and society of the GDR and of postwar German history, while pointing to perspectives of further debate and discussion. The general thesis of the following account is summed up by this book's original German title: the "Mielke Concern," which builds on colloquial terms for the Stasi such as "VEB Horch und Guck" (People's Own Enterprise "Listen and Look") or "die Firma" (the Firm). State Security is taken here as a central pillar of the power structure of communism viewed as a historical formation. The self-understanding and methods of this institution originated in Soviet Stalinism, but it was only during the post-Stalinist phase, starting in 1957, that the MfS developed into a "mixed concern" (*Gemischtwarenkonzern*) for security issues, into a "general enterprise for power maintenance and repression" that extended well beyond its classic secret-police and intelligence-gathering functions of the initial years.[8] The breadth and variety of tasks the MfS assumed over the years and the depth of its penetration into all spheres of society resulted in its exceptionally strong position in the East German party-state.

The widely branching apparatus with its varied concrete tasks was held together inwardly by the elitist self-understanding of its employees, who viewed themselves as "Chekists"—that is to say, as successors to the revolutionary "Extraordinary Commission for Combating Counterrevolution and Sabotage" (abbreviated in Russian as Cheka), founded in 1917 by the Russian Bolsheviks. As part of this tradition, the ideological mission of the MfS was to secure the "dictatorship of the proletariat" and protect it from all forms of enemy attack via a covertly operating executive organ invested with state instruments of force. Chekism ensured its legitimacy as a militant class warrior on a global and national (in the German case, dual-state) scale. This will to fight with the aid of a "special machine of suppression"[9] had gone from being a potentially reversible means to an end in the Soviet Union of the 1930s, something that would gradually "wither away" alongside the state in the utopian perspective, to a self-perpetuating institution, a given of the Communist system.

The potential for repression strongly influenced social relations in state-socialist society. In the early years, manifest physical violence was an offensive instrument for shaping society in the period of Communist transformation. Once the system was consolidated, repression mainly served to secure positions of power. This was also true—at least for the threat of repression—in later years, years we now know had caused Party leaders and the strategists of State Security monumental headaches, embarking as they had on a sociopolitical path fraught with deep and varied contradictions between a form of rule propped up by force and the ever more urgent need to modernize and adapt.

There has yet to be a systematic analysis of the role of the MfS in state and society beyond the studies of its general significance as the "shield and sword of the Party" within the apparatus of domination. In particular, the sociopsychological effects of its activity in the immediate social context of family and friends, neighbors, and coworkers have not yet been sufficiently investigated. The public debate in

Germany alone and even more so the strong emotions that the catch-word "Stasi" triggers in almost every East German are an indication of the extent to which State Security was always close at hand, in both subjective and objective terms.

This book will likewise address the wholesale claims that the MfS controlled virtually everything, calling the shots and manipulating at will, both during the GDR's existence and after its demise, within its borders and outside as well, or—conversely—that it was an insignificant part of the system of rule, of little import for the "real lives" of common people, and ultimately not worth investigating. Rather, I would like to show and to argue that State Security was indeed of great importance for the history of the GDR and the people who lived it—as a direct and indirect factor, as a social, political and economic agent, as a calculated risk, or as an instrument exploitable for personal gain, with intended or unintended consequences.

My account begins with the formative period of East German State Security through 1956, when it was still under a strong Soviet hand. It was during this phase of Stalinism "draped in the colors of the GDR" that the MfS apparatus took shape inside and outside, permanently forming its perception of the world and the enemy. Chapters two through six are thematically oriented, covering the period from the aborted de-Stalinization of 1956 into the 1980s. These five chapters will illustrate the effects of Stasi "corporate expansion" in its main spheres of activity, as well as the political and social consequences thereof. Special emphasis will be placed on the structural development of the apparatus and its full-time employees. The unofficial informers will be viewed against the backdrop of recent historical research into the phenomenon of denunciation, while addressing the consequences of the Stasi's mission to provide pervasive security and exploring the real extent and effects of surveillance of the whole of East German society. The classic secret-police struggle against the internal opposition in the GDR will be investigated alongside the Stasi's varied Western and foreign-intelligence work.

The book is rounded off by some thoughts on the circumstances and conditions surrounding the surprisingly quiet collapse of SED rule and the MfS apparatus in the fall of 1989, while addressing some of the burdens that continue to plague reunified Germany. A comprehensive overview of the history of the Ministry for State Security of the GDR is not yet possible due to the disparate state of current scholarship in many areas and the lack of historical perspective in general, which is to say, the still very recent nature of the events in question. My account attempts, here and there, to bridge the gap—characteristic of much historical research—between the history of SED power structures and of GDR society on the whole. The actual depth of the MfS's penetration in East German society plays an important role here, as do its echoes at the grassroots of society which reverberated back to the apparatus and affected its course of action.

This volume is indebted to countless discussions with colleagues and friends, who for reasons of space cannot be mentioned here by name. I profited enormously from discussions held at in-house research colloquia of the Federal Commissioner for the Stasi Archives, as well as at the colloquium on East German and Eastern European history led by Christoph Klessmann, Axel Schildt, and Bernhard Schalhorn. I owe a deep debt of gratitude to Clemens Vollnhals, who encouraged me to write this book; to Helmut Müller-Enbergs, who shared his endless knowledge of unofficial collaborators and MfS operations in the West with me; to Roger Engelmann and Walter Süss, who read the manuscript and offered constructive criticism; and to Stefan Meyer from my German publisher, DVA, who gently and patiently prodded me on.

The English edition was made possible by Helge Heidemeyer, who paved the way for generous translation funding from the Federal Commissioner for the Stasi Records, by the manifold support of my assistant Ute Gross, and of course by my longstanding translator – and in a sense co-author – David Burnett.

Finally, it was Ulrike, Rasma, and Tjark Knigge who bore the brunt on holidays, weekends, and countless evenings.

Chapter 1

ANTIFASCISM—STALINISM—
COLD CIVIL WAR

Origins and Influences, 1945 to 1956

East Berlin, 8 February 1950

On the wintery Wednesday evening of 8 February 1950, the representatives of the Provisional Volkskammer of the GDR convened in East Berlin. It was their tenth session since the founding of the republic the previous October. After more than seven hours, just a few minutes past 9:00 p.m., the minister of the interior, Dr. Carl Steinhoff, took the floor and gave a short speech, introducing a bill to expand the East German government, the Council of Ministers, by adding a fifteenth department. There had been repeated bombings of late, claimed Steinhoff, in national industries and on state farms, in transportation and on newly established private farms (*Neubauerngehöfte*). Spies, subversives, and saboteurs were becoming ever more active: "The detailed reports, whose basic contents you will have gathered from the press, offer proof of the activities of criminal elements in the employ and under the direct guidance of the Anglo-American imperialists and their henchmen."[1] The Main Administration for the Protection of the National Economy (Hauptverwaltung zum Schutz der Volkswirtschaft) in the Ministry of the Interior was to be transformed into the "Ministry for State Security" in order to put a stop to these criminal activities.

After the minister of the interior it was the representatives' turn to speak. They refrained from comments, committee discussions, abstentions, and dissenting votes, thereby allowing one of the most momentous decisions in the history of the GDR to be passed in a matter of minutes, and to "great applause," as the SED's official organ, the Party daily *Neues Deutschland,* reported.[2]

Indeed, in the preceding week these representatives could have read in the newspapers about the sabotage, subversion, and spying that "American imperialism, the chief enemy of our republic and our people,"[3] was using to assail the young republic. On 26 January, the Council of Ministers had received detailed reports from state authorities which it passed on to the press. The director of the Central Commission for State Control, Fritz Lange, bemoaned the immense production losses caused by sabotage and fraud emanating from the gentlemen in the West whose businesses had been expropriated and who wanted to force the new "people's own" enterprises into submission. The director of the East German criminal police, Chief Inspector August Mayer, described fires, especially in the countryside, seemingly due to negligence, but which he claimed were really caused by wealthy peasants who were out to harm the mayors, functionaries, and above all the beneficiaries of land reform, the "new farmers" (*Neubauer*). The most strident in tone was the general inspector of the Main Administration for the Protection of the National Economy, Erich Mielke. He denounced the struggle of "gangsters and murderers"[4] against the GDR. Terror and espionage organizations, steered by the West and often run by old Nazi cadre, were blowing up production sites under the orders of British and American intelligence services, he claimed, agitating for war with incendiary pamphlets, planning for the assassination of East German functionaries, and inciting innocent youths. Mielke had one solution to offer:

Do the facts not force us to take action and put an end to the doings of these hostile elements? The Constitution of the German Democratic Republic says in Article 6: "Incitement to the boycott of democratic institutions and organizations, incitement to the murder of democratic politicians, the propagation of religious, racial, and national hatred, military propaganda and the incitement to war, and all other acts directed against equality of rights are offenses according to the Criminal Code." To preserve the full effectiveness of our Constitution it is necessary to put this article into practice through the creation of suitable organs for waging a battle against agents, saboteurs, and diversionists, as well as through relevant criminal laws which give the judiciary the possibility to justly punish the perpetrators apprehended and found guilty by these organs.[5]

It was some time before more detailed laws would come into force, but the "incitement to boycott" article cited by Mielke was the blanket clause that would serve in the ensuing years to put real or supposed enemies of the GDR behind bars or even on the scaffold. A day after Mielke's allusion to an impending intensification of the struggle against "enemies of the state," the SED's official newspaper finally announced what the Volkskammer would pass just a few days later: the government of the GDR had resolved to establish a Ministry for State Security to put a stop to the insidious activities of enemies of the republic.[6]

The Provisional Volkskammer passed the law quickly and eagerly. This body, having originated in the German People's Council (Deutscher Volksrat), which in turn had merely been constituted on the basis of a previously determined, unified list of candidates, was by no means a parliament chosen by free elections, but purely a body of yes-men for the Soviet Union's *Deutschlandpolitik*, its policy toward Germany. Nevertheless, the circumstances surrounding the establishment of the MfS were anything but self-evident, even under the prevailing conditions.

The speaker of the Provisional Volkskammer, Johannes Dieckmann (LDPD), expressed doubts about its legality, as the bill, unlike the law on the establishment of the Provisional Government on 7 October 1949, did not mention the new cabinet members by name. Mentioning the names, he argued, was necessary according to the Constitution of the GDR, Article 94, which stipulated that the cabinet and "each of its members require the confidence of the Volkskammer for the conduct of office."[7] Yet the legal advisors in the Council of Ministers apparently preferred not to mention any names, deciding that, if need be, a vote of no confidence of the Volkskammer would be sufficient once the government had appointed the minister and state secretary—otherwise there was reason to believe that the confidence required by the Constitution was given.

The actual appointments were made about one week later. On 16 February 1950, Walter Ulbricht, in his capacity as deputy minister-president of the GDR, appointed two veteran Communists, Wilhelm Zaisser and Erich Mielke, to the positions of minister and state secretary, respectively. With that a further, albeit primarily symbolic, focus had been set. The carefully calculated balance of parties in the Democratic Bloc hitherto adhered to in forming the government had suddenly shifted, the majority of cabinet members now coming from the SED. On 24 February, East German President Wilhelm Pieck swore in Zaisser and Mielke. Only on this occasion did the public learn who was to head the new ministry.

The appointments to the new ministry degraded Minister of the Interior Carl Steinhoff to the role of bystander. The real power was now vested in a reliable Communist underground cadre, individuals who had long since determined domestic and police policy in the Soviet Occupation Zone and the GDR anyway: Zaisser as the former minister of the interior of Saxony-Anhalt, then as director of the Main Administration for Training (Hauptverwaltung Ausbildung) in the Ministry of the Interior (MdI), responsible for the building up of protomilitary units; and Mielke as the vice president of the German Administration of the Interior and director of the Main Administration for Protection of the National Economy. Both men had most recently served as deputies to the minister of the interior. Steinhoff, by contrast, as an erstwhile Social Democrat, doctor of jurisprudence, experienced Prussian ministry official, and former minister-president of Brandenburg, was mainly just a figurehead in the new government, despite his loyalty to the SED. He was soon relegated to the sidelines entirely, losing his seat as a candidate member of the Politbüro just a few months later and thus visibly demoted relative to Zaisser, who in being appointed head of the MfS became part of the Party's highest administrative body and hence occupied a higher position in the SED hierarchy. In 1952, with the Ministry of the Interior being expanded into the umbrella institution for the remilitarization of the GDR, Steinhoff was forced to abandon his ministerial office altogether, being shunted off to a chair of administrative law at Humboldt University in Berlin.

Thus the founding of the Ministry for State Security of the GDR was a highly symbolic act, despite the attempts to play it off as a kind of self-defense against the supposedly relentless attacks and harassment of British and American "imperialism" and its West German minions. It signaled that, for all its borrowings from the practices of German parliamentarism, the aim here was clearly different: the transformation of the GDR into a "people's democracy" of the Stalinist type and alignment of its political system to the power structures of the Soviet Union.

Though none of the members of the Provisional Volkskammer spoke out against this momentous step, some voted on the new course of the government with their feet—such as former Saxon finance minister and CDU delegate Gerhard Rohner, whose mandate expired on this "great day in the Volkskammer,"[8] having opted, like so many bourgeois and social-democratic politicians, to leave the GDR. Others resigned themselves to the situation, such as Deputy Minister-President Otto Nuschke, likewise a member of the Eastern CDU. Two years later, on 19 September 1952, when asked by a journalist in Bonn whether the State Security Service was subordinate to the government of the GDR, he answered, as aptly as unconstitutionally: "No, it is an authority in its own right. This is commensurate to its great importance and to the difficult circumstances we have to reckon with."[9]

The founding of the MfS was not the only sign of a tightening of the reins in domestic politics. In early January, the director of the Party Training Department (Abteilung Parteischulung) in the Executive Committee of the SED, Professor Kurt Hager, declared in *Neues Deutschland* that "heightened vigilance" was the foremost task of party training. He compared supposed plans of the Japanese to use germ warfare against China with the alleged machinations of former Hungarian foreign minister László Rajk and the second-highest Bulgarian Communist Party functionary, Kostov. Accused of espionage and forming fascist sabotage troops, both men were sentenced to death in show trials then executed—Rajk in October, Traycho Kostov in December 1949. Hager threatened: "Can one assume that the Anglo-American warmongers will be less aggressive and perfidious towards the German Democratic Republic? To assume this would be an unpardonable, even downright criminal folly."[10] He mentioned high-placed politicians arrested just weeks earlier in Saxony-Anhalt: the minister for economic affairs, Leo Herwegen (CDU), as well as the former Social Democratic ministry official Willi Brundert (SED), who were accused of making off with 100 million marks worth of assets from expropriated enterprises. Just a few months later, in March 1950, they were both sentenced to long prison terms. The parallels drawn by Hager were clear. They indicated that bloc politicians and former Social Democrats would continue to be the targets of political persecution. The high phase of Stalinism had begun in the GDR, in which even the highest Communist functionaries could be the victims of purges on trumped-up charges of being fascist, imperialist, or Titoist agents and spies.

Looking Back: Soviet Persecution in the SBZ

The advent of the Ministry for State Security was not the beginning of political persecution in the GDR and its predecessor, the Soviet Occupation Zone (SBZ). In the five years after the unconditional surrender of the Third Reich, it was primarily the security organs of the Soviet occupying power itself that—under varied circumstances—engaged in the purges and political persecution that informed the experiences of the people living under it.

As early as 1945, in the course of its military advance, the Soviet Union began "cleansing" the territories it occupied. It agreed in principle with the Western Allies that Nazis and war criminals needed to be identified and punished, and that the roots and foundations of the Nazi regime should be eradicated from German society. There were disagreements from the very start, though, as to how this was to be done. Concrete objectives differed due to varied social and theoretical assumptions about the nature of National Socialism. According to the Marxist-Leninist version, the Nazi regime was a form of fascism, which in turn was just a variety of capitalism. The USSR therefore concentrated their de-Nazification efforts from the very beginning on the economic basis of the Third Reich, whereas the Western Allies focused on the political system in the narrower sense. These different approaches were also due to vastly different experiences of war in a very concrete way. Unlike the war it waged in the West, the Third Reich had conducted a racially motivated war of extermination against the Soviet Union, with devastating effects. The massacre of the civilian population and the systematic starvation of more than half of the nearly 5.3 million Soviet prisoners of war, in blatant disregard of the conventions of war and international law, had a formative influence—beyond mere political differences—on the way Soviet troops and commanders, as opposed to, say, the U.S. Army, dealt with the Germans after the war. Moreover, the Soviet approach visibly and increasingly reflected the Stalinist practice of persecuting all manner of domestic political "enemies," a practice which had claimed the lives of millions in the Soviet Union ever since the 1930s. Communist ideology, the barbaric experiences of war, and the secret police's habitualized practices of Stalinist persecution all made for a different starting position in the Soviet-occupied part of Germany as compared to the Western zones.

The widening differences in de-Nazification practices were evident immediately after the war, first and foremost in the different forms of camps set up for captured Germans. Soviet POW camps differed drastically from those of the Western Allies and resembled its system of forced-labor camps, the Gulags. In reaction to the Nazi war of extermination, the Soviet Union made no distinction between Wehrmacht soldiers, SS and SA members, or concentration-camp and prison guards, treating them all as prisoners of war. The majority of them had to work as forced laborers in the Soviet Union until 1948–49, as a kind of reparation. Soviet captivity went beyond the standard framework of international law and served as a kind of punishment against Nazi "ideological warriors" (*Weltanschauungskrieger*). Moreover, Soviet military tribunals condemned about 15,000 to 20,000 prisoners of war as war criminals, meting out long camp sentences in often arbitrary proceedings. The last 6,500 of these captives returned to Germany only after Federal Chancellor Konrad Adenauer's famous visit to Moscow in 1955. The uncertain fate of POWs, who often had to wait many years before being allowed to give any sign of life to their next of kin, put a strain on relations between the German populace and "the Russians."

The practices of Soviet security organs in the SBZ made for even more grim experiences, especially in the notorious "special camps" for "active" Nazis and war criminals, as well as increasingly for political opponents. To this day it is still a matter of debate who was interned in these camps and to what extent they were really the perpetrators the Soviets claimed them to be or whether they were merely innocent victims of Soviet despotism locked up behind barbed wire. According to the Soviet basic decree of 18 April 1945, that was instrumental in setting up these camps, internment in the camps was initially intended as a kind of preventive detention for dangerous civilians. Thus the main targets were supposed "forces of diversion [i.e., subversion]," whom the Soviets feared would act as "werewolves" in the hinterland of the Red Army, carrying out acts of terror and reprisal, as well as the mass of low-ranking Nazi functionaries: *Ortsgruppenleiter* (local party group leaders), *Zellenobleute* (cell heads) of the NSDAP and their secondary organizations, etc. There were similar camps in the Western zones, albeit with a distinctly different thrust. Whereas severely incriminated SS perpetrators made up the bulk of prisoners in the American camps, such men did not figure prominently in the Soviet camps, being treated as simple prisoners of war and generally not winding up in special camps. For this reason alone the inmates of these special internment camps tended not to be Nazi war criminals. They were mostly "active" Nazi Party members and low-ranking functionaries, usually somewhat advanced in age. About three-quarters of the prisoners in Buchenwald Camp No. 5, for instance, were over forty years old, and 40 to 50 percent were members or functionaries of the NSDAP. The recollection of many former inmates that there were hardly any "real" Nazis there is reflective of this difference. Added to this were adolescents picked up for being "werewolves" or possessing a gun, and not least of all the victims of arbitrary denunciations and arrests. From 1945 to 1950 the Soviet security organs interned about 154,000 Germans and 35,000 foreigners in special camps. By October 1945 alone they had arrested about 82,000 Germans. One in three of them died during internment, whereas the death rates in Western camps were no higher than in the population at large.

Despite detaining different kinds of prisoners, the Soviet Union could rely at first on a kind of inter-Ally consensus. As long as it was instituting ad-hoc measures against the threat of uncontrolled attacks by the presumably ubiquitous system supporters of the Third Reich, it could claim a certain legitimacy for its internment practices, treating them as anti-Nazi protective measures. Allied internment policies went separate ways once and for all in 1946–47, however. Diet and housing in the Western camps were equivalent to the (rather low) levels of the overall population in war-ravaged Germany—in other words, they were relatively ordered and humane for the most part. The occupiers' obligation to care for their internees sometimes even resulted in a higher standard of living for those in the camps than for those outside. What's more, during this phase the Western Allies released most of their internees if their Nazi involvement was deemed insignificant, or instituted court proceedings against them in the case of seriously incriminated individuals.

The Soviet leadership, on the other hand, let its malnourished captives vegetate under deplorable living conditions. At the start of the harsh winter of 1946–47, they lowered the daily rations for most foodstuffs to the minimum level of the Soviet Gulags, resulting in a wave of mass deaths due to hunger and disease. Faced with foreseeable consequences, even camp commanders and officers of the Soviet Military Administration in Germany (SMAD) pleaded in the fall of 1946 for releasing 35,000 of the 80,000 detainees, given their minimal complicity in Nazi crimes and the low security risk they posed. But Stalin turned this suggestion down, demanding instead that 27,500 able-bodied prisoners be sent to the USSR as forced laborers to replace debilitated POWs. The fact that camp doctors could not even round up 5,000 able-bodied prisoners speaks volumes about the disastrous conditions.

The Moscow leadership wouldn't budge, neither allowing the internees to be sentenced for their supposed or actual crimes, indeed not even taking the trouble to launch investigations in most cases, nor setting them free in obvious cases of lesser incrimination. Internment was, in effect, unlimited punishment without trial. Many prisoners perished from starvation and epidemics. To a certain extent this stubborn refusal to put an end to the deaths in special camps seems inexplicable even from Moscow's perspective, the Soviet occupiers having sent out a deliberate signal in August 1947, in the form of Order 201, that de-Nazification was coming to a close in the civilian sector of the Soviet zone of occupation as they began reintegrating the less incriminated into social life. Though a considerable portion of the internees undoubtedly could have been classified as "less incriminated," their condition remained unaffected.

Beyond the categories of individual guilt was an apparent will to revenge, paired with the dynamics of excessive "vigilance" as a technique of securing power—the elixir of Stalinist mass persecution in the 1930s. The internees, moreover, served as reserve workers for forced labor in the Soviet Union, although no work was done in the special camps themselves, the prisoners there being condemned to agonizing inactivity. What began in the guise of a military occupation measure as a reaction to the barbarism of German warfare was slowly coming to resemble the inner-Soviet conditions of the Gulag system.

Only after the SMAD's repeated insistence did a commission under the direction of the Soviet leadership begin to investigate the cases of internees. It would take until the summer of 1948 for a larger number of prisoners to actually be released from the special camps, and only in 1950 were the camps dissolved by the Soviet occupying power. Soviet military authorities handed over 3,432 internees to the judicial authorities of the newly founded GDR. That very same year they were summarily convicted in the notorious Waldheim trials, sentenced mostly to lengthy prison terms and, in 32 cases, to death. The SED and occupying Soviet power even tried to capitalize on the dissolution of the camps for propaganda purposes: in the very weeks they were launching the Ministry for State Security, they publicly paraded newly released prisoners and church dignitaries in an effort to contradict Western reports and rumors describing the catastrophic conditions of incarceration.

The actions of Soviet security organs in the SBZ were not only characterized by the lack of even minimal legal guarantees and brutal ignorance about mass deaths in the special camps; the range of individuals subject to political persecution gradually expanded or shifted as well. Alongside real or supposed war criminals, Nazis, and "werewolves," the arrests increasingly targeted the representatives of other political currents and social forces: Social Democrats who opposed the fusion of the SPD and KPD into the SED; bourgeois politicians who refused to be coopted by the united-front tactics of the bloc parties; or entrepreneurs and tradesmen who came into conflict with the policy of nationalization. An "anti-imperialist" thrust gradually replaced or eclipsed the initial impulse—aimed against German pacifists—in the early phase of the Cold War. There was no democratic program behind "liberation," just the concept of "Stalinist antifascism."[11]

The main motivation was a Communist strategy of seizing and maintaining power. A comparison with the Baltic states and Poland, where Soviet security forces took similarly vigorous measures starting in 1944 in order to neutralize all political forces resisting "people's democratization," confirms this objective. The main victims there, apart from Germans who were arrested and interned in the course of expulsion, were the fighters of the Polish Armia Krajowa (Home Army), who originally banded together in the resistance against German occupation and were loyal to the Polish government-in-exile in London. They were persecuted as nationalist gangs or bandits. The Soviet state police, the NKVD, offered tens of thousands of soldiers for "the combating of banditry." In Lithuania alone, 12,500 "bandits" were arrested and 2,500 killed by late 1944.

Internment without trial in SBZ special camps mainly affected those who were charged with crimes committed before 1945. But Soviet military tribunals did pass sentences in the occupation zone. These proceedings, too, were originally intended to punish war and Nazi crimes, yet the majority of verdicts were handed down for "crimes" against the Soviet occupying power committed after the collapse of the Third Reich: possession of firearms and the alleged formation of terror groups ("werewolves"), dissemination of political pamphlets, and later "Social Democratism" and "Titoism." The formal legal basis for this was usually Article 58 of the Criminal Code of the Russian Socialist Federative Soviet Republic (RSFSR) with its list of fourteen offenses, which made "counterrevolutionary crimes" punishable by law and also served as the most important legal foundation for Stalinist mass persecution in the Soviet Union. Soviet military tribunals quickly took on the character of special political courts, which hardly targeted Nazi offenders anymore but went after political forces of any stripe, "Edelweiss Pirates" as well as the simple victims of denunciation who were caught in possession of firearms during the last days of the war. They were therefore an essential instrument of political Sovietization in the SBZ.

A great many Social Democrats as well as Liberal and Christian Democrats were convicted for "counterrevolution" because they resisted being coopted by the SED and tried to engage in independent politics. According to the Russian military prosecutor's office, which deals with rehabilitation today, approximately 40,000 people had been sentenced by the tribunals by 1955, more than 17,000 of them by the end of 1946. About 16,000 Germans convicted by Soviet military tribunals served their predominantly routine sentences of ten to twenty-five years forced labor in SBZ special camps but were strictly separated from the others there. Others ended up in Soviet "corrective labor camps," which formed part of the Gulag system in Siberia or in other inhospitable regions. Even after the founding of the GDR in 1949, Soviet military tribunals continued to sit in judgment on people whose "anti-Soviet" activities affected the interests of the still-present occupying power, doing their part to fuel the atmosphere of repression in the 1950s. Only in 1955 did they pass their last sentence.

The practice of releasing prisoners in the following years sheds some light on the arbitrariness of sentencing. Of those convicted by Soviet military tribunals and detained in special camps, more than 5,000 were released in 1950 when the camps were dissolved, whereas more than 10,000 had to continue serving their sentences in GDR prisons. Moreover, in the early 1950s, the Soviet Ministry of the Interior transferred many German prisoners from Soviet Gulags to GDR penitentiaries. About half of the prisoners were set free in 1954, and most of the remaining prisoners in 1956, in the course of de-Stalinization. Most of the convicts were therefore released before their sentences expired, but this did nothing to change the arbitrariness of their persecution or the trauma of camps and prison cells—not to mention the fate of those for whom justice and clemency would never come, having died from the harsh prison conditions or suffered execution before being amnestied.

What do the camps and arrests mean in the experience of postwar Germans? Erich Kuby's oft-quoted claim[12] that the Soviet soldiers could have behaved like "the heavenly hosts" while occupying Germany and it would have done nothing to change the hostile attitude of the German population is certainly warranted: racist propaganda had left its mark and, what's more, many were well aware of the German atrocities committed in the East and reckoned with bitter revenge because of it. And yet "the Russians" hardly behaved like heavenly hosts. Even well-disposed Germans who had greeted the Red Army as liberators were shocked by all the raping and pillaging—"the encounter became an assault," as Bertolt Brecht noted, capturing the mood in 1948.[13] The Germans' perception of their occupiers was formed by a mixture of stereotypes inherited from Goebbels propaganda, the fear of retribution for German crimes, uncertainty about the fates of husbands, brothers, and sons in war and captivity, the humiliation caused by the raping of women and girls as well as other mistreatment of civilians by Soviet soldiers in the course of occupation, and finally the despotic regime of Soviet secret organs. Those arrested generally just disappeared or were summoned to the local commander of the Soviet Military Administration under some pretext or another. Inquiring family members received no news as to whether their loved ones had been arrested, where they were being held, and what was in store for them. The sheer number of detainees aided the proliferation of reports and underground rumors about torture and death in "silent camps" (*Schweigelager*) and "GPU [i.e., Soviet secret police] basements." Officers of the occupying army and politicians of the "Russian party"—the SED—were well aware how arbitrariness and the lack of even the most elementary legal guarantees damaged their reputations in the eyes of the people. Soviet Military Administration commanders repeatedly pleaded with Soviet leaders for a more lenient approach. In November 1948, for instance, the head of the Soviet Military Administration in Thuringia, Ivan S. Kolesnichenko, appealed in Moscow for a solution to the protracted problem of internees. He reminded them that even in the Third Reich relatives had been informed about arrests and that the latter required a court warrant:

> Our Soviet security organs, on the other hand, are waging the battle against political criminals with completely different methods. I'm not even talking about 1945, when we let such arbitrariness reign that even today it is hard to call some cases closed; but the "disappearance" of people because of the activities of our Operational Sectors is still arousing major discontent among the German population and providing every hostile element with ammunition for anti-Soviet propaganda.[14]

His counterpart in Saxony-Anhalt, Mikhail A. Shlyakhtenko, and the prosecutor general of the USSR, Gorshenin, warned Soviet leaders that this was only fueling anti-Sovietism in the population. But for the time being, the will to exercise unrestrained power and the self-perpetuating machinery of persecution prevailed.

For the German populace this impenetrable complex inadvertently evoked associations with the recently defunct Nazi regime. With the approach of the Cold War, the Western press began to make analogies to National Socialism, repeatedly referring to the "new" or "Red Gestapo." Such observations were prompted by the obvious similarities, unhindered as these "extraordinary" apparatuses were by the binding rules of a normative state, as well as the fact that a number of special camps were set up on the sites of former Nazi concentration camps, such as Sachsenhausen and Buchenwald. When news leaked to the West that a Ministry for State Security would be formed, the West Berlin radio station RIAS (Radio in the American Sector) promptly reported on the formation of an apparatus "similar to the earlier Reich Security Main Office."[15] The comparison to a totalitarian state was especially credible given that former opponents and victims of Nazism now found themselves caught in a new machinery of repression.

On the other hand, this rhetoric had an exonerating function, for the double dissociation from Nazis and the Soviet Union made it easier to overlook the fact that Nazi organs of persecution had found a broad and enduring base of support in regular state and police organs as well as in the overall population of the Third Reich, and that even in 1947, according to Western surveys, more than half of Germans considered National Socialism a fine idea poorly implemented.[16]

Despite devastating effects on the mood of the population and the attendant negative impact this had on any all-German perspectives in the Soviet Union's *Deutschlandpolitik*, the USSR held fast to its course. Several factors were apparently at work here. For one thing, the trauma of German invasion strengthened the Soviets' resolve to secure a victory over National Socialism with every available means and not to take any risks with the German population. Retribution and reparations in the form of forced labor were particularly severe. At the same time, the respective Soviet administrators transferred the political rule of Stalinism to their occupying regime. They made "vigilance" toward the "imperialist class enemy" a cornerstone of their policy, with all the internal dynamics of repression that resulted from this. With their prior experience in Soviet domestic politics, it seemed wholly normal to them to forcibly eliminate supposed political and social adversaries. Indeed, for many years this had been the day-to-day business of officers in Soviet state security. This was the climate they grew up in. What's more, measured against the deathly silence of Soviet society following the great purges and given the still-existent and relatively well-organized opposing political forces, they felt all the more compelled to resort to drastic measures. A human life was not worth much—this was the unfortunate attitude inherited from decades of civil war, terror, and war.

Into German Hands?

A network of Soviet apparatuses, variously linked to the regular military administration but also with their own, officially prescribed channels to Moscow, established themselves in the Soviet Occupation Zone as institutions of terror. As of 1946, the USSR's Ministry of State Security (MGB) was in charge of secret-police investigations, arrests, interrogations, and the like, whereas the special camps and prisons themselves were subordinate to the Ministry of the Interior. These apparatuses in the Soviet zone played an exceptionally important role.

The highest-ranking officers there—Colonel-General Ivan A. Serov until 1947, then Colonel-General Nikolai K. Kovalchuk—were also deputy Soviet ministers of the interior. In early 1946, the Department of the Interior had a staff of well over 2,200 and the Soviet security service about 400 employees stationed in the SBZ, distributed in Operational Regions and Operational Groups in every larger city. Torture and extorted confessions were the order of the day in the administrative departments of the *opergruppy*, or Operational Groups, whose basements generally contained cells for detainees. Added to this were about 15,000 men of the Inner Troops.

Germans initially played a subordinate role in this system of persecution, the Soviet authorities recruiting them at first as undercover informers. The network of informers comprised about 2,300 people in 1946 and grew to more than 3,000 by 1949. Even later, Soviet state security was never willing to forego its own unofficial network in the GDR. Small groups of trained KPD members had entered Germany along with the Red Army and Soviet security organs. These German Communists supported the Soviets in making arrests and conducting investigations, but the formation of a German secret police was still a long way off. Militating against this were the Allied Control Council's ban on the creation of political-police agencies, the Soviets' mistrustfulness, and a precarious staffing situation.

Though the ban on political police was later purely a façade, it nonetheless continued to play an important role in the blame game of the Cold War. More fundamental, however, were the premises of Soviet police policy, marked as it was by "vigilance" and the mistrust of any German self-initiative. With the collapse of the Third Reich and the concomitant end of German executive power, the SMAD pursued an extremely restrictive policy; it was reluctant to give even German Communists armed executive powers, purging them of undesirable elements and veteran police officers. This was particularly true for the political police. Cadre was recruited from the groups of German partisans and underground specialists attached to the Red Army and NKVD troops, and was reorganized by the police in the states and provinces of the Soviet Occupation Zone. This began at the communal level, in Dresden, for instance, where the members of a former partisan group became part of the city administration, assigned with the task of hunting down Nazis and other suspects. Little by little, starting in 1945–46, regular regional and provincial police forces were built up, and in 1946 the German Administration of the Interior (DVdI) was created as the headquarters of a zone-wide police policy. Branches for political crime were set up at each local police station.

These had various designations and were weakly staffed to begin with. The DVdI later standardized the structures of the political police. As a department of the criminal police it was called K-5, a name that would soon become notorious. Working alongside the Operational Groups of the MGB, it carried out investigations on assignment, took part in searches and arrests, and passed on political cases uncovered on its own to Soviet secret-police officers.

The character and role of K-5 remained ambivalent. The pursuit of political "criminals" was still the absolute prerogative of the Soviets. The occupying power's overriding need for security was a handicap to German policemen, who had to wait ages for adequate supplies and equipment, such as firearms and telex machines. Thus they were hardly capable of combating the rampant criminality of a "society in collapse" (Zusammenbruchsgesellschaft)—black marketeering and theft, for instance. Whereas keeping law and order and the criminal prosecution of nonpolitical offenses became more and more the responsibility of the German police—the People's Police (Volkspolizei), as they were regularly called as of 1948 and officially as of 1949—the tracking down of political offenders would remain more firmly in Soviet hands. It is therefore quite correct to view K-5 as an auxiliary organ of the Soviet secret police. K-5 policemen, of course, could be zealous and extremely harsh in carrying out these auxiliary tasks. Thus, from the very start, K-5 was considered a special police unit with significance well beyond that of a subdivision of the criminal police.

Yet K-5 lacked the personnel to meet the high demands that were placed on it. Whereas care was taken to present a certain semblance of pluralism in filling positions in the various departments of local, regional, and provincial governments, as well as in the central administrations of the SBZ, other criteria applied to the Department of the Interior with respect to its staffing, security, and policing responsibilities. The top positions there were consistently filled by Communists who enjoyed the confidence of the occupying power. These key positions were a kind of security, to protect against unpredictable developments in a state administration still in the process of rebuilding. At the same time, these "commanding heights" enabled the occupying power to effectively influence the course and speed of transformation of state and social structures in line with the current strategic aims of Soviet Deutschlandpolitik and using minimal personnel. This concept of "cadre policy" imported from the Soviet Union was a proven method for accelerating social transformation from a minority position using forcibly seized powers of the state.

The radical police-staffing policy was somewhat wobbly at first. The top positions were occupied by Germans returning from emigration in the USSR, partisans, and Communist prisoners from Nazi jails and concentration camps. The K-5 department in the German Administration of the Interior, for instance, was headed as of 1948 by Erich Jamin. Jamin had been held in concentration camps and prisons since 1933, had defected to the Red Army in 1944 after joining the Dirlewanger SS penal unit, and was placed in the German Administration of the Interior immediately upon his release from Soviet captivity in 1947. The K-5 in Saxony and Thuringia was headed by Rolf Markert and Jean Baptiste Feilen, two former prisoners from Buchenwald concentration camp, and the K-5 in Mecklenburg was put under the command of Rudolf Wunderlich, a former prisoner of Sachsenhausen concentration camp. In Brandenburg, by contrast, affairs were conducted by former partisans: Emil Wagner, a young Wehrmacht soldier who had wound up in Soviet captivity in 1943 and become a partisan and Soviet agent after antifascist training; and the Sudeten German Martin Weikert, who had attended the Moscow Lenin School in 1934–35, been a functionary in the Czech Communist Youth until his emigration to the Soviet Union, where he had then worked as a mechanic in Stalingrad and Kazakhstan, and as of 1944 had been a radio operator at the partisan general headquarters in Slovakia before resettling in the SBZ in 1946 and starting his police career. Cadre with similar biographies filled the leading positions in the entire police force of the Soviet Occupation Zone. As so-called underground cadre and prisoners they had gone through the school of hard knocks, embodying at the end of the war the will to an uncompromising departure from the bourgeois state that had so thoroughly compromised itself in the preceding twelve years and therefore seemed to confirm the doctrine of the "inevitable" (*gesetzmässig*) victory of socialism and the historical mission of the working class.

And yet there were very few experienced Communists left after the ravages of Nazism and war, not to mention appropriately trained professionals. The new Communist police leadership had driven nearly all social-democratic and bourgeois policemen from their posts by 1948–49 but only managed to replace them in a rather makeshift fashion. This went for the staffing of K-5 as well, which was given special priority. On the one hand, a veritable hodgepodge of more or less dubious forces entered the ranks of the police force, many of whom were merely looking for a way out of postwar hardship and left the force as quickly as they joined it. The turnover rate during these years ran between 20 and 50 percent. On the other hand, the police recruited many young men and a small number of women from underprivileged families who had found a new spiritual and political beginning in the Free German Youth (FDJ) after the traumatic experiences of their world collapsing under National Socialism. The "real" workers among these recruits often had serious difficulties getting used to unaccustomed office chores.

And yet none of these internal deficiencies prevented K-5 from quickly acquiring a notorious reputation. This was due not least of all to the visible ambition of Communist Party leaders and their police experts to make their mark with their own political police force, which, acting as loyal disciples of Soviet security organs, would spearhead the so-called social transformation being implemented by a variety of institutions. This can be seen particularly clearly in the SMAD's De-Nazification Order 201/47. In the course of implementing this decree K-5 was granted a range of exceptional powers. They could conduct proceedings themselves, in lieu of a state prosecutor, until the indictment was drawn up; they could take incriminated persons into custody without an arrest warrant from the court; and they retained control over the punishment of condemned Nazi perpetrators. This clustering of competencies was much to the detriment of regular judicial bodies, whose "transformation" and Sovietization, though energetically pursued by the SED, proved to be a difficult task with the strong presence of bourgeois lawyers in the judiciary and even SED-oriented judges and prosecuting attorneys turning out to be *rechtsbewusst*—acting with respect for the law. Time and again Erich Mielke condemned the allegedly inflationary number of acquittals and tried to influence the selection of jurors. The minister of the interior of Mecklenburg-Western Pomerania, Hans Warnke (SED), seconded ventures like this with recourse to Gulag tactics. He suggested assigning prisoners in pretrial detention to tasks such as peat cutting or chalk and limestone quarrying. Mielke welcomed these plans for "useful but hard and heavy labor."[17] The political police and its spokesmen, with the obvious backing of Ulbricht, presented themselves in this context as the reliable agents of accelerated Sovietization, purged of all bourgeois thinking.

It was in 1948 that SED leaders first expressed their wish for an independent secret-police apparatus. SED Chairman Wilhelm Pieck complained to the SMAD that cases involving sabotage and anti-Soviet youth gangs, especially the so-called "Edelweiss groups," were being taken away from K-5, which was certainly capable of handling them itself. Walter Ulbricht appealed to Soviet authorities for the continued expansion of K-5. On a visit to Moscow in December of that year, SED politicians presented their suggestions to Stalin in person. A "Main Administration for the Protection of the Economy and the Democratic Order" was to take the place of K-5, no longer as a subdepartment of the criminal police but directly subordinate to the president of the German Administration of the Interior as well as, of course, the Soviet secret service.

The proposal aroused the suspicions of the Soviet minister of state security, Viktor S. Abakumov, who apparently saw the position of his ministry jeopardized. He complained to Stalin that German secret police were not sufficiently reliable or experienced to replace Soviet forces in the SBZ, and furthermore they could count on an immediate reaction from the Americans and British, who would set up German secret services of their own in their respective spheres of influence. The Anglo-Americans would even be at an advantage because, unlike the Soviets, they would have no scruples in using experienced secret-service agents and police officers from Nazi organizations.

But Stalin sided with the German comrades and agreed to the creation of a new directorate or "main administration," in the course of founding an East German state. To be sure, he made the formation of this new apparatus subject to the strict control of the MGB, so he didn't mind when Abakumov was several weeks late in delivering the concrete suggestions he had requested for creating the apparatus. Thus the actual go-ahead for the creation of the subsequent MfS coincided almost exactly with the founding of the Federal Republic. On 6 May 1949 the German Administration of the Interior officially detached K-5 from the criminal police. Erich Mielke, in the guise of DVdI vice-president "for general affairs," simultaneously assumed the task of constructing the new main administration. The MGB had an additional 115 officers transferred to the SBZ for staff-selection purposes. They made every effort to support the reserved attitude of their minister and allowed only about 10 percent of K-5 personnel to switch to the new main administration or its branches in the states and districts. The mass of employees came from other criminal police departments or often from key positions in other parts of the People's Police. The vetting was in full swing by the time the main administration became the Ministry for State Security, in February 1950. Recently transferred police officers were sometimes removed from the new apparatus when screening results turned out "negative," for example, when it turned out they had "contacts in the West" (*Westkontakte*).

The last step in establishing the State Security Service—the transformation of the main administration in the Ministry of the Interior into an independent cabinet department—was taken by the German side in the form of an SED Politbüro resolution on 24 January 1950, two days before the publicized Council of Ministers meeting. It is safe to assume that this occurred with the consent of Moscow, although there is still no evidence of this. Why a full-fledged ministry was created instead of sticking to a division within the Ministry of the Interior (as in the case of the other people's democracies, the GDR's socialist "brother nations") is unclear, as is the rather precipitate nomination of its minister. Although it was Erich Mielke who was busy all year in 1949 building up the apparatus in terms of organization and personnel, Soviet decision-makers ultimately opted for Wilhelm Zaisser, one of their veteran agents, famed as International Brigade commander "General Gomez" in the Spanish Civil War. One of the most "Russianized" cadre members in Communist émigré circles, Zaisser had gone to Moscow as early as the 1920s and been deployed in several countries as an underground cadre, but was only loosely connected to the KDP leadership-in-exile around Pieck and Ulbricht. Mielke, by contrast, seemed suspicious to Soviet MGB leaders, his conduct in Belgium and France during the war being hard for them to verify. The head of the Soviet Control Commission, Colonel-General Vasily I. Chuikov, and his political advisor Vladimir S. Semyonov wrote to Stalin that Mielke had "allegedly escaped" during the German invasion in France, "but the length of his stay in the camp and the date of his escape are not known."[18] It is also unclear what Mielke did during the last year of the war, when he was conscripted into the "Todt Organization." He was thus one of the so-called Western émigrés, who seemed less reliable to them than the ones who had spent the war in the Soviet Union. The Field affair in the early 1950s made things even harder for these individuals, as they fell under the general suspicion of being in the employ of the Americans. It is one of the great ironies of Mielke's biography that in subsequent years he put many of these Western émigrés behind bars and tried to extort confessions from them that they were American or British spies. Perhaps the theory of historian Wolfgang Kiessling, an expert on Communist émigré circles, is not so far-fetched after all: that Reichsbahn (East German railway) director Wilhelm Kreikemeyer, who was arrested in August 1950 and died under mysterious circumstances in MfS custody, paid with his life for his candidness, claiming before the Party Control Commission that Mielke, too, under his nom de guerre "Fritz Leistner" in France, had received money during the war from American organizations through the offices of Noel Field.

Cooperation and Competition Between Apparatuses

Unlike later periods, when the State Security Service not only acquired a monopoly on political persecution in the GDR but also assumed a great variety of other tasks and extended its powers into numerous walks of society, in their first years of Communist rule Soviet power and the SED set up—in addition to K-5—a bewildering range of overt and clandestine organs with surveillance, persecution, and espionage functions. Whether this multitude of bodies was a calculated strategy—serving both a means of camouflage and a way to leave open as many avenues of influence as possible with respect to intra-German policy—or a product of competing interests in the leading apparatuses has yet to be resolved.

Instrumental in the policy of expropriation directed against private entrepreneurs was the Central Control Commission (ZKK) of the German Economic Commission (DWK) formed in 1948 and which since the establishment of the GDR was called the Central Commission for State Control in the Council of Ministers. The commission criminalized entrepreneurs in a targeted manner in order to confiscate businesses and combat bourgeois and social-democratic forces in the economic bureaucracy. It too was filled with reliable SED comrades, operated in disregard of the regular justice system, and was granted many special privileges. Its first big performance was in 1948, in the show trial against textile manufacturers in Glauchau-Meerane, who were charged with "black marketeering" for the then quite common practice of bartering ("compensation transactions"). The ZKK had leading ministry officials of social-democratic or bourgeois extraction condemned as American or British agents. The same "spectacle" took place in 1949–50, this time in proceedings against the Deutsche Continental-Gas Gesellschaft.

The SED—or, to be more precise, its Communist wing—began screening its members with regard to their pre-1945 activities not long after its founding. A well-camouflaged party-internal counterintelligence apparatus under Bruno Haid was set up for this purpose, hunting down crypto "Schumacher men" (i.e., Social Democratic opponents of the merge as well as Communist deviants) and probing the pasts of former SPD and KPD members for statements made under the Nazis, e.g., to the Gestapo. The SED likewise set up a secret network of agents in the Western occupation zones. This Western apparatus served as the foundation of the newly formed Foreign Political Intelligence Service (Aussenpolitischer Nachrichtendienst) of the GDR, in 1951–52. Admittedly, few of these agents were of any use for further deployment, having either proved unreliable or been exposed by Western intelligence services.

Finally, there were smaller institutions that were supposed to take on subordinate tasks in the surveillance and persecution apparatus but apparently had only limited success. These included the Offices for the Protection of National Property (Ämter zum Schutz des Volkseigentums), often confused in the literature with the subsequent Main Administration for the Protection of the National Economy, and the information offices of the regional governments, which apart from their tasks as press offices and media controllers were also supposed to gather reports on the mood of the population (Stimmungsberichte). The latter offices were apparently intended to be the successor to "Ifo-Dienst," which was run under the aegis of the SED by Walter Ulbricht and his wife-to-be, Lotte Kühn, but effectively exposed in 1947 by Western publications. These state information offices and the central "Office for Information" did actually compile such reports, but these were only moderately realistic and had a marked tendency to whitewash and idealize. Thus there was no great future in store for them in the secret-service domain. Their director, Gerhart Eisler, a "Western émigré," got caught in the machinery of the purges at the instigation of the Soviets, and the central office was ultimately dissolved in 1953.

It remains a mystery to what extent this agglomeration of more or less short-lived, frequently renamed, and often minimally staffed apparatuses was a deliberate camouflage or simply the product of chaotic circumstances. Cooperation and competition overlapped, and there was a surprising interlinkage of employees as well. An institutional clarification process set in, however, after the founding of the Ministry for State Security and only really came to an end in the early 1960s, even though most rivals had already been neutralized by the early 1950s. As of 1953, the ZKK only served as a supervisory body for internal administration. The information offices were likewise dissolved, and the Western apparatus of the SED was absorbed by the Foreign Political Intelligence Service.

Many organizational changes were the direct result of Soviet provisions and models. This can be seen with particular clarity in the case of the Foreign Political Intelligence Service (APN) during the early 1950s. In December 1950, the CPSU Politburo informed Ulbricht that it had no objections to the SED's Western espionage network being handing over to the MfS. In July 1951, however, the same body announced the creation of the APN as an independent institution under the deputy chairman of the Council of Ministers and later the Foreign

Ministry. In 1953 the APN was incorporated into the State Security Service. Each of these moves corresponded to the respective organizational state of Soviet foreign espionage.

State Security in the High Phase of Stalinism

In the early years—prior to February 1956—State Security established itself as an instrument of "bureaucratic terror" in the context of SED social policy and the inter-German (German-German) conflict between competing ideological systems. This was its formative period. Its leading figures— State Secretary Erich Mielke, in particular—set to work exercising the full range of Stalinist Soviet repression in their half-country. With that they stirred up an atmosphere of cold civil war which, feeding off the system conflict between the two Germanies, had a lasting influence on the apparatus and character of State Security. Step by step the Stasi staked out its fields of activity and thus established the relentless logic of its "all-round battle against the enemy" (*allseitige Feindbekämpfung*).

The top priority was still the battle against organized political opponents of the SED—and indeed there was no lack of these: the Eastern bureaus of the SPD, CDU, and FDP (Free Democratic Party), as well as of the trade-union organization DGB; the Investigating Committee of Free Jurists (UFJ), which as a point of contact for judges, prosecuting attorneys, and administrative officials removed from their posts; and the militant Combat Group Against Inhumanity (KgU), to name a few. Added to this were outfits of the Western Allies, such as the Berlin radio station RIAS and—of course—the Western secret services, including the Gehlen Organization, the precursor to the Federal Intelligence Service (BND), West Germany's foreign intelligence agency. Also considered "enemy bases" (*Feindzentrale*) were companies headquartered in the Federal Republic whose assets in the GDR had been expropriated and transferred to state ownership. All of these organizations denounced these infringements of the law and the lack of democracy in the East and tried to weaken SED rule. They found support in the form of the U.S. policy of "liberating captive peoples," which aimed at destabilizing the Soviet Union's position of power throughout the whole of Eastern Europe.

In this respect, the Eastern concept of the enemy and Western policy-making actually overlapped. But the SED, State Security, and the Soviet security officers still steering things in the background were not content to leave it at that. Following a fatal logic, they declared as a matter of principle that anyone with dissenting opinions or views or who became a target through no fault of their own would be considered a secret agent, saboteur, or bandit in the service of these enemy bases. Thus, for all intents and purposes, the SED was waging a cold civil war on two separate fronts: against domestic and Western enemies. In terms of practical investigative work, it was simply a matter of "proving" it—which, following the Soviet Chekist model, generally meant extracting confessions from detainees by means of sleep deprivation, isolation, and outright violence. The principal aim of this policy was to eliminate all forces that posed a potential threat to SED rule and its course of political and social transformation. State Security, for example, arrested high-ranking bloc politicians such as Foreign Minister Georg Dertinger (CDU), who was taken into custody in December 1952 and, after being convicted as a spy, was not released from prison until 1964, as well as the minister of trade and supplies, Karl Hamann (LDPD), who was given life in prison for his alleged "sabotage of the systematic supply of the population," and was pardoned and released in 1956. Similar fates were suffered by many Social Democrats who opposed the course of the Unity Party or were slated for removal from their offices. Many young people were arrested as well, such as nineteen secondary-school students from Werdau, in Saxony, in May of 1951, for repeatedly distributing and posting pamphlets in protest of Volkskammer elections or the death penalty. The courts accused them of maintaining ties to the Combat Group Against Inhumanity. The students, almost all of them under twenty years of age, received prison sentences of two to fifteen years.

But eliminating opponents and rivals from the political domain was not enough for the SED. The crackdowns went further. Hence religious minorities such as the Jehovah's Witnesses were persecuted once again, being deemed American spies as well. In the run-up to the Volkskammer elections of 15 October 1950, they ran afoul of the regime, refusing for religious reasons to take part in the elections and thereby jeopardizing the aim of achieving the (henceforth standard) 99 percent approval at the polls for the unified list of the "National Front." By 31 August 1950 the minister of the interior had already prohibited the "Watchtower Society" for its allegedly unconstitutional aims, claiming that it had agitated against the existing state order, disseminated illegal pamphlets, and was serving imperialist secret services. The members of this religious community were removed from public offices, and more than 500 of them were arrested. Seven of them were convicted of espionage in a show trial, being sentenced by the Supreme Court to lengthy prison terms. Between 1950 and 1955 the

State Security Service put nearly 2,800 Jehovah's Witnesses behind bars. It is unknown how many cases there were of the Soviets taking matters into their own hands.[19]

The larger religious communities came under pressure as well. One point of contention was the remilitarization of the GDR through the formation of the so-called "People's Police in Barracks," or Kasernierte Volkspolizei. The SED and FDJ pressured thousands of young men into "voluntary" military service. Organizations such as the Junge Gemeinde, a Protestant youth group whose open and youth-friendly atmosphere of pacifism provided a refuge to teenagers traumatized by World War II, came into conflict with the SED and were severely persecuted. The high point of domestic terror came in the wake of the Second SED Party Conference, in July 1952. It was at this conference that Walter Ulbricht declared the "Building of Socialism" in the GDR, heralding the start of a new phase in the transformation process. The party conference resolved: "It must be kept in mind that the intensification of class struggle is inevitable and the working people must break the resistance of enemy forces."[20]

The SED sounded the attack on the last bastions of the private economy by introducing draconian commercial criminal laws. The remaining private entrepreneurs were put under enormous pressure, and the collectivization of agriculture, workshops, and small-scale manufacturing began. Many farmers, craftsmen and tradesmen were taken to court for alleged "economic crimes." The GDR likewise adopted the harsh disciplining of industrial workers of the kind introduced in the Soviet Union in an effort to increase productivity. The "Law on the Protection of National Property" enabled severe punishment for minor offenses. A worker stealing a single coal briquette or half a pound of sauerkraut, for example, could be sentenced to one year in prison. More serious cases of theft could result in the notorious "twenty-five years" meted out by Soviet courts—albeit in a penitentiary as opposed to the Soviet "corrective labor camps." In just a matter of months, by the end of March 1953, East German courts initiated such proceedings against more than 10,000 people.

The culmination of this high phase of Stalinism was the aforementioned inner-Party terror announced by Kurt Hager in late 1949 and the anti-Semitic campaign of early 1953. The SED and State Security began preparing show trials modeled after the ones in Moscow during the 1930s and the proceedings in Hungary and Bulgaria of 1949, when leading Communist functionaries were sentenced to death for allegedly being fascist, imperialist or Titoist agents. Among the first to be arrested were the deputy chairman of the West German KPD,

Kurt Müller; the chief producer of "Deutschlandsender" radio station, Leo Bauer; the director of the Deutsche Reichsbahn, Wilhelm Kreikemeyer; and eventually Müller's successor in the KPD, Fritz Sperling. The hunt mounted by the SED Central Party Control Commission and the MfS was primarily aimed at former Western émigrés, whom they considered "loose cannons." Mielke conducted a number of the interrogations personally and bragged to the captive functionaries that as an "old Chekist and pupil of Beria" he had "already liquidated a number of people" and had even been present at the first Moscow show trials.[21] Yet the plans for show trials in the GDR were postponed time and again. Perhaps the functionaries being detained were not sufficiently prepared to play their assigned role of repentant sinners in a staged trial. Or perhaps there were tactical considerations, part of the Soviets' *Deutschlandpolitik.*

Under the banner of "intensified class warfare" the Party and secret police took aim once again in the fall of 1952. In December 1952 the former general secretary of the Czechoslovak Communist Party, Rudolf Slansky, was sentenced to death in the Czechoslovak Socialist Republic for allegedly being recruited as a U.S. agent by the American Noel Field, during the war. Every German Western émigré who had come into contact with Field was now suspected of being a spy. In the GDR, the highest functionary to be affected was former Politbüro member Paul Merker, after Slansky mentioned him in his "confession." Merker had been expelled from the SED back in 1950 but had not been arrested. The MfS apprehended him in December 1952. The SED abstained from a show trial after Stalin's death but nonetheless sentenced him to eight years in prison in 1955. Merker was released in February 1956, being acquitted and legally rehabilitated by the same court in July of that year. He would never return to politics. Leo Bauer was sentenced to death by a Soviet court, his sentence later being commuted to twenty-five years of hard labor in Siberia. Kurt Müller received just as many years. Both of them returned from the camps to the Federal Republic in 1955. Others did not survive persecution, such as the aforementioned Kreikemeyer and longtime Communist functionary Paul Bertz, who took his own life while in custody, as well as Lex Ende, erstwhile editor-in-chief of *Neues Deutschland,* who, banished and put on "probation in production," died of heart failure in a smelting factory in Saxony.

With the persecution of Merker, a vigorous defender of the rights of Jews, the purges in the GDR took on an anti-Semitic tone. Stalin had specifically targeted Jewish physicians in his campaign against the so-called "Doctors' Plot." In the Slansky trial as well, eleven of the fourteen defendants were Jewish. Yet the SED was less than zealous in pursuing this new "anticosmopolitan" line—whether due to its scruples after the Nazi persecution of Jews is unclear. It went about dissolving the Association of Persecutees of the Nazi Regime (VVN), cautiously mentioned the first Jewish names that turned up in connection with the Field affair, and even summoned the chairman of the Council of Jewish Communities in the GDR, VVN Volkskammer deputy Julius Meyer (SED), for questioning before the Central Party Control Commission. But it never came to large-scale arrests. About five hundred Jews, including Meyer and nearly all of the leaders of local Jewish communities, fled to West Berlin a few days later. Though aware of their escape plans, the Party and MfS did not intervene. Perhaps they were pleased to be rid of these "cosmopolitan" elements.

The persecution soon lost its anti-Semitic edge after Stalin's death. "Anti-Zionism," however, remained an integral component of the MfS's concept of the enemy, with all of its attendant undertones. The aura of urbane Communist Party intellectuals of Jewish descent remained deeply suspect to Mielke and his men. Merker, during his interrogation by leading investigative officers of the MfS, had to put up with being derided as a "Jew-lackey" (*Judenknecht*) and "King of the Jews." "World Jewry" (*Weltjudentum*) and the "World Zionist Organization" were standard Chekist vocabulary well into the 1980s.

Structure of the Apparatus

The MfS managed in just a few years to rapidly expand its apparatus and fulfill its active function in the radical transformation of GDR society. By the time Stalin died in March of 1953 it already had around 10,000 employees. In the previous year alone it had more than doubled its staff, thereby surpassing the Gestapo in its Reich-wide staffing levels of the prewar period. There was no end of personnel expansion in sight. Three years later, in early 1956, more than 16,000 individuals were working for State Security. In this sense, the GDR was on par in this phase with the other East-Central European people's democracies. Communist parties everywhere were setting up powerful bulwarks with Soviet backing to establish and consolidate their power. Czechoslovakia, for example, had an estimated 10,000 to 11,000 employees during these years. Poland achieved a similar level in 1953, with about 33,000 employees against a total population of 38 million.

These Communist secret-police forces not only had the rapid expansion of their staff in common but a similar employee makeup as well and, with that, their characteristic "Chekist" atmosphere. Whereas each apparatus was led by a small group comprised of old Communist underground fighters—mostly longtime Soviet émigrés, Comintern agents, and partisans—along with persecutees of the Nazi regime, the mass of employees was made up of extremely young men from socially underprivileged families with a markedly low level of education. It was this social milieu that provided cadre recruiters with the people they needed for the rough-and-ready business of arresting and interrogating, men who were particularly susceptible to the worldview and image of the enemy propagated by Stalinism. Indoctrinated in political training schools, they absorbed the requisite ideas and mentally equipped themselves with the tools they needed for a lifelong orientation. The future director of MfS foreign espionage, Werner Grossmann, for instance, bears witness to this even today, describing in downright effusive tones his educational experience back then—in his case, at the school of the Foreign Political Intelligence Service, which soon thereafter was absorbed by the MfS:

> Our classwork was powerful and intense. In lectures and seminars as well as self-study we dealt with the Marxist classics. Including Stalin, of course. Each idea of Lenin we discussed was followed by the instructor's question: What did Stalin say about that? We reacted fast and added Stalin's view without being asked.

Though well aware of Stalin's deeds and the consequences of his teachings, he adds: "None of us had ever thought such a comprehensive study of the social sciences was possible."[22]

The sheer number of employees undoubtedly explains the considerable clout of the apparatus in persecuting apparently ubiquitous "enemies" and "spies." The mass of employees was meant to compensate for their lack of quality, because MfS staff was far from being the ideal of a firmly disciplined, elite vanguard. Elementary skills and the most basic techniques of policing, such as taking down an interrogation protocol, were often wanting. What's more, the "Chekist" attitude of omnipotence promoted a tendency toward disciplinary lapses, which the Stasi paid for with an exceedingly high turnover rate in the form of early dismissals. Besides which, the open border in Berlin enabled employees who ran afoul of their superiors and disciplinary authorities to leave the country with relative ease. By 1961, about 400 active or previously discharged MfS employees had fled to the West. The ministers repeatedly reacted with severe threats, and acted on them too, repatriating 108 of these men through cunning or force and executing 7 of them in order to set an example. The rest of them generally received long prison terms, which they mostly served in MfS detention centers. The lack of general and professional skills meant that the desired statements and confessions in interrogations were often extracted by violent means—wholly in the manner of Soviet "advisors," who generally came from a lower social background as well but who had the advantage of years or decades of "hardening" through the experience of Chekist class warfare.

For all the elitist self-drama of the "Chekists" and their general contempt for the People's Police, the MfS was still dependent on it. Indeed, the People's Police was every bit as involved as the MfS, for example, during the great waves of arrests, in 1952–53. State Security was also greatly dependent on the cooperation of the Party apparatus, which had a much more broadly developed organizational network to start with, even down to the factory level.

The number of informers rapidly grew. Between 1950 and 1952 alone the Stasi recruited about 30,000 people for unofficial collaboration as "secret informers" (GI) or "secret collaborators" (GM), as they were called, using Soviet terminology. MfS leaders calculated in 1954 that at this rate one in two East German citizens would be recruited by 1963. The quality of these informers, however, left much to be desired. What's more, the often young and inexperienced State Security staff had trouble recruiting informers where they needed them most. Recruiting Guideline 21/1952, the first detailed instructions of their kind, stated:

> The search for suitable persons to work against the so-called "Free Jurists," for example, must be conducted among the group of persons from which the agent headquarters itself selects its agents. Of the criminals from the so-called "Investigating Committee of Free Jurists" convicted in the last trials
>
> 32 percent were in ministries and the state apparatus
>
> 31 percent were engineers and designers in state-owned enterprises and
>
> 10 percent were department heads in state-owned enterprises;
>
> 10 percent were self-employed craftsmen and businessmen, and
>
> 17 percent were jurists, lawyers, and legal consultants.[23]

The list continued for other organizations, citing former Hitler Youth leaders and SS officers, regular soldiers in the Wehrmacht, criminals, "morally depraved" juveniles, engineers, technicians, and managing employees of state enterprises. In other words, the old elites—abundantly present in the GDR—were considered potential enemy bases and were therefore the most important recruiting pool for unofficial collaborators. But these elites were considerably more difficult to enlist for volunteer work than, say, SED members. Though MfS employees represented state power, they couldn't hold a candle to potential recruits with a "bourgeois" political mindset. The actual success rate behind the often aimless and crude mass recruiting was rather low, in other words. Many bowed to open or concealed pressure then turned out to not be very cooperative later, broke off their collaboration at the next opportunity, or avoided it altogether by fleeing to the West. Thus, for example, by 1961 more than 1,500 people whom the MfS had tried to recruit as stool pigeons had contacted the Investigating Committee of Free Jurists in West Berlin. MfS leaders reacted in 1955 and curbed these mass recruitment efforts. By 1957 enlistment had been cut in half. Instead of 30,000 new and reenlistments (as in 1954) there were now only about 15,000.[24]

There is no question then that, with respect to State Security's full-time apparatus and network of informers, the SED and Soviet hegemonic power had installed an extensive power apparatus to harass the opponents of their rule and accelerate social transformation. Considerable staff resources, however, were not only an indicator of vigorous policy but were also a response to the weakness of their social base.

Little by little the Ministry for State Security took over from the Soviets, acquiring ever new powers and authority. Until 1955 the occupying power reserved the right to try and condemn Germans before Soviet military tribunals. The last verdict of this kind was reached on 16 September 1955, just four days before the GDR was granted formal sovereignty. The reporting channels between the central ministry and administrative offices at the state or regional and district levels were handed over to the Germans in 1952. Soviet advisors and instructors were present at all levels of the MfS apparatus, and Soviet state security still had about 2,200 employees stationed in the GDR for operational work, some under their own command, some directed by the MfS. The Soviet minister of the interior, Lavrentiy Beria, originally wanted to reduce this apparatus to 328 employees after Stalin's death, but his successor Kruglov relaxed this measure after Beria's arrest. Hence 450 KGB men would continue to be active in the GDR and were still in a position to give MfS comrades orders. As of 1958 only 32 liaison officers were responsible for the MfS. Formal acceptance on an equal footing into the ranks of the East European "brother organs" came in March 1955, when the MfS took part in a conference in Moscow attended by the secret-police forces of the USSR, Czechoslovakia, and Poland.

Stalin's Death, June Crisis, De-Stalinization

The more narrowly defined high phase of Stalinism came to an end in the GDR about nine months after the Second Party Conference, with the death of the Soviet dictator. The ensuing months were not only marked by turmoil regarding the Soviet Union's *Deutschlandpolitik*, but also by the USSR's massive criticism of the SED's extreme policy of confrontation (initially supported by the Soviets). The SED offensive on nearly all fronts of society had overtaxed the strength of the Communists and pushed the patience of their grassroots opponents to the breaking point. The number of people fleeing to the West skyrocketed as a result. In March 1953 alone, 58,000 people left the GDR. All of this called for a new approach. Thus the hard line taken against private ownership and self-employment, farmers, and Christians was to be toned down, "measures to strengthen the rule of law and guarantee civil rights"[25] were to be taken, and excessive punishments were to be reviewed. The intended "New Course" included downsizing the People's Police in Barracks and secret navy and air-force units from 117,000 to 93,000 men, and the reduction of Soviet military advisors from around 1,000 to between 250 and 300. Those condemned under the Law on the Protection of National Property were generally supposed to be set free if the sentences they received were under three years, and the same applied to those in pretrial detention for the same offences, the Politbüro announced in its famed communiqué of 9 June 1953. But these concessions were not enough, especially considering that no relief was in sight for the largest and most important group lending the SED its legitimacy: the workers. It was they who began the riots on 17 June, when the ruling state party refused to lower work norms.

The uprising was a fiasco for State Security. Perhaps the announcement of the New Course had succeeded in unnerving and disorienting its employees, so that it was not class warfare they sought but class peace. Whatever the case, the force of protest surprised them. They turned out to be more or less helpless in the face of thousands of demonstrators, especially at a number of district offices that were besieged and ultimately stormed. Their hands were tied by conflicting orders from Zaisser: they were supposed to hold the administrative offices at all costs but were not to use firearms. This was virtually impossible given the forces arrayed against them, especially considering that no precautionary measures had been taken to use riot-control gear such as water cannons, tear gas, or truncheons. In the mind of the Chekists, the political conflict on the streets was an armed civil war, but their commanders did not risk the crucial step towards confrontation. MfS headquarters in Görlitz, Niesky, Jena, Bitterfeld, and Merseburg, as well as twelve prisons and thirteen police stations of the People's Police wound up in the hands of the rebels, who released prisoners and destroyed or walked off with files. Only when Soviet troops intervened did the tables turn. They dispersed the rebels and shot at least twenty protesters under martial law.

MfS employees were apparently only too pleased to adopt the theory of a "fascist provocation" proclaimed by Ulbricht and the editor-in-chief of *Neues Deutschland,* Rudolf Herrnstadt, on 18 June, although in industrial centers such as Halle and Bitterfeld it must have been sufficiently clear to them that this hardly squared with reality. Political officers of the guards regiment reported that in the days after the attempted revolt a "thirst for adventure and sensation" had taken hold of the soldiers. Forces deployed at the sector border had even toyed with the idea of abducting West Berlin policemen and taking them to the East. This wanton exuberance arose from the relief at having survived thanks to Soviet assistance. One soldier summed up the mood as follows: "We were lucky they arrived in the nick of time; we owe a lot to them."[26] The experience of 17 June was indeed profound for this generation of MfS employees. It reminded them how dearly their role as secret police would cost them should the tables turn some day—a traumatic scenario that forever preyed on the minds of the Chekists and suddenly materialized in crisis situations. The events of June had made painfully clear to the Communists how slim their power base really was.

To be sure, very few quit the service after this experience. Most threw themselves into their work with militant zeal in an effort to forget the disgrace they had suffered. The first task was to put behind bars as many of the demonstrators and their leaders as possible. By 7 July alone, the Stasi had hauled in 4,816 individuals. The People's Police made nearly as many arrests. Most of the arrested were released by the security organs after a short time.

The crisis had two very symbolic consequences for the Ministry for State Security, the causes of which were only indirectly related to its failure during the June riots but which now invariably seemed like punitive measures. On 18 July 1953 the Politbüro decided to downgrade the apparatus to a state secretariat and incorporate it into the Ministry of the Interior under the leadership of Willi Stoph. The SED was following the example of the Soviet MGB, which Minister of the Interior Beria took back into his department after Stalin's death, though the CPSU went one step further and arrested its notorious police and state security chief on 26 June. Only in November 1955 did State Security become a ministry again. The second consequence was Minister Zaisser's dismissal by the Politbüro, likewise on 18 July. Zaisser was the victim of a power struggle in the upper echelons of the SED, the winner of which, paradoxically, was none other than Walter Ulbricht, the man who had been expected to fall. A supposed "German Beria," Zaisser was accused of having removed the MfS from the Party's reach and isolated it. Zaisser and his alleged cohort Rudolf Herrnstadt were expelled from the Central Committee at its Fifteenth Plenary Session, and were later expelled from the Party in January 1954.

Public degradation was followed by an embarrassing internal investigation by the Central Commission for State Control (ZKK) concerning dubious financial conduct among the entire MfS leadership. Leading MfS cadre had set up an "extremely well-appointed and luxurious"[27] weekend house for themselves in a former hunting lodge of Hermann Göring on Wolletz Lake and heavily enriched themselves with misappropriated funds and goods. The ZKK discovered unauthorized payments and loans of at least 230,000 marks in the case of Zaisser, almost 63,000 marks in the case of State Secretary Erich Mielke, and just under 37,000 marks for Party Secretary Otto Walter, the ministry's "third man," in addition to abuses other deputy ministers and state or regional leaders. Erich Mielke seriously reckoned with the end of his career and, in response to the MfS chief accountant's discoveries after Zaisser's fall, "noticeably endeavored . . . to settle his outstanding debts, expressing the opinion on several occasions that the availment of these loans was not defensible under the law."[28] But the finance inspectors had overshot the mark. Apart from Zaisser, all of the incriminated functionaries kept their posts thanks to Ulbricht's intercession.

The new head of the State Secretariat for State Security was Ernst Wollweber, a longtime expert in maritime sabotage. Thus Ulbricht was once again forced to accept a staffing decision of the Soviets. His beleaguered right-hand man Mielke remained a deputy and needed some time to reconsolidate his position after Markus Wolf joined the ministry as head of foreign espionage and likewise entered the circle of deputies.

That criticism focused on the dismissed minister was good for State Security on the whole. The failure of 17 June could be blamed on his misguided leadership, thus sparing the rest of the apparatus from the consequences. Under such conditions, there was naturally never any fundamental criticism of State Security's role as an organ of terror.

Quite the opposite, in fact: the Politbüro charged State Security with the task of "proving," after the fact, its theory that the uprising had been a "fascist provocation." The Western organizers of the "putsch" were to be unmasked and, if possible, arrested. This "exterritorialization" of the problem was one way out of an apparent crisis of legitimacy. The search for the wire pullers in the West and their agents in the GDR opened up a wide field. The chairman of the Party Control Commission, Hermann Matern, reminded his Stasi cadre—as if nothing had happened—that the "strengthening of state power," and thus State Security, in line with the Second Party Conference of 1952, was still the "main instrument" for creating the foundations of socialism. The criticisms of the SED during the preceding months did nothing to change this:

> We have to hit hard and ruthlessly. There is no room in our ranks for weak-kneed pacifists and dreamers [Mondgucker]. Comrade Ulbricht once proclaimed at a Central Committee meeting: "We must make the German Democratic Republic a hell for enemy agents." Comrades, this is your principal task.[29]

A number of "concentrated blows" to a range of Western organizations with alleged or actual contact persons in the GDR followed. A first wave in October–November 1953 with over one hundred arrests, "Operation Fireworks" (Aktion Feuerwerk), was aimed against the Gehlen Organization and other Western secret services, as was a second in August 1954, "Operation Arrow" (Aktion Pfeil), with nearly 550 arrests. A third operation under the code name "Lightning" (Blitz), which netted more than 500 arrests, was aimed at political organizations such as the Eastern offices of political parties, as well as targeting West Berlin journalists who were critical of the GDR. Although only one MfS line was in charge in each instance (in the first two operations Line II/Counterintelligence, in the third one Line V/Political Underground), the MfS arrested any suspects whose cases seemed sufficiently advanced, regardless of their presumed connection to Western organizations. The MfS planned kidnappings as well. West Berlin journalist Karl Wilhelm Fricke, for instance, was captured during the last wave and sentenced in East Berlin to four years in prison. The attempts to kidnap SED-critical journalist and former U.S. agent Carola Stern failed.

From a strategic point of view, operations of this sort were not necessarily expedient. Conceivably, the MfS would have been better off secretly infiltrating enemy organizations and paralyzing them, instead of going after known contacts and risking the buildup of new, unknown structures. But the Stasi wanted to use these actions to dismiss the claim that it had degenerated into a "study association," denouncing as shrilly as possible the machinations of Western organizations in the GDR. To this end, the large number of widespread arrests was not without a marked effect. The operations were followed up by press conferences and show trials at which "repentant sinners" and "scrupulous criminals" were put on display. Wollweber, Mielke, and other top Chekists gave dozens of speeches to workers at major factories to popularize these actions.

Even from today's perspective it is hard to neatly characterize these waves of arrests. They were primarily aimed against organizations which, though not responsible for the events of 17 June, were nonetheless avowed opponents of the SED regime, fighting it however they could, sometimes with the help of contact persons in the GDR. In this respect these "concentrated blows" did indeed constitute "some noteworthy counterintelligence successes"[30] in the covert intra-German secret-service war. Since the number of arrests and their diffusion were every bit as far-reaching as those of the "intensified class warfare" in the wake of the Second Party Conference, these operations had the air of a new wave of universal terror potentially affecting anyone—regardless of whether or not this person was actually an opponent of the regime, let alone an enemy agent. State Secretary Wollweber was well aware of this. In November 1953 he explained to leading employees that the operations should indeed have a "shock effect on the agents" but that it was imperative to avoid a "shock effect on the population, . . . which could give the impression that a wave of arrests was under way where random suspects are being apprehended and where the occasional wavering individual might think he could be taken for one."[31] This distinction was in line with the official interpretation of the June revolt and the attempt to exonerate "the people" in retrospect. The warning also fit the critique of excessive severity expressed at the Second Party Conference. It is more than doubtful, though, that the people made such a distinction and hence if this was a realistic assessment of the actual effects of the arrests. Rather, the June strikers and demonstrators seemed to view the operations as an act of revenge, confirming the bitter lesson that political protest came at a high price, even if the Party was now willing to offer some limited material concessions in exchange.

Despite its "successes" in battling the enemy, East German State Security had to reorient itself "after Stalin." The war of succession in the CPSU leadership and its groping for a new mode of rule had a constant effect on the GDR and State Security. The death of the dictator in 1953 apparently thwarted another impending purge of the Party leadership and put a bloodless end to the "Doctors' Plot." The execution of Beria in December 1953 and of Abakumov—the minister of state security from 1946 to 1951—in 1954, marked the end of a Chekist "tradition" as well: that secret-police chiefs themselves met their end through a bullet in the back of the head.[32] A sigh of relief was felt, and a "thaw" was in the air that finally arrived in February 1956 with Nikita Khrushchev's famous "secret speech" at the Twentieth Party Congress of the CPSU.

Ulbricht endeavored to limit the damaging effects of the speech, claiming that the excesses described by Khrushchev had never existed in the GDR and that, besides, State Security had already corrected its course back in 1953. But the pressure of expectations mounted in the GDR too. Karl Schirdewan presented Khrushchev's speech at the Third Party Conference, so that word spread to Party organizations. One important practical result was the formation of a "Commission of the Central Committee for the Inspection of Affairs of Party Members." Apart from cases of inner-Party purges, the body concerned itself with other political prisoners and ordered many of them to be released. Among the committee's members was Ernst Wollweber. Erich Mielke was present as a permanent participant. In the course of 1956 about 25,000 prisoners were freed, including 400 functionaries of the bloc parties, nearly 700 SPD supporters, and several hundred individuals convicted by Soviet military tribunals.

De-Stalinization and the release of political prisoners produced a sense of insecurity in the ranks of the MfS. Its employees found it harder to make new arrests. They also showed a deep lack of understanding for the sudden profanation of Stalin, whose words and writings had served them as guiding principles. The "disturbance" lasted little more than six months, however. With the suppression of the Hungarian revolution in the fall of 1956, Ulbricht regained the upper hand and was able to put a stop to de-Stalinization before it really began. On 5 November 1956 he wrote to MfS employees:

> The militarists and monopolists in West Germany, disappointed and foaming with rage about the defeat of the Hungarian counterrevolution, will leave nothing undone in the days and weeks to come to distract from the defeat by causing provocations in the GDR. For this reason, comrades of State Security, heighten your revolutionary vigilance and combat readiness. Allow no wavering in your own ranks and strike the enemy wherever he dares to rear his head.[33]

Wollweber came into conflict with Ulbricht during the tightening of the political course. With the arrest of dissident philosopher Wolfgang Harich it came to an open break. Ulbricht had gained access to Harich's investigation files through Wollweber's first deputy, Erich Mielke, before the minister himself had seen them. Wollweber reacted by issuing a reporting regulation that bound his deputies to channel all information to the state and Party leadership directly through him. Ulbricht accused Wollweber of wanting to place himself above the Party—the very same verdict that had brought down Zaisser. Thus Wollweber was eventually forced to declare the order invalid. During the course of 1957 he had to accept a range of organizational changes in the ministry that seriously restricted his influence. In July 1957, after months of absence the year before on account of a heart attack, he went on convalescent leave, effectively stripping him of his power.

Wollweber was certainly no liberal; he was a Communist relatively independent from the leading man in the Party and who tried to set his own course, which after 1956 meant a relaxation of repression. In 1956–57 he set out to trim down the apparatus and, though not making all the changes he wanted, this was nonetheless the only phase without a constant growth of MfS staff. In the final showdown with his opponents in the MfS leadership, he admitted that he had "set the goal of proving that the tragedy in all socialist countries with their state securities is not inevitable [*keine Gesetzmässigkeit*], but rather that the inroads [*Übergriffe*] that occurred are avoidable."[34] Apparently he was referring to the inner-Party purges of the early 1950s. It was under his watch in 1955–56 that interrogation methods and prison conditions were first relaxed somewhat. Before that, all-night interrogations, sleep deprivation, and solitary confinement were part of the standard repertoire of extracting forced confessions. Beatings and other torture methods, despite all the superficial warnings to uphold the "democratic rule of law," were at least tacitly considered legitimate from a Chekist point of view. All of this now was slackening. On the whole, Wollweber's story shows that in 1956–57 there was no consensus in the GDR on how to react to Soviet de-Stalinization. It also shows how much energy the group around Ulbricht had to expend in order to come out on top. After months of illness, Ernst Wollweber officially gave up his position as minister on 1 November 1957. In January 1958 the SED Central Committee expelled him for forming a faction, along with the SED cadre chief, Karl Schirdewan. His successor, Erich Mielke, was already preparing Wollweber's day of reckoning in court, but the era of inner-Party show trials was now a thing of the past. Unlike Zaisser, his predecessor, Ernst Wollweber was not even expelled from the Party.

The experiences of a single decade, from the collapse of the Third Reich to the brief period of thaw in 1956, had left their mark on a whole generation. On the one hand there was imprisonment and conviction by Soviet occupiers, the restructuring of state and society by means of secret-police executive powers, expropriation, expulsion, and frequent escapes to the West, the revolt of June 1953 and its suppression by Soviet tanks. Hundreds of thousands of individuals ended up in prison for short or long periods; tens of thousands paid with their lives. On the other hand there was an ardent minority of Communists and those who sympathized with the "workers' and peasants' state," about 17,000 German Chekists among them. These people had drummed the idea and image of an enemy into their heads—the imperialist threat from the West—through training and hands-on experience, had begun their ascent as a new elite but had also come to know the fragility of their power, their dependence on the protective hand of the Soviet Union. In the future they would be equipped with the self-assurance of power and a rigid methodology for fighting the enemy, with a new strongman at the helm, who even after the turning point of 1956 made no secret of his personal admiration for the profaned dictator Stalin, despite—or precisely because of—his atrocities. Thus in the Ministry for State Security the spirit of Stalin survived like nowhere else in the GDR.

Chapter 2

THE SAFEST GDR IN THE WORLD

The Driving Forces of Stasi Growth

Forty Years of Expansion—Staff and Budget Figures

In its first developmental phase, the Ministry for State Security took on and fulfilled the classic functions of a political secret police and intelligence service. The impulses of these early years, the high phase of Stalinism, the image of the enemy as omnipresent imperialist forces threatening with encirclement, the theory of a constant "intensification of class warfare" under the dictatorship of the proletariat, the formation of a stable base of cadre with Chekist ruthlessness, and an elitist self-understanding—all of this had a lasting impact.

Yet the Stasi apparatus acquired a new quality in the late 1950s and early 1960s. It developed into a widely ramified, barely transparent security bureaucracy with manifold tasks, an enormous staff, and a network of informers, spies, and agents unparalleled in history. Even for a Communist secret-police force this development was not inevitable, as seen by a glance over the fence. In Poland, for instance, the Służba Bezpieczeństwa, or "Bezpieka," had already passed its peak as a violent agent of transformation by the mid-1950s and never again regained its former size or status—not even in the early 1980s, with the emergence of the Solidarity movement and the imposition of martial law. Even the Soviet KGB, the mother of all Communist secret-police organizations, with its approximately 500,000 employees at the end, had a considerably lower ratio of agents in proportion to the overall population.

With nearly 17,000 employees, the MfS was not exactly small even at the end of the Wollweber era. Its expansion, however, was only just beginning. In rough terms, East German State Security doubled its staff each decade until the early 1980s. In 1961, the year the Berlin Wall was erected, it had around 20,000 employees; in 1971, when Honecker advanced to the position of first secretary of the SED Central Committee, it had more than 45,500; in 1982, in the midst of the Polish crisis and against the backdrop of the GDR's growing foreign debt, it had about 81,500. Its growth decreased considerably thereafter. In late October 1989, as the personnel planners in the Main Department for Cadre and Training (Hauptabteilung Kader und Schulung) began to tally the figures for the last time under normal conditions, the Ministry for State Security had exactly 91,015 employees. This figure comprised 71,233 regular employees (career officers and career noncommissioned officers), 2,232 officers on special assignment, 2,118 full-time informers ("unofficial collaborators"), 143 so-called "unknown officers," 185 civilian employees, 13,073 regular soldiers (*Zeitsoldaten*), and 2,031 employees on temporary leave. This meant that there was one MfS employee for every 180 East German citizens—a truly exorbitant figure. In the Soviet Union the ratio was 1 to 595, in Czechoslovakia 1 to 867, and in Poland 1 to 1,574.[1]

The highest growth rates were between 1968 and 1982. It was during the year of the Prague Spring that the annual increase first surpassed the mark of 3,500 additional employees set in 1952. The annual average during this phase was 3,239; the highest number was in 1973, with 3,921 new employees. In terms of the budget, as of 1966 annual growth was consistently over 15 percent, achieving an initial highpoint in 1969, with an additional 241 million marks. Subsequent annual growth rates were generally more than 100 million marks, and between 1976 and 1978, as well as in 1981, exceeded the 200 million threshold again. The only ever budget cut was in 1983, with a reduction of 25 million marks of state funding. Shortly afterward, in 1985, the final peak was reached, with a growth in expenditures of 322 million marks. In 1989, budget expenses were 4.195 billion marks, of which 2.355 billion marks were payroll costs for full-time staff. Though surely not the decisive factor in the collapse of the East German state budget—the army and a socially motivated policy of state subsidies on basic foodstuffs, rents, etc. were considerably more of a burden—the GDR's "defense and security organ" was nonetheless an enormous self-imposed burden.

Was there an unwritten "law of perpetual Chekist prosperity" that blessed State Security with these enormous institutional resources? If so, what was its content? A plethora of theories emerged after 1990, when the true extent of the MfS apparatus became known and the first figures were released concerning the massive expansion of the "long 1970s." Armin Mitter and Stefan Wolle, in their weighty general account of the "downfall in installments" of the GDR, maintained that the Stasi had been expanded in direct response to acute system crises (the June uprising in 1953, construction of the Berlin Wall in 1961, the Prague Spring in 1968). A decisive reorganization of the MfS apparatus in July and August 1953 was merely followed by its "continual refinement."[2] So did the apparatus never really change its ways but simply expand its operations? A counterthesis was offered by Klaus-Dietmar Henke, Clemens Vollnhals, and Roger Engelmann. According to them, the MfS developed a "historically new form of exercising power [*Herrschaftsausübung*]" during the Honecker era which, apart from performing the classic function of repression as a secret-police apparatus, gave rise to a hitherto unknown "extensive covert steering and manipulation function."[3] State Security therefore may have become so bloated because it assumed ever new functions in society, down to the level of families and friends, helping in this capacity to offset built-in systemic deficits through covert techniques of intervention. This would indeed mark a new, quasi-Orwellian quality, having left behind the primitive, violent methods of the 1950s and the period before and created a new dimension of totalitarianism quite different than Nazi genocide.

This totalitarian *Vervollkommnung*—the "perfectioning," in GDR terminology—of the system of rule had a defensive aspect as well. Could it not be possible, asked Engelmann, that the increased personnel outlays of the 1970s were a direct response to the policy of détente? The concessions made in the international and inter-German sphere had made it harder for the SED to react to resistance in the population with overt repression, for fear of negative headlines in the Western media and possible deadlocks in negotiations. Hesitant to put their power at risk, they took great pains to keep the internal situation under control by means of less visible surveillance and discipline. "There is an obvious connection between these covert—and much more labor-intensive—forms of fighting the opposition and the increasing personnel outlays of the 1970s and early 1980s."[4]

Hypotheses like this take a certain inherent efficiency of the MfS for granted. They claim that its supposedly "refined" methods made the MfS particularly effective in propping up SED rule, helping to keep the system alive in a better way than with the use of overt repression. But the huge staff of the MfS can also be interpreted the other way around: as the expression of a hypertrophied security bureaucracy run totally off the rails, of an increasingly self-absorbed entity that could no longer deal with the mountains of information it produced. From this perspective, the inflationary costs of the apparatus not only ruined the GDR, but the apparatus actually killed itself—choked to death, so to speak. One argument supporting this hypothesis is the fact that there was "no correlation whatsoever between the size of the MfS and the size of the opposition."[5]

The argumentative sweep of these theories alone shows that there is more at stake here than a simple explanation for the increase in personnel, that is to say, the question of State Security's role in Honecker's GDR in the first place. Thus while these theories figure prominently in the following chapters, they will first be examined in relation to the driving forces and mechanisms of MfS personnel development.

The reconstruction of staff data was hardly complete when researchers began to posit the first hypotheses. Only later did some basic trends essential to carrying on a discussion become evident. The first finding was that the Stasi grew not only during the 1970s and 1980s but throughout the whole forty years of its existence, save for the brief episode, outlined above, under Wollweber in 1956–57. A second finding revealed that it consistently grew in all of its parts: in the various specialist branches, its headquarters, and the regional and district offices. The exceptions here are the few units that were drastically downsized or shut down entirely: Department VI in the early 1960s, for example, responsible among other things for the GDR's short-lived aeronautical industry, or the separate administration for Wismut, the Soviet-German uranium-mining company, in 1982. The third important aspect, which has yet to be fully explained, is that the strongest period of growth really began in the 1960s and came to an end in the 1980s.

The Battle Against "Political-Ideological Diversion"— The Security Doctrine of Post-Stalinism

With the abrupt end of de-Stalinization, Erich Mielke—officially appointed minister in November 1957, but for all intents and purposes the actual head of the MfS in the preceding weeks and months as well—went about reorganizing the apparatus. He rescinded the employment moratorium imposed by Wollweber and encouraged his main department and regional administration heads to quickly make up for the personnel development neglected in the last two years. A new staff plan was drawn up and took effect in 1959. The plan contained a staff expansion of 3,643 employees—a 25 percent increase compared to the previous plan. Almost as many additional employees, exactly 3,521, were hired by the MfS in the first three years after the change of minister in 1956. The 20,000 mark had nearly been reached by 1961, not including the 4,395 men in the guards regiment, almost twice as many as in 1956.

The expansion strategies were an immediate reaction to de-Stalinization: compensation for the period of insecurity it caused and, in the case of the guards regiment, the establishment of a new system for defending against internal disturbances after the experiences of the Hungarian revolution and its suppression. At the same time Mielke began to reformulate the struggle of the SED Central Committee against "revisionism" into a strategy of its own. He made "political-ideological diversion" the key component of the MfS's concept of the enemy, even giving it its own acronym: PID. Unlike direct acts of espionage and sabotage by enemy organizations of the West carried out by their agents in the GDR, which might traditionally be termed acts of subversion, the SED and MfS used the specifically East German term "political-ideological diversion" to denote the covert weakening or "softening up" (*Aufweichung*) of the GDR population in general, and SED membership ranks in particular, through nonconformist ideas.

It was no coincidence that this new accent was set at this particular moment. De-Stalinization had allowed a variety of anti-Stalinist concepts of "Third Way" socialism to emerge among Party intellectuals who were now being attacked as "revisionist" and "opportunist." The imperialist strategy, or so the thrust of PID theory, aimed at promoting such currents on the sly through covert intellectual influences, thereby stabbing socialism in the back.

What began as the reaction to an immediate crisis developed into the key guiding principle of the surveillance state and the lifeblood of the MfS's existence, for there was certainly no lack of Western ideas in the GDR, with or without secret agents. Mielke turned this into an ambitious agenda of secret-police presence in all areas of life, detecting and combating deviant thoughts and actions, even those of subjectively loyal East German citizens.

None of which means that State Security neglected its original mission. The collectivization of agriculture, the growing number of escapees to the West (known in MfS jargon as "human trafficking") and, finally—the latest focus of persecution—the countless protests against the construction of the Berlin Wall in August 1961 all called for the MfS to function in its classic role as a secret police. Though the number of political prisoners did not reach the levels of 1956, there were still about 6,000 in the summer of 1961, a figure that skyrocketed in the second half of the year. In the three weeks following the erection of the Wall, a steady "supply of arrests" (*Zuführungen*) was made by the People's Police and State Security, 6,041 of them by 4 September. Half of those arrested were taken into pretrial custody. By the end of the year there were more than 18,000 convictions for "state crimes." The MfS's aim after the erection of the Berlin Wall was the "fastest possible liquidation of all enemy bases."[6]

But the MfS was on the road to undermining its own legitimacy, because if closing the border in Berlin had really and fundamentally improved the security situation of the GDR, it would have made sense to appreciably downsize the costly control apparatus behind the Wall. The MfS reacted to this situation with some curious arguments, claiming that by building the Wall many hostile elements could no longer leave the GDR and would therefore strengthen the "political underground." Another argument asserted that with the usual and well-known channels of contact and influence through Berlin now blocked, increased efforts were required to sniff out and foil the enemy's attempts to set up new contacts and networks.

But the MfS was already making sure it had another leg to stand on. As early as 1960, Mielke had wanted to make his ministry into a kind of chief controlling body for the state and economic apparatus. The move was triggered by a coordination and control group set up in the Council of Ministers under its chairman Willi Stoph, in which undercover MfS agents were to monitor the state apparatus. The minister told the inner circle of MfS leaders: "No other organ in the GDR has such an opportunity to support the Party, to help it and give it advice as to where it needs to tackle problems and which methods to use in doing so."[7] Whether problems with spring planting or the frontier police, concerns about the number of sick employees or the warehousing practices of state-owned enterprises, cost reduction at construction sites or the communication system of the People's Police—the MfS always had something to report and was able to make its influence felt.

At first glance, these additional responsibilities were only indirectly related to fighting the enemy in the conventional sense: if the deficiencies were caused by enemy activities, remedying them was the job of State Security anyway; if the problems had other causes, the MfS had a new field of activity where it could bring to bear its apparent strengths—its own covert information network, for example, and its ability to keep a low profile in the event of sensitive issues.

On the other hand, many of the problems it uncovered were caused by objective factors which required specialists to solve them or that were the direct result of system defects in the planned economy. The MfS lacked both the technical knowledge and the will to critically analyze the system in order to really be of any help here. Instead it followed the conventional pattern of trying to trace back any problem to the hidden influence of the enemy. If no evidence could be found of deliberate sabotage by Western agents, the theory of "political-ideological diversion" could always be called upon, tracing the source of the problem back to inscrutable intellectual influences.

This agenda of all-round responsibility did not meet with the general approval of the Party leadership to start with, and was seriously questioned after the Wall went up. In December 1961, Mielke had to curb the wave of arrests. A large number of the recently condemned political "offenders" were soon released, and Mielke announced before his ministry's top brass: "It is not possible to keep up the present high number of arrests."[8] Enemy activity had to henceforth be fought with other means. The minister also used the opportunity to promote his new universal interventionist policy. Until then State Security had offered "good and useful suggestions" for the work of the state apparatus; now it was time to go over to "the control and implementation of these suggestions."[9]

An important, perhaps decisive, factor for the new reservedness of its methods of persecution was the Twenty-Second Party Congress of the CPSU in November 1961, which unleashed a second wave of de-Stalinization in the Soviet Union. The "democratic" or "socialist rule of law [*Gesetzlichkeit*]"—that is to say, a stronger regard for the written criminal law and criminal trial law and a generally more lenient treatment of prisoners—received more attention, and the cultural world of the USSR could now address such topics as Stalinist terror in works like Solzhenitsyn's *One Day in the Life of Ivan Denisovich*.

In the GDR this course corresponded to the discourse on a "socialist human community" (*sozialistische Menschengemeinschaft*) and the attempts of longtime dictator Ulbricht to recast Party policy along new lines, with economic reforms and new initiatives in youth policy. The chairman of the Central SED Party Control Commission, Hermann Matern, one of Ulbricht's most trusted confidants and a longtime partner of the MfS in inner-Party purges, formulated the consequences for East German State Security at an internal MfS conference in December 1962. He relied on a voluminous, unsigned paper, presumably from the Central Committee's Security Issues Department. Matern likewise demanded that the MfS adhere to the laws. The Central Committee paper had called for the MfS to abstain from using illegal methods during arrests, house searches, and interrogations. Matern seconded this: state prosecutors had to finally live up to their oversight functions vis-à-vis the investigating bodies, whereas the MfS, for its part, in effect had to monitor state prosecutors. "Extraordinary" methods had to be abandoned, he said, because they were no longer necessary under the new social reality.

Matern was by no means talking about dissolving State Security, for it was still supposed to uncover and liquidate real enemy activities. But he did criticize Mielke's agenda of general control. The MfS should not be putting a large circle of citizens under surveillance, he said, just as it should not be trying to influence the state and economic apparatus. Its main task was to fight those who were organizing state crimes against the GDR out of hostility to the state.

> A number of comrades need to change some things about their way of thinking, their ideology. These comrades think that the organs of State Security have a privileged position compared to all the other state organs, that they are not a part of the state apparatus but are themselves an organ of the Party. This is wrong. State Security is a centrally governed state organ, a part of the state apparatus which is given clearly defined tasks by the Party and government.[10]

MfS comrades were taken aback. The traditional "shield and sword" an ordinary part of the state apparatus? The "knights of the revolution" an administrative employee bound by the law? Mielke openly heckled the speaker. Others apparently didn't know whose lead to follow and refused outright to discuss the issues addressed by Matern, as noted in the conference report of the Security Issues Department.

The conflict was no longer restricted to the dais at this point in time. The National Defense Council of the GDR had already caused a stir in September when it decided to make considerable cuts in the budgets of the armed forces. The move was intended to relieve the economy in order to ease the planned reform of the system of planning and management announced at the Sixth Party Congress in 1963. It also confirmed the argument that the erection of the Berlin Wall had helped lower expenses for internal and external security. The three ministers for national defense, state security, and the interior were given two weeks to make suggestions on how to reduce their budgets.

Mielke followed the new line at first. He pointed out to his regional bosses that imperialism had to be defeated in the "material sphere," through increases in productivity and the accompanying improvement in overall living conditions. The MfS, too, had to save on materials and personnel now that "the Republic" had "consolidated" itself; it also had to "seriously reconsider its structure and working methods." His list of recommendations was long. Tasks such as fire prevention were to be handed over to the respective bodies, and situation reports were to concentrate on security issues. He even put the entire Line VII up for negotiation, whose task it was to "secure" the People's Police and other institutions of internal administration, which for their part were supposed to provide for order and security in the country:

> Is it necessary to have an apparatus to keep tabs on the People's Police? Does it not make sense to solve security tasks with the help of the People's Police in such a way that it lightens our workload, that another apparatus is not needed to secure it?[11]

As a sign of the new importance of the economy, full-time employees of district offices and factory units (*Objektdienststellen*) could be demoted to the rank of "secret main informers" (the precursors of full-time unofficial collaborators) and transferred directly to the respective plants. The officers on special assignment were to concentrate on combating spies and underground movements instead of the widely scattered assignments they had just undertaken, whereas incompetent and older employees were to be dismissed or retired from the force. The minister also wanted to trim down midlevel positions of the hierarchy, the division and department heads, along with countless deputies.

Mielke's listeners probably suspected that his words, though drastic-sounding, were not really meant that way. The directors of the regional administrations immediately indicated that they saw no margin of maneuver for cutting costs, because a "strict standard" had always been applied to the staff plan and additional tasks were waiting. In secret, the minister seems to have agreed. He told his regional "princes" that they should not breathe a word about the planned austerity measures upon returning to their work, that instead they should take time to think it over. As it soon turned out, Mielke was right in not abandoning hope that his empire, still in the process of being built up, would be spared these unreasonable demands to downsize.

Whereas the Ministries of the Interior and Defense had to accept some massive cuts following the Defense Council's decision, State Security went untouched. The MfS was in a good position for this. It was still relatively small, and with a state subsidy of 431 million marks it utilized less than 10 percent of the total (1962) security budget of 4.9 billion marks. The two other ministries, in other words, had much more fat to cut. The Ministry of Defense had to slash 232 million marks from its budget in the two subsequent years, and the Ministry of the Interior lost a total of 499 million marks between 1962 and 1964, nearly a third of its state funding.

Mielke needed all of 1963 to loosen his ministry's belt. Its state subsidy increased by only 3 million marks, to 434 million that year, and its staff was expanded by a mere 35 employees. It is unknown what arguments Mielke used to persuade decision-makers in the Defense Council.

The tables turned, in any case, in 1964. Staff and budget were beefed up considerably, offsetting almost completely the scarcity of the year before. The MfS received 52 million marks more from the state (a 12 percent increase), and it hired an additional 2,700 employees (an 11 percent increase). Added to this was the change in atmosphere: In 1964–65 the SED broke off its brief phase of liberal social policy in the GDR when influential representatives of the Party and security apparatus in the Soviet Union ousted Khrushchev and put Party conservative Leonid Brezhnev in power.

For the MfS this meant that the constant state of insecurity since late 1961 was over. In the long run it became apparent that Erich Mielke had succeeded in 1962–63 in setting the course for the Stasi's rapid growth, as well as divorcing it from the institutional development of the other armed organs and the state apparatus in general. The apparatus grew relentlessly in the following years, developing in terms of personnel and budget into the third, independent pillar of East German state security, alongside the police and the army.

There are a number of indications, though, that at this point in time a new coalition of interests had already formed between the Party apparatus under the leadership of Erich Honecker and the secret-police apparatus under Erich Mielke. Both organizations were reluctant to accept the plans for economic and social reform that Ulbricht initiated during this phase. The security apparatus apparently played a key role in the run-up to the so-called "clean sweep" (Kahlschlag) plenary of the Central Committee in 1965, cooperating with the Party apparatus and arming reform opponents with its portrayals of teenage hooliganism (Rowdytum). Honecker was instrumental here too as Central Committee secretary for security issues and secretary of the National Defense Council. It is hard to say when exactly he began to see Erich Mielke less as a rival for the favor of Party patriarch Ulbricht and more as a partner and fellow climber. The subsequent relationship between these two most important representatives of conservative post-Stalinism was forged during this period, at any rate.

Its bureaucratic superstructure was the main benefactor of MfS growth, particularly the ministry's Berlin headquarters and its Main Department for Cadre and Training, whereas regional administrations and district offices developed disproportionately less. Personnel-intensive tasks not specifically related to the responsibilities of a secret police and secret service also gained in importance. The Main Department for Personal Security (Hauptabteilung Personenschutz) tripled its size to more than 1,600 employees by late 1967. This department, moreover, was well on its way to becoming much more than a bodyguard. With the construction of the Politbüro compound in Wandlitz, it took on the role of an all-round service provider for the top brass of the SED. By ensuring them a pleasant lifestyle, it effectively made itself indispensable to these functionaries and their families—an approach very much in line with Mielke's style of politics.

Another powerful sideline was added to the ministry in 1962, when passport control at border checkpoints was taken over by the MfS. In Berlin alone more than 1,100 people were employed in this line, not to mention the passport inspectors at the other border crossings. Both of these new activities are symptomatic of the diversification of the MfS's range of security duties.

The fastest-growing of the classic units were Main Departments VIII and IX—that is to say, the cross-functional branches for arrests, observation, etc., as well as for criminal investigations. This goes to show that, for all the new functions it acquired, State Security did not slacken in its classic role as an organ of repression, that indeed it redoubled its efforts to gather "evidence" and launch investigations to make sure its targets were punished. The mere extraction of confessions was no longer sufficient.

The heightened attention paid by Party leaders to problems of economic efficiency prompted State Security to react by expanding its network of security officers in factories, most of whom worked as unofficial collaborators. Their hunt for hostile activities in the manufacturing sector gave them the opportunity to intervene in many aspects of factory management. More than 450 of these security officers in the Inspection Department of the Council of Ministers, as well as in the ministries of industry and the Association of State-Owned Enterprises and Combines (VVB) were even full-time "officers on special assignment." Thus the MfS assigned extensive tasks to its core secret-police apparatus and began to expand itself into the state apparatus and economy as a guardian of general security interests.

The new, broadly defined definition of responsibilities found its semiofficial expression in the secret statute of the Ministry for State Security passed by the National Defense Council in 1969. According to this document, the activities of the MfS focused on "reconnaissance and counterintelligence for the exposure and prevention of hostile plans and intentions of the aggressive imperialist forces and their cohorts," while also serving in general to "consolidate and strengthen the socialist state," as well as to "secure the formation of the developed social system of socialism." The MfS was granted the express right to "contribute in close cooperation with the working people"—that is to say, with the help of unofficial collaborators—to the "substantial reduction and exclusion of interfering and inhibiting factors in the development of all social spheres." It was authorized to "take a stance and make suggestions" with regard to all "problems of state management affecting issues of state security."[12] The curtailment of MfS responsibilities proposed by Matern had utterly failed.

MfS leaders found an important confirmation of their expansion course in the Prague Spring of 1968. The events in Czechoslovakia made plain from their perspective the kind of uncontrollable developments that could result from domestic liberalization policies—an object lesson in "political-ideological diversion." Yet the events in Prague were not the direct trigger for a renewed expansion of staff. Indeed, preparations were already well under way in the years leading up to 1968.

Détente and Expansion

There were two driving forces to the expansion of the MfS that began in the 1960s: first, its strategic orientation as a "general enterprise for security, power maintenance, and repression"[13] with a basically unlimited scope of activity; and, second, its uncoupling from rational economic and budget criteria as limiting factors in its funding. A third impulse was added in the 1970s, when the MfS gradually assumed the role of a key guarantor of domestic political stability under the conditions of détente.

The direct initial effect of inter-German contacts on MfS personnel expansion can be seen in the microcosmos of 1960s Berlin. There, in late 1963, for the first time since the Wall went up, an agreement was reached about West Berliners visiting East Berlin. Seven such agreements on frontier-crossing permits were signed by 1966, in each case permitting short visits of a few days around Christmas, Easter, and Pentecost. More than 1.2 million people rushed to enter the eastern part of the city at the very first opportunity. Though boosting the prestige of the GDR, State Security viewed these frontier-crossing agreements as an enormous risk, fearing all kinds of enemy activities and secret-service contacts as a result. It therefore mobilized thousands of MfS employees for special assignments during the holidays in East Berlin. Shortly thereafter it established a new unit, the Working Group on Securing Tourist Travel (Arbeitsgruppe Sicherung des Reiseverkehrs), and armed itself little by little for its new field of operation.

The MfS faced similar problems when Willy Brandt, the Social Democratic federal chancellor, visited Erfurt in March 1970. It apparently underestimated the security situation. Though they did make a concerted effort to keep potential sympathizers away from the city center, the situation soon spun out of control for security forces under the command of Major-General Franz Gold, the head of the Main Department for Personal Security. Several thousand citizens of the GDR cheered on the West German head of state at Erfurter Hof hotel. The chancellor's visit turned into a debacle for the Party. The Politbüro declared that in future such events were to be safeguarded according to the rules of "inner mobilization."

What that meant would become clear at the latest in 1981, during the visit of Federal Chancellor Helmut Schmidt to Hubertusstock Castle and Güstrow. The scenario was downright eerie, with Schmidt walking across the town square of Güstrow next to Honecker, cordoned off by a thick line of uniformed men and hand-selected "passersby." No less than 34,000 members of the People's Police and the MfS were called out by the SED to quell any spontaneity. This precautionary siege took place against the backdrop of the Polish crisis. The night after Schmidt's visit to Güstrow, General Jaruzelski declared martial law in Poland.

The Stasi was able to mobilize forces in a targeted manner for such isolated occasions or for special tasks of a limited duration, thus upholding the surveillance standards of a walled-in closed society. This changed with the partial opening of the GDR in the course of the inter-German agreements of the early 1970s. From that point on, many channels of East-West contact closed since 1961 or extremely hard to use were now suddenly open. Erich Honecker explained his strategy in 1973, in an article in *Neues Deutschland*:

> We always keep two things in mind: making our contribution to détente in Europe and at the same time foiling any attempt to encroach—under whatever circumstances—upon the security and stabile development of our German Democratic Republic.[14]

Erich Mielke made himself clearer to the men inside his ministry. In November 1972, just before the signing of the Basic Treaty between the two German states, he declared at an internal conference:

All in all we are facing the difficult task of tracking down the negative political-ideological effects on a certain part of our citizenry resulting from diverse and more extensive contact opportunities.[15]

The treaties created many new contact opportunities between East and West that were considered suspicious on principle, because the West would use them, or so they feared, to "intensify its counter-revolutionary, subversive activities."[16] Total surveillance of the transit corridors from the Federal Republic to West Berlin was certainly work enough, and required enormous human resources. On top of this came the monitoring of travel in and out of the GDR. A typical case was when East German citizens traveled to the West in the case of urgent family matters. Though not many trips were permitted, given the rather narrow definition of "urgent," they nevertheless constituted a sore spot for the MfS's preventive security doctrine, as travel requests in the event of a death or serious illness in the family could naturally only be made and granted on short notice. In any case, there was a large number of East German citizens who could have potentially applied for a travel permit, since many had relatives in the other Germany. There was simply not enough time for lengthy routine inquiries and controls if the applications were to be taken seriously. Mielke therefore gave orders that the MfS was to know about such travel plans "prior to the police application and approval procedure" in order to conduct the preliminary investigations it considered necessary. The only real way to achieve this was to keep all East German citizens with Western relatives under constant surveillance in their day-to-day lives through intensive mail and telephone monitoring and unofficial collaborators.

Considerably more numerous were the trips made by West Germans and West Berliners to the GDR. In this case it was possible to screen the applicants during the visa-issuing procedure but not to keep them under total surveillance during the actual visit. Thus the minimum Mielke demanded from his people was that all West German visitors and East German hosts of "politically operational" significance be kept under "operational control," along with all "concentration points," as popular travel destinations were referred to in MfS jargon. "We are well aware that the organization of operational controls of these groups of people poses complicated problems for our operational units due to their diversity and considerable size."[17]

The travel figures illustrate the enormity of its new tasks. Private trips to the West were still a rarity: from 1973 to 1982 about 40,000 East German citizens a year traveled to the "class enemy." Given the preventive investigations ordered, the MfS had a colossal task in this domain alone. Added to this were about one and a half million pensioner and business trips a year. But it was the other direction that was really an open field. Between 1972 and 1982 there was an average of five million visitors to the GDR annually, an almost equal share from West Germany and West Berlin.

The international recognition accompanying the German treaties was the GDR's greatest foreign-policy achievement. The concessions this entailed, however, were a considerable burden to the MfS and challenged the surveillance standard achieved by it to date. Mielke therefore endeavored to find the "correct" interpretation of these negotiations with the "imperialist class enemy." They were part of a "tough class struggle" marked by diverging interests.[18] Many employees directly suffered from this development, being transferred, for example, to less attractive border areas under extremely makeshift conditions in order to bolster passport-control units.

In institutional terms, however, the Stasi was not in the worst of positions as a result of the treaties. Dealing with the hidden consequences of them was the task of all State Security units, Mielke repeatedly emphasized. And again it was Stasi headquarters that grew the most: with 55.1 percent of all State Security employees in 1982, it had the highest share in the whole apparatus in the entire history of the MfS. The personnel administration department at MfS headquarters quintupled between 1968 and 1982—an autogenerative effect, but also a reaction to détente, because its own employees now had to be more strictly controlled and shielded from Western contacts. The large "operational" branches grew too, above all Main Department II, whose nominal responsibility for "counterespionage" (*Spionageabwehr*) now included the surveillance of numerous new Western diplomatic missions and newly accredited Western journalists.

The classic secret-service task of defending against foreign-intelligence attacks became blurred with the function of general surveillance, as employees of the classic counterespionage branch were also supposed to monitor all contacts between these (predominantly West German) foreigners and East German citizens. In 1982, 1,746 employees were working at main headquarters in the counterintelligence line—well more than twice as many than in 1968. Other important branches (the so-called "lines") of the overall preventive surveillance strategy grew less vigorously but still had a good-sized staff in 1982: Line XX (state apparatus, culture, opposition, churches) with 1,271 employees, as well as Line XVIII (economy) and Line XIX (transportation, infrastructure), with a total of 2,143. Another 8,764 MfS employees at district offices and factory units were responsible for local surveillance.

In purely numerical terms, however, the biggest division was Line VI, with 7,123 employees. Line VI conducted passport controls and "secured" the entire tourist traffic of the GDR. At first glance this branch took on routine border-police duties, but its mission was highly symbolic, combating as it did the most significant threat to the "state security" of the GDR: "the policy of imperialist contacts" along the frontier of divided Germany.

The process of détente reached its peak in the second half of the 1970s with the Conference on Security and Cooperation in Europe (CSCE) and the signing of the Final Act of the Helsinki Accords in August 1975. The GDR basked in its international recognition—and paid the price in the form of concessions that would preoccupy it until its final days. In the years to come, more and more East Germans would appeal to the basic human rights and liberties set down in the accords, especially "freedom of movement" (*Freizügigkeit*)—the right to leave one's own country temporarily or permanently. The number of "applicants for permanent emigration" citing the CSCE Final Act as their authority grew appreciably. These would-be emigrants increasingly banded together and made their demand public. The emigration movement was beginning to form.

State Security understood the fight against the emigration movement as the job of all its units, as applicants came from all "security areas," but reacted by expanding the organization even more. Coordination groups at headquarters in Berlin and at the regional level recently formed to fight *Republikflucht*, or "flight from the Republic" (i.e., escape to the West), took on the additional task.

MfS leaders drew up a three-stage program. Since the phenomenon of *Republikflucht* was considered to be the work of the West, top priority was given to the fight against its supporters in the Federal Republic—the anti-Communist emigration organization "International Society for Human Rights," for instance. Second, the applicants were to be thoroughly "scouted out" (*aufgeklärt*) to determine their motives and find ways of getting them to abandon their plans. Third, all potential applicants were to be identified and investigated before they took the decisive step that would plunge them into social isolation. This required more personnel.

It would be an exaggeration to claim that the policy of détente prompted MfS expansion. The course was already set by virtue of the fragile power base of SED socialism in "half a country," which for all the Party's efforts to establish a more consensual mode of rule was ultimately only tenable by means of repression. This basic setup paved the way for the MfS to establish a position of power and influence unique even in the socialist bloc. These conditions would have persisted even without détente. But the Western policy of "change through rapprochement" (*Wandel durch Annäherung*) did help undermine the SED's policy of isolationism and (re)awaken the presumably predominant Western orientation of East German citizens. In this sense it struck the nerve of the SED's security doctrine and played a part in Honecker and Mielke carrying MfS personnel expansion to unheard-of extremes.

The law of perpetual Chekist prosperity—that is to say, the certain expectation of a continually growing and ever more influential internal security apparatus—was thus based on the assumption that the GDR could only hold its own in the inter-German system conflict by constantly redoubling its efforts to control and fight the influence of the West on the East by means of its secret police. The retrospective ironic remark of one MfS officer that Mielke's ideal of a socialist society would be achieved when every East German citizen was working for the Stasi as a full-time employee or informer reflects the hypothetical target of this "inevitable" development. The MfS came to occupy an extremely strong position in the course of the 1970s, which seemed to ensure an almost automatic growth of personnel.

By the early 1980s, however, this notion of absolute security had reached it rational economic limits. The GDR had lived beyond its means, invested too little and too inefficiently, while channeling too many resources into consumption, the social system, and, of course, its State Security apparatus. The reduction of oil supplies from the Soviet Union and the resultant loss in hard-currency revenues for the GDR, as well as the credit boycott by Western lenders due to the de facto insolvency of Poland and Romania, put the GDR's state finances in dire straits.

By 25 January 1983 the financial crisis had reached the Ministry for State Security. It was clear that the MfS had to economize. The minister sent a formal memorandum to the directors of his units instructing them as follows: "The number of employees may, as a matter of principle, not be exceeded as of February 28, 1983." The "Guidelines on Expanding the Volume of Permanent Posts for 1983–1985" valid to date were thereby rendered obsolete. Mielke explained to his leading cadre-administration officers:

> In recent years the MfS, too, has had to face inevitable reductions in planned material and financial resources. Further reductions are to be

expected. This will naturally affect the future handling and development of salary and bonus funds, the provision of office space, apartments, accommodations, and other social benefits.[19]

The first and only budget cut was in 1983, with a reduction of 25 million marks of state funding. Given the overall budget of nearly 3 billion marks, this was a minimal but nonetheless symbolic cutback.

The ensuing years were marked by contradiction. The symptoms of crisis in the GDR were mounting; the emigration movement and internal opposition were beginning to develop—hence State Security really did experience the oft-invoked "increase in tasks."

At the same time, however, they were to work more efficiently and avoid overlapping authorities. In April 1983 the MfS cadre chief came to the conclusion that "nothing essential for performing the security duties of the MfS can be rationalized out of existence."[20]

Thus while there was some reshuffling and a certain downsizing of the central bureaucracy in favor of the district offices, which bore the brunt of day-to-day responsibilities, there was never a real reduction in staff with any attendant cutback in personnel costs. The pressure to cut costs slackened in the following years, and there were once again budget increases into the hundreds of millions.

The last rise in the old manner occurred in 1985, with State Security's budget allocation increasing by 251 million marks—apparently a direct result of the billion-mark loans from the Federal Republic brokered in 1984 by West German politician Franz Josef Strauss. The money not only allowed for the recruiting of another 1,600 employees, it also helped finance a substantial hike in salaries, with Honecker's personal stamp of approval. But the "golden years" were a thing of the past, and overall growth rates lagged considerably. Personnel statistics registered a net loss of 23 employees in 1987 and 297 in 1988.

"Shield and Sword of the Party" or "State Within a State"? The MfS Apparatus and Its Institutional Position in the GDR

When the intellectual "clean-up work" began in 1990, after the revolution of the previous fall, it was the longtime "crown prince" and SED general secretary during the *Wende* period, Egon Krenz, who coined the phrase "state within a state" to describe the MfS. The term was his attempt to eschew responsibility for the security apparatus and its outgrowths—and this from a man who since 1983 had been secretary for security issues in the apparatus of the Central Committee of the SED, the seat of power of the East German state, responsible for political oversight of the GDR's armed forces. At the Round Table talks he complained about his powerlessness:

> In reality the Ministry for State Security increasingly developed into a state within a state, shielded from the outside world and which even kept Party members under control. . . . Questions of state security and the concrete operational work of the Ministry for State Security, with the exception of cadre decisions and investments, were essentially discussed and decided by the chairman of the National Defense Council and the minister for state security, in violation of all democratic principles. . . . The conclusions or so-called "central decisions" reached in the discussions between the chairman of the National Defense Council and the minister for state security were then passed on to those responsible for carrying them out.[21]

Erich Honecker himself later agreed that this description aptly depicted the role of the MfS. In contrast to Krenz's version, though, he maintained that as chairman of the National Defense Council he had had little insight into the inner workings of the apparatus and had relied entirely on the information provided to him by Mielke, who withheld the most vital information from him, he claimed:

> I have to say I highly value the activities of the Ministry for State Security. They were responsible comrades. But to develop such an all-encompassing [*flächenweit*] system of the kind that has become apparent now, this contradicted every decision of the Politbüro and the National Defense Council with regard to full-time and volunteer workers and can only be explained, in my opinion, as the attempt to develop a state within a state modeled after the Cheka. . . . This was endemic to the tradition of the state-security system in the socialist countries.[22]

Erich Mielke wouldn't hear of it. Sitting in prison in Berlin-Moabit, awaiting trial for the murder of two policemen in 1931, he stated for the record his version of the relationship between Party leaders and the ministry:

> The image of shield and sword of the Party is not a mere ideal. The MfS was under the Party's control until the very end. We were accountable to the general secretary, the National Defense Council, and the Council of Ministers. . . . Honecker was informed of the number of full-time employees. He also received the figures for the Viennese negotiations on conventional disarmament. It may be that he did not know the exact figures regarding the number of unofficial collaborators. But in prin-

ciple here, too, he knew the extent of the ministry's activities. It was even like this: when something in the country happened which aroused the General Secretary's disapproval, he would say: And State Security didn't report anything either. . . . It did not exist independently. The MfS was not a state within a state.[23]

To be sure, behind these thinly veiled attempts to evade responsibility are some central questions regarding the role and function of the secret-police forces in state-socialist systems. How independent was an apparatus like the Stasi in its institutional position, and which internal dynamics could it develop? How strongly did the monolithic, totalitarian state structure bind the executive apparatus of the Communist Party? And how serious can its self-fashioning as the "shield and sword of the Party," as the unconditional bodyguard of the Party leadership, be taken?

The preceding analyses of personnel growth have shown that the real development of the MfS cannot be reduced to one extreme of the debate or another. The ministry never questioned the leading political role of the SED. In that respect it really was the "shield and sword of the Party" and remained so throughout its existence. At the same time, however, some essential processes within the apparatus were largely insulated against external influences, thus exhibiting features of a state within a state. So was State Security both in one?

The experiences of other totalitarian dictatorships show that behind the centralized and hierarchical communication and decision-making structures, apparently so clearly ordered by way of Party or dictators' decrees, lurked considerably more complex processes and structures. Under National Socialism there was a polycratic jumble of competing institutions and organizations (Wehrmacht, economy, NSDAP, SS). It was characteristic of Hitler to go long periods of time without making any clear-cut decisions or to circumvent these decisions by building new institutions.

The polycratic model is irrelevant to the debate about the GDR, however, and this for one simple reason: the almost antithetical historical origins of the two systems. The Nazi polycracy rested on the mixed power base of the system—on the one hand the National Socialist movement, represented by the NSDAP itself, as well as the SA and, later, the SS with the security apparatus under its control; on the other hand the traditional elites, especially in the Wehrmacht and the economy, who allied themselves with the Führer state. There was no such diverse power base in the GDR. Rather, as a product of the Soviet occupying authority it founded its system on a power monopoly pushed through by a "revolution from above." Thus none of the traditional elites assumed the role of an independent pillar of social power—not least of all because they had fundamentally discredited themselves in the eyes of the new authorities on account of their role under National Socialism. At best, parts of this "old" society could continue to carry on a more or less stable existence as tradition-oriented milieus, in niches and nooks of East German society, even enjoying a privilege or two, the hard scientists and technicians so important to the economy being one such example. But they had nothing to do with the decision-making structures of the political system.

Sovietologists and peace researchers came to a different conclusion with regard to the Soviet Union as a military superpower. The USSR had a weighty military-industrial complex comprising the army, arms industry, and the attendant planning bureaucracy, and which had a strong influence on the country's arms policy. These scholars therefore talk about "interest groups" competing within the system and a shared ideological framework, and which tried to tie up as many resources for themselves as possible. Canadian political scientist H. Gordon Skilling argued in 1970:

> [I]n the seventeen years since Stalin's death the Soviet political system has been passing through a period of transition, characterized among other things by the increased activity of political interest groups and the presence of group conflict. Although decision-making in its final stage still remains in the hands of a relatively small group of leaders at the top of the party hierarchy, there has been, it is assumed, a broadening of group participation in the crucial preliminary stages of policy deliberation and in the subsequent phase of implementation.[24]

After the end of Stalinist terror, which time and again had targeted leading cadre in the Party and mass organizations, in the planning bureaucracy and state apparatus, in the army and secret police, these important pillars of the Soviet state were able to stabilize themselves internally. They had grown quite large in terms of staff and formed the core group of the socialist service class which steered the fortunes of the country as loyal functional elites. At the same time, certain sociomoral milieus sprang up which, consolidating themselves around these apparatuses, increasingly differed in their values and aims. All of the members of the socialist service class played the part of loyal Party servants, yet the particulars of this self-understanding could greatly vary. These apparatuses and milieus acted as interest groups vis-à-vis the Party leadership. They used information channels to convey news and reports that suited their interests by highlighting certain problem areas. They suggested various solutions and tossed in facts wherever they could. In effect, they were in a kind of competition when it came to deciding on a political course or allocating resources. They also formed a common sociopolitical bloc whose interests the Party leadership could not ignore. The growing significance of these apparatuses probably first became evident with the ousting of Khrushchev in 1964. Historian Manfred Hildermeier writes:

> Brezhnev and N. V. Podgorny, Central Committee secretary since 1963, were pulling the strings, and could rely on the eager assistance of KGB chief V. Y. Semichastny and his predecessor A. N. Shelepin (who had meanwhile entered the Politburo). . . . It was not incorrigible old-guard Stalinists who forced Khrushchev into retirement, but his own protégés. They were not motivated by the attempt to reestablish the dictatorship of yesteryear, but by a peculiar mixture of the old and a new mentality: a commitment to the interests of some powerful organizations the socialist state had meanwhile brought forth. . . . In some respects a legacy of Stalin had manifested itself, which for all the justifiable attention paid to terror, industrialization and totalitarian rule should not be overlooked: the enormous growth of institutions in state, economy, society, and army.[25]

The Khrushchev era and its demise thus symbolized the "transition from a personal to an institutional dictatorship,"[26] which in the Soviet Union was built on three pillars: the Party; the state and economic apparatuses (including the security service); and the army.

Compared to Stalinism prior to 1953, the power position of the secret police in this new situation was rather limited and relativized. An agency of social-revolutionary terror under Stalin directly linked to the dictator, under Khrushchev it had become one powerful institution among others, beside or behind the Party apparatus and army. On the other hand, it was much more stable than in the 1930s, and this in a double sense: the dynamics of a young generation of social climbers, which Stalin himself had profited from on his rise to power, subsided, and the unrest caused by internal purges no longer existed either.

In the opinion of Sovietologist Frederick C. Barghoorn, the KGB was more strongly identified with the system than any of the other apparatuses in the 1960s and 1970s: its personnel had "their own vested interests in the maintenance and growth of Soviet authority" on account of "what must be an acute sense that they might well be the prime targets of any successful revolution against the political order they have served loyally and harshly."[27] It therefore reacted ultracritically to potential attempts at "liberalization" and rapprochement with the West—not least of all as this jeopardized their material privileges.

The inner workings of the KGB and its role in the decision-making processes of the state and Party leadership were necessarily a kind of empirical black box at the time of Barghoorn's analysis in the early 1970s. The obvious parallels to East German State Security in the take-off phase of the 1960s and the heyday of the 1970s are therefore all the more remarkable. In the GDR, however, the military-industrial complex had nowhere near the same importance as it did for a military superpower like the USSR with its highly developed and extremely costly strategic nuclear weapons. Whereas about 8 percent of national income was used for internal and external security in the GDR, in the Soviet Union the same figure was a staggering 30 percent.

From this perspective, the conflicts of the 1960s can be interpreted as a crisis of institutionalization in which the "conservative" coalition of interests between the Party apparatus represented by Erich Honecker and Mielke's security apparatus replaced the more personal relationship between Ulbricht and his loyal pupil Mielke. However controversial Ulbricht's personal role in the reform discussions of the 1960s may be, it is rather clear that the Party apparatus and the MfS used their information policy to dramatize the potential consequences of a more liberal youth and cultural policy, effectively torpedoing it with their horror scenarios of waywardness and "beat" decadence.

The improved institutional situation with the transition of power from Ulbricht to Honecker was reflected in the personal advancement of Mielke. Following the example of the Soviet KGB chairman, Yuri Andropov, the minister for state security climbed to the rank of SED Politbüro candidate in 1971, and in 1976 to full membership. In mystery-shrouded tête-à-têtes after the weekly Politbüro meetings, the minister informed the general secretary about the security situation and received instructions. The close cooperation between the two men was not based on any personal affinity but on coinciding interests and a shared, security-centered view of the world. Deputy Colonel-General Markus Wolf was probably not far off the mark when he characterized them as "hostile brothers"[28] who had teamed up at the right time.

State Security's stronger position resulted in several potential avenues of influence of a lobbyist nature. It had a substantial influence in drawing up the political line. Though it didn't have a say in every matter, as soon as "security"-related issues came up the MfS was on board. With the expansion of Western contacts and the increase in applications to emigrate, it assumed the role of a "compensation agency" in ever new fields, with the task of making up for damage in the area of security policy. When in doubt, it always pleaded for the harsher option without ever seriously challenging the political course vis-à-vis the West.

Inwardly the MfS was able to accumulate enormous resources thanks to its successful pressure-group policy, putting itself in a largely unassailable position in the rivalry between apparatuses. The MfS was barely accountable to the State Planning Commission and the Finance Commission, and if need be took recourse to agreements with the general secretary.

Abundant material and financial resources as well as the development of its own branches enabled the MfS to carry out projects without the consent of regular planning organs. Thus, for instance, the MfS had its own "subsidiary" of a construction company in the 1960s, operating under the name "VEB Spezialhochbau" as of 1974. The chairman of the State Planning Commission, Gerhard Schürer, recalls the plan negotiations for the armed forces:

> The ministers for defense and security were there and had a strong position. Hoffmann and later Kessler were Politbüro members, Mielke too. Only Dickel, the minister of the interior, wasn't in it, which is why he always fared the worst, since they cut the most from his budget. . . . On the whole it was always a struggle for the greatest possible amount of resources, especially by the Ministry for State Security, because in my opinion they made the most excessive demands, which of course we found out about and tried to cut back. When this gigantic State Security building was built on Frankfurter Allee, for example, we tried to prevent something just as big or bigger from going up around Biesdorf, the regional administration of State Security. Even Honecker agreed once the shell had been erected that it should be closed down, that construction work should stop or be "rounded off," as we used to say, meaning it would be used in the state it was in. Even so, construction continued unaided. We couldn't control it, because State Security had its own construction crews and they didn't ask us.[29]

At the same time, cohesion in the State Security milieu became stronger among employees and their families. While the MfS still nominally held aloft the banner of the proletariat, the majority of the more than 40,000 members recruited between 1968 and 1982 came from the families of "workers, *honoris causa*," meaning their parents were only working class on paper and were mostly from the police, army, and State Security, or from other branches of the Party and state apparatus. This junior staff was considered loyal to the system by nature, was easy to screen, and generally did not have taboo contacts in the West. A sampling of people hired in these years revealed that 17 percent had a father working for the MfS; the police and army were represented by an additional 22 percent of parental homes; 11 percent were leading economic and administration cadre, and 7 percent Party functionaries. Only 30 percent of the new recruits were actually from working-class homes. The share of SED members was correspondingly high. The employees themselves were almost always in the Party, but even four out of five fathers and two out of five mothers of these recruits were SED comrades.

In other words, they tended to be more and more among their own kind. This created favorable conditions for preserving and cultivating the atmosphere of Chekism, both elitist and crude, that unfolded in the 1950s. Though there was a considerable professionalization in the 1960s thanks to more extensive training, the basic qualities of the Chekist milieu essentially remained intact: a worldview strongly influenced by certain concepts of the enemy coupled with an overall modest level of education and a pugnacious, anti-intellectual and antibourgeois attitude. To quote Erich Mielke: "We don't smell good, but we have a good nose." This work was honored by the Party with above-average pay and other privileges, such as the ability to purchase Western goods with East German currency.

The Stasi never overstepped its predefined role as an armed security organ of the ruling Communist Party. It subordinated itself to the will of the Party leadership, i.e., the first secretary or general secretary, and accepted the fact that the full-time Party apparatus was a no-go zone for its "operational" work. In this respect, its self-fashioning as the "shield and sword" had a kernel of truth. But within this predefined framework, of course, State Security developed into an apparatus with enormous powers and considerable sway in resource allocation and political decision-making processes.

State Security from a Comparative Perspective

The enormous size of the Ministry for State Security in absolute numbers and in relation to the GDR's population is striking. In order to gain a more nuanced picture, though, some basis for comparison is required. As a result of its successful pressure-group policy, the Stasi, as seen above, was able to take on a variety of tasks that in other countries were performed by the police, army, or civil institutions.

Characteristic of the system of internal security in the GDR, in other words, was an extreme centralization of tasks under the broad umbrella of the MfS, buttressed by a universalist security doctrine which took what seemed like quite normal state tasks, utterly devoid of a political controversy, and "Stasified" them, as it were, declaring them to be sensitive areas from a secret-police perspective.

It also duplicated many tasks of other institutions, helping to "homogenize" (*entdifferenzieren*) the social institutions of the GDR. Spheres such as law, the economy, science and research, or the maintenance of public safety and order, which had already lost their independence due to the primacy of SED policies, were saturated by the Stasi in its search for ever-present security risks traceable to enemy influences.

In 1989, Berlin headquarters alone had about sixty service units. Most branches were also represented in the regional administrations and district offices in the form of departments, divisions, or individual employees. The core secret-police tasks were handled by foreign espionage (Main Administration for Reconnaissance[30]), military counterintelligence (Main Department I, operating under the name "Administration 2000" in the National People's Army), civilian counterintelligence (Main Department II), and radio intelligence and counterintelligence (Main Department III). These branches of the service were never "pure" intelligence services, however, but also took on domestic surveillance functions. Thus military counterintelligence, for example, also kept tabs on the opinions expressed by recruits and did its best to enlist them as unofficial collaborators. After being discharged from the National People's Army they were passed on, if possible, to other units. Added to this were the units for routine tasks such as protecting secrets, cryptography, and government communications of the GDR (Central Working Group for the Protection of Secrets, Main Department XI, Department N). Finally, of particular strategic importance was the Working Group on the Area of Commercial Coordination, whose task was to safeguard and supervise the trade in weapons and embargoed goods run though the Ministry of Foreign Trade as well as the hard-currency business of MfS Colonel on Special Assignment Alexander Schalck-Golodkowski.

The core tasks as a secret police continued to play a central role under post-Stalinism. Since there was no institutional separation between intelligence service and police, the MfS itself made arrests and conducted observations (Main Department VIII), as well as criminal investigations (Main Department IX), and even had its own detention centers (Department XIV). The main "operational" load in terms of internal surveillance was with Main Departments XVIII (economy), XIX (transportation, postal services, infrastructure), and XX (state apparatus, social organizations, churches, culture, and political underground). Added to this was the Central Coordination Group for Flight and Emigration (ZKG). These surveillance offices also included Main Department VII, which controlled the entire portfolio of the Ministry of the Interior, including the People's Police. It was these branches, in particular, that had a strong "substructure" in the regions and districts.

Several service units were specialized in various forms of armed combat, mainly for war or crisis situations. These included the "Felix E. Dzerzhinsky" Guards Regiment with over 11,000 soldiers, and "terror defense" with its own special paramilitary units for sabotage and terror attacks behind enemy lines in the event of war (Main Department XXII). The Minister's Working Group (AGM) was responsible for the building of shelters and preparing mobilization. The classic policing tasks of the MfS were already detailed above: the Main Department for Personal Security, Main Department VI for passport controls and controlling tourism, and Department XVII, the visitor offices for West Berliners applying to enter the East.

All units had technical auxiliary services at their disposal in the form of telephone and postal monitoring, the Operational-Technical Sector and the Weapons/Chemical Services Department. The Central Evaluation and Information Group (ZAIG) as well as numerous other units (the secretariats of the minister and his deputies, management office, international relations department, central file archive, data processing center, legal office, central operational staff) did a variety of legwork for East German leaders. In the background loomed a massive "rearward" bureaucracy made up of service units for general administration, finances, cadre and training (including medical services and an in-house university), and SED Party organizations. Finally, the MfS provided employees for the central management office of the "Dynamo" sports club, whose offshoot, the Dynamo soccer team of Berlin, was the dread of every East German referee.

Such an accumulation of surveillance and security powers under the roof of a single secret-security apparatus was unusual even for a Communist dictatorship. The most similar in structural terms was the Soviet KGB, the role model of East German State Security in many organizational aspects. None of the other East European secret-police forces had this size or level of institutional independence, being much more strongly integrated into their respective ministries of the interior and having considerably fewer employees relative to their populations.

The peculiar accumulation of authorities in the East German secret-security apparatus makes it hard to find enough common ground to enable a system comparison with West Germany—even putting aside the more fundamental differences, i.e., that there was no comparable "Chekist" brand of loyalty to a "vanguard Party" and its revolutionary claims in the Federal Republic, and that the rule of law and the constitution there largely succeeded in circumscribing the radius of action of West German secret services. Any realistic comparison has to take into account the other, non-secret parts of the East German security apparatus. In the late 1980s there were about 218,000 full-time employees deployed in the internal-security sector of the GDR. Apart from the 91,000 MfS employees, this included nearly 80,000 people in the service of the German People's Police (including transport and riot police, but not including firefighters) and the border troops of the GDR under the aegis of the Ministry for National Defense, with a strength of approximately 47,000.[31] Thus, in purely statistical terms, there was about 1 police officer or secret-police employee per 77 East German citizens.

In the Federal Republic of Germany, by contrast, there were about 258,000 employees working in internal security in 1989. About 209,000 officers and staffers were employed by state police forces. Added to this were the federal police agencies: about 8,500 employees in the Federal Criminal Police Office (BKA) and the Railway Police. The Federal Border Guard had a staff of around 25,000, and the secret services of the Federal Republic (Office for the Protection of the Constitution, Federal Intelligence Service, and Military Counterintelligence Service) a total of about 15,500 employees. That amounts to a ratio of 1 security-staff member for every 241 West German citizens.

In other words, the personnel outlay of the GDR for internal security—relative to population—was more than three times that of the Federal Republic. What's more, a considerably smaller share of these employees in the West was assigned to national-security and secret-service tasks, which unlike in the MfS were distributed among a multitude of agencies. To take just a few examples, the federal and regional police forces of the West Germany included the not entirely quantifiable but relatively small national-security departments, various bodyguards (the Bonn Security Group, for instance), and other areas of responsibility which in the GDR were in the purview of the MfS. The Federal Border Guard supplied the passport inspectors at border crossings and the terror defense troops of Border Guard Group 9. Secret-service tasks were shared by the three intelligence services and separated by police executive authorities. However warranted it may be to criticize the noticeable tendencies among all of these institutions towards expanding their authority, as well as towards an esprit de corps and a "law and order" mentality, we are nonetheless dealing with two fundamentally different approaches to security.

Even more problematic methodologically is a comparison with the terror apparatus of National Socialism. A juxtaposition with the Gestapo confirms the MfS's enormous size. In 1937 the Gestapo had about 7,000 employees; in 1944 it had a little more than 31,000, albeit for the entire territory of the Third Reich, including its occupied areas. Two things must be kept in mind, however. First of all, the Gestapo was only one of several terror institutions of the Nazi regime. Other organs played a role in different phases and with staffs of various sizes—the storm troopers, or *Sturmabteilungen* (SA), which acted as thugs and torture squads in establishing the Nazi system and eliminating political opponents up until 1934, later the SS Security Service, or Sicherheitsdienst (SD), which acted as an intelligence service for monitoring the mood of the population, as well as various other branches of the SS and the Reich Security Main Office (Reichssicherheitshauptamt). Moreover, the Gestapo and other Nazi organs of persecution were a much more serious threat: the persecuted had to fear for their lives, either in the form of a death sentence meted out by a court or being sent into "protective custody" in a concentration camp. A strictly numerical comparison is therefore untenable.

Second, Nazi power was not only based on the special apparatuses of a prerogative state, but to a large extent on perfectly ordinary institutions inherited from the Weimar Republic. Thus the Gestapo recruited to a large degree from the ranks of police detectives and cooperated with the Criminal Police and Order Police (Ordnungspolizei) along with other state offices in many areas of repression. There they often found zealous supporters in their business of murdering people. This was especially true during World War II and the Holocaust. According to estimates by historian Konrad Kwiet, a total of more than 500,000 people were actively involved in the extermination machinery of the Final Solution, working at desks jobs or at various locations in a variety of institutions and organizations.

All indications suggest that the Third Reich did not need a strictly disciplined and centrally steered apparatus like the MfS, as there was more than enough interest and spontaneous willingness to take part in persecuting Jews, Communists, homosexuals, or Sinti and Roma. From this perspective, a comparison reveals how weakly anchored the MfS was in the East German population, because the security of the SED state could apparently only be provided by an apparatus that was held together by a high degree of ideologization and pressure. This finding is of no small importance in analyzing the methods of State Security and how they transformed over time.

Chapter 3

THE UNOFFICIAL COLLABORATOR
A New Type of Informer

"A Nation of Traitors"?

The abyss that opened in 1990 when the first spies were unmasked has continued to affect the Stasi debate right down to the present. The official abbreviation "IM" (*inoffizielle Mitarbeiter*) became a symbol of universal collaboration, of the loss of confidence in interpersonal relations and what people thought they knew about each other. Suddenly it seemed that the GDR had been populated by a "nation of traitors," as the newspapers wrote. "Him too?" or "How could he?" were the questions repeatedly asked, given the revelations about well-known and respected figures working under code names such as *Torsten* and *Donald, Notary* and *Secretary*.

In the scholarly debate, the discovery of a vast IM network brought a renewed interest in denunciation as a historical, social, and psychological phenomenon. The bureaucratic perfection with which the Stasi expanded its network of informers and agents, regulating the handling of this network in hundreds of pages of guidelines and unwittingly documenting for posterity's sake the daily interactions of case officers and informers with a sobering attention to detail, laid bare an unparalleled wealth of knowledge about normally hidden worlds.

Indeed, denunciation was not the preserve of real socialism. Voluntarily reporting to the authorities the supposed or actual misconduct of one's neighbor has been a constant feature of human coexistence. We need only think of the betrayal of heretics and witches to the medieval Inquisition, the reporting of homosexuals to the municipal authorities of Venice in the fifteenth century, or the first instance of professionally hiring starving artists as informers by the Paris police in the eighteenth century—a list that could easily be continued. In Germany the interception of correspondence and casual tip-offs to the local police played an ever-larger role with the expansion of the state's monopoly on the use of force as of the late eighteenth century and with the creation of a secret "higher police" force for the pursuit and surveillance of bourgeois revolutionaries. During the Vormärz period, agents from Metternich's Mainz Information Office spied on fugitive liberals and Republicans in Paris, Geneva, and other places of exile; since the 1840s they set their sights on Communists scattered throughout the continent. It is no coincidence that Hoffmann von Fallersleben's oft-cited lines, "The greatest scoundrel in the land is and remains the informer," were penned during this period, showing how the liberal bourgeoisie ostracized the informer.

It would be wrong, of course, to view denunciation as a kind of anthropological constant of human behavior and close the books, as it were. Who reported whom to a higher authority for political reasons, when, how, and why, was and still is subject to different social and cultural conditions. In this respect, the system of IMs seems to be a culture of its own, the specifics of which will be examined in more detail below.

In order to give a historical answer to the moral question, "How could they have done it?" we will first take a look at the current state of knowledge about IMs to better appraise the type and extent of their activities and enable a comparison with other, more fundamental aspects of the SED dictatorship. Second, some findings from the two most important areas of research in this field, Nazi Germany and Stalinism, will be sounded out with a view to East German State Security, the peculiarities of the highly formalized IM system being contrasted with the phenomenon of spontaneous informing. Third, and finally, a typology of motives for IM work will be outlined in order to facilitate an understanding of concrete situations of recruitment and cooperation.[1]

The IM Network

Unofficial collaborators were instrumental in the work of the MfS. The last valid directive on IM work, Guideline 1/79, spoke of them as the "main weapon in the fight against the enemy."[2] The "love of IM work" was the "most effective Chekist weapon," wrote three leading MfS officers in their joint doctoral thesis at the MfS university in Potsdam-Eiche.[3] They praised in downright effusive tones the merits of human intelligence, as work with informers is called in the lingo of secret-service professionals:

> The ability to penetrate the thought processes of others can only and exclusively be done by humans themselves. Despite highly developed devices and mechanisms to relieve and sometimes replace the physical and mental work of human beings, there is nothing in the age of modern technology comparable to the art and capacity of a human being to probe into the train of thoughts of another. . . . There is and will be no equivalent substitute to the Unofficial Collaborator working along these lines.[4]

Unofficial collaborators had generally reached a written agreement with State Security to work for it conspiratorially, i.e., in a covert and secret manner. From the perspective of the MfS, their activities served to gather information, support the "fight against the enemy," exercise an influence on social developments, or support these functions through logistic assistance.

Even the term "unofficial collaborator" was part of a language-hygiene program which attempted to conceal the disreputableness of snitching while at the same time trying to avoid the traditional bourgeois terminology of "confidants" (*Vertrauensleute* or *V-Leute*) and "informers" (*Informanten*). Though the term IM was already in common usage in the early years, the official designations were "secret informer" (*geheimer Informator*—GI) and "secret collaborator" (*geheimer Mitarbeiter*—GM). Both coinages came directly from Soviet secret-police jargon, whose *sekretnye sotrudniki*, shortened to *seksot*, were notorious ever since the 1920s. They described the actual function quite precisely: whereas the main task of secret informers was to keep their ears and eyes open, gathering information and capturing the mood, the secret collaborators were to carry out "active" MfS assignments as well. A new guideline in 1968 put these functions in a softer light by calling them both "unofficial collaborators." Certain motives for working as a spy also acquired a less unsavory ring. Thus instead of career advantages and cash payments, there was now talk of "personal or material interestedness," and instead of recruitment "under pressure," using "compromising material" to blackmail prospective informers, the MfS spoke of "promoting the will to make amends" (*Förderung des Wiedergutmachungswillens*).[5]

The term "collaborator" also suggested a close, formalized, and nearly equal cooperative relationship between the full-time case officer and his informers. This suggestion upgraded the informer to the role of an acknowledged partner while serving the self-dramatization of the MfS as an organ in the service of the "working people," with whom it cooperated in a "trusting" manner.

The statute of the MfS, adopted by the National Defense Council in 1969, was likewise formulated in this vein. Paragraph 4 contains the authorization to work as an IM, according to which the MfS carried on its fight "in close cooperation with the working people . . . on the basis of the trust and conscious responsibility of citizens" in the spirit of "revolutionary mass vigilance."[6] This idea resurfaced in the much-ridiculed Volkskammer speech of Erich Mielke on 13 November 1989, when he claimed that his employees had an "exceptionally high contact with all working people."[7]

His deliberate equating of full-time MfS employees and the network of IMs still reverberates today, blurring the qualitative difference between secret policemen and their accomplices—albeit with a different conclusion, the IMs receiving the bulk of the attention nowadays and, hence, most of the blame.

From the perspective of the MfS, the linguistic enhancement of unofficial collaborators was part of the psychological guidance of an IM by his case officer. The in-house *Dictionary of Political-Operational Work* describes this supposedly trusting relationship as follows:

> In political-operational work there is generally talk of the T[rusting] R[elationship] between operational employees [case officers] and IMs, the aim being that the IM shows his full trust in the operational employee, whereby the operational employee in his relationship to the IM must always bear in mind the security and control aspect.[8]

No trace of equality, in other words. In reality the IMs were no more and no less than an instrument of secret-service work, just like observation, bugging, making inquiries with the beat patrol officer (*Abschnittsbevollmächtigter*) of the People's Police, or postal surveillance, though admittedly it was the most important of these.

The spectacular exposures after the disbanding of the MfS quickened the statistical imagination. There was soon talk of many hundreds of thousands, even one to two million IMs. As always when figures like this come into play, it is important to keep definitions in mind, as well as the manner of counting: which groups are included, and what point or period of time is covered?

The quantitative dimensions have since been clarified by and large—with precise figures or at least solid educated guesses. The IM network in the mid-1950s comprised as many as 20,000 to 30,000 people, on paper. This says nothing, however, about the practicability of this cooperation, especially considering that there was a professed tendency to recruit "under the gun," and that the pressure to achieve positive results had a distorting effect on statistics. The IM network grew in the 1960s and 1970s, parallel to the full-time apparatus. Around 100,000 IMs had been signed on by 1968. State Security continued its massive expansion until 1975, increasing the number of IMs to about 180,000, after which point in time the figures essentially remained constant until the end of the GDR. There was, however, a continual turnover rate of about 10 percent. In 1988–89 about 173,000 people were working as IMs, about 85 to 90 percent of them men.

This figure comprises about 93,500 individuals (54 percent) listed as classic informers under the designation "unofficial collaborators for securing an area of responsibility" (inoffizielle Mitarbeiter zur Sicherung des Verantwortungsbereiches—IMS); almost 4,000 top IMs with "enemy contact" or Feindberührung (IMB, a good 2 percent), like the well-known cases of Ibrahim Böhme, Wolfgang Schnur, etc; approximately 7,200 so-called expert IMs (IME, 4 percent) who, among other tasks, wrote reports on assignment for the MfS; and finally 4,600 "controller" IMs (Führungs-IM—FIM, almost 3 percent), each of whom was in charge of several IMs to lighten the load of the full-time apparatus. Two special groups can be added to these various categories: first the approximately 33,300 "social collaborators for security" (gesellschaftliche Mitarbeiter für Sicherheit—GMS, 19 percent), who were publicly known to be loyal functionaries and, second, a good 30,000 IMs for the logistical support of conspiracy (IMK, nearly 18 percent). These two groups volunteered their apartments as safe houses for meetings between case officers and IMs or served as contact points with cover addresses or telephone numbers.

These figures include the unofficial collaborators in the so-called "counterintelligence units" (Abwehrdiensteinheiten), which mainly operated on the domestic front. The following groups are not included in the sum total of 173,000: the IMs working inside and outside the GDR for the HVA (Main Administration for Reconnaissance/foreign espionage), the so-called border and cell informers (prisoner recruits),[9] as well as the so-called contact persons who were not formally recruited.

The apparatus, organized according to the division-of-labor principle, had "only" about 12,000 case officers controlling IMs in 1989, most of them in regional administrations and, for the most part, at the district offices. Fifty-one percent of unofficial collaborators were linked to the district offices, especially the IMSs. There were 11 to 12 IMs per case officer at the district level as opposed to 1 case officer for every 4 to 5 IMs at the Berlin headquarters of the ministry.[10] Depending on the region, the Ministry for State Security had managed to achieve a ratio of 1 unofficial collaborator per 80 to 160 inhabitants.

This decentrally organized network intended, in particular, for daily surveillance was a powerful instrument for State Security to carry out its all-encompassing task of control. The majority of IMs worked on Lines II, XVIII, XIX, XX, and VI, the classic areas of control (state apparatus and public life, economy and infrastructure, churches and all manner of Western contacts). Other important mainstays were the IMs in the other armed forces: military counterintelligence (Main Department I/Administration 2000 in the National People's Army) and Line VII (Ministry of the Interior/People's Police).

Just like its number of full-time employees, the Stasi's extensive IM network was largely unique in kind. To be sure, there are no reliable figures to enable a comparison with other organizations, e.g., in the other East European states. In reality, such global data are only an initial clue to the function and social consequences of the system of informers in the GDR. This becomes clear when compared with the research on Nazism and Stalinism.

A rough glance at the statistics reveals that the Stasi had set up a highly formalized network of informers, as exceptional in its scope as the full-time apparatus. And yet the scenario of a "nation of traitors" rings hollow, however much MfS leaders might have wished it to be so. Compared to the 2.3 million SED members, the flock of informers was relatively small. Moreover, we still need to consider how efficient this unofficial network really was and which functions it actually performed.

Denunciation: Dictatorships in Comparison

One of the great strides made in research on National Socialism is the effective debunking of the "Gestapo myth"—that is to say, the idea that National Socialism had a gigantic apparatus and a basically ubiquitous network of informers at its disposal and could therefore uncover and nip in the bud any undesirable developments. Not only was the number of full-time Gestapo employees relatively small, as indicated above; the informers formally recruited and entrusted with assignments were surprisingly small in number as well. Thus the Gestapo office in Frankfurt am Main, for instance, employed only about a hundred informers—a ridiculously small number, given the area under its surveillance. Nazi informers were most significant in the early years of the dictatorship, until 1935–36, especially in persecuting political opponents on the left. The Gestapo managed with the help of these spies to crush virtually every attempt to illegally reorganize the KPD and SPD in the resistance.

But the pressure applied by the Gestapo was less the result of its own organizational strength than of the broadly based cooperation with other police units, as well as with local NSDAP functionaries and their secondary organizations—and in certain key areas was thanks to the considerable volume of spontaneous denunciations among the population. These were crucial for infiltrating "Red working-class districts," but especially important in the Gestapo's day-to-day affairs later on. The denunciations mainly concerned violations of racial policies and anti-Jewish discriminatory laws, especially "racial defilement" (*Rassenschande*—sexual relations with non-Aryans) as of 1935–36, and in wartime the so-called "radio crimes," i.e., tuning in to enemy stations, the expression of dissenting opinions ("malicious practices" or *Heimtücke*), and attempts to avoid being drafted into the Wehrmacht.

About 60 to 80 percent of these cases were pursued by the Gestapo as a result of spontaneous tip-offs from the population, mostly reported to Nazi functionaries or local police stations. These percentages were comparable to the reporting rates for nonpolitical offenses. The willingness to report on others and the acceptance of this practice were therefore extraordinarily high. More recent research estimates that about 5 to 10 percent of Germans under the Nazi regime were willing to make political denunciations or actually did so. The level of support thus went well beyond the hard core of active Nazis.

Two motivating factors can be distinguished here. On the one hand, there were the ideology of the national community (*Volksgemeinschaft*) and the belief in the Führer, both of which had a deep effect on society. This is particularly evident in the case of denunciations born out of a sense of patriotic duty and which brought no real personal gain to the denouncer—reporting on a fellow passenger on the train, for instance, for making a "disrespectful" comment about the Germans' chances of winning the war. On the other hand, many denouncers did have their own interests in mind. Those denounced therefore included an above-average number of neighbors, coworkers or higher-ups at the workplace, and other individuals from the immediate social surroundings of the denouncer, excluding close family members. There was usually a status discrepancy between denouncers and the denounced, meaning the denouncer was usually turning in his boss, landlord, or similar persons in higher positions. In other cases denunciation resulted from direct competition—at the workplace, between businessmen and workmen, or among the residents of a building. Whereas it was almost exclusively men who denounced others on the job, women played a considerable role in denunciations arising from neighborhood feuds or family quarrels. Gerhard Paul summarizes his findings for Schleswig-Holstein as follows:

> The Gestapo was functionalized by "national comrades" [*Volksgenossen*]—as Heydrich correctly observed—into an instrument of private conflict resolution. Family feuds, neighborhood strife, unpleasant business competition, social envy, old political rivalries, and problems at the workplace could seemingly be sorted out by means of denunciation.[11]

Denunciation was the "little power of 'national comrades,'"[12] who were often pursuing personal aims but were evidently in sufficient agreement with the political contents of National Socialism to not consider their actions reprehensible from a political or moral standpoint. This astonishingly low inhibition threshold and the high level of approval, or at least indifference, we can deduce from it made Gestapo persecution so effective, because, in principle, anyone could be reported. Direct complicity, indirect involvement, or consenting acceptance of repression went well beyond the narrow circle of active Nazis.

Two conclusions can be drawn from this for the situation in the GDR. First, it seems there was never such a willingness among East Germans to denounce other people to the secret police. Second, the high occurrence of "apolitically" motivated denunciations in similar historical contexts gives reason to question the frequent claim that ideological motivations were paramount in the GDR.

A more accurate picture can also be gained from the situation in the USSR, even if the research into organized and spontaneous forms of denunciation in the Soviet Union of the 1930s to the 1950s is making sluggish progress due to barely opened or resealed archives.

A functional model of denunciation was inherited from Tsarist days. Subjects in the countryside would report local officials, landowners, and other superiors to the higher authorities for corruption, mismanagement, embezzlement, or similar offenses. This tradition is sometimes explained as a substitute for democratic procedures and the rule of law, and in this respect has a decidedly neutral or even positive connotation. The tradition is claimed to have continued seamlessly under communism, even being vitalized under the egalitarian claim of Soviet power.

Alongside this traditional form of denunciation, aimed entirely at higher-placed persons outside the immediate personal sphere of the denouncer, there was a second, quasi-totalitarian form: the reporting of possible "enemies" of the Soviet order during the mass terror of the 1930s. This type of denunciation was widely propagated in the martyr figure of Young Pioneer Pavlik Morozov, who allegedly reported his father for hoarding grain and was murdered by his uncle in retaliation.

This type of denunciation reached its climax in the preventive self-indictment of the Marxist-Leninist ritual of "criticism and self-criticism." Here we can find all the classic features of ideological hysteria provoked by constant calls for vigilance in the face of Trotskyist and fascist agents, as well the totalitarian attempt to intervene in immediate family environments. To be sure, intrafamilial denunciations played a subordinate role despite all the propaganda hype.

The internal dynamics of mass terror during these years likewise produced the preventive type of denunciation: so as not to become victims themselves in the general climate of suspicion, people cast aspersions on the people around them. Many denouncers apparently tried to gain a personal advantage this way, a common case being to report a fellow occupant of the same apartment as suspicious under some pretext or another in order to get his room. There is therefore good reason to believe that such denouncers were not only acting out of ideological fanaticism but just as often for pragmatic reasons, fending off unreasonable politically motivated demands or simply trying to survive. Sovietologist Sheila Fitzpatrick calls these denunciation strategies a "sociocultural equivalent of the Stalinist 'second economy' or black market," the shadow economy beyond the reach of the Plan.[13] The comparison to Nazism and Soviet Stalinism therefore shows that while totalitarian intervention and personal motives could indeed go hand in hand their intentions were by no means identical.

Formalization as Strategy

East German State Security, too, owed its disciplinary and intimidating effect to its image among the population as an omnipresent force with unlimited powers of intervention. We know today that this "Stasi myth" had a kernel of truth in the form of a lavish apparatus. Even the number of spontaneous denunciations under National Socialism, not to mention the downright infinitesimal number of Nazi informers, seems small when compared to the size of the IM network. In other words, there was a highly formalized "informational metabolism" between State Security and the society under surveillance.

This expansion of the unofficial network over the course of many years was apparently—like so many things—in keeping with the Soviet model. According to the research of Russian historian Irina Sherbakova, already in 1917 the Cheka was investing a lot of energy in building up a dense network of informers. This push for the largest circle of organized informers possible seems to have resulted from a deep-seated fear of supposedly ubiquitous class enemies and the call for vigilance. It was also a response to the ambivalent position of seeing oneself as the objective executor of the historical mission of the working class—the majority of the population—while constantly being confronted with the seemingly obvious fact that the real basis of support was more than fragile.

Given the basic setup of secret-service surveillance in a Communist dictatorship, the high degree of formalization would seem to be explained by the fact that the MfS could not necessarily rely on an unsympathetic population for spontaneous tip-offs about nonconformist behavior and dissidence, and that it therefore had no choice but to groom and bind its informers systematically. Acceptance among the population, in any case, was much higher in the Third Reich, and the threshold of inhibition there was much lower than in the GDR. Not without reason did the selection of IMs aim to constantly protect the GDR from hostile intruders, to make the GDR immune from any surprise initiatives from below, and to contain or fight the widespread inner affinity with the West in all of its varied manifestations. The high number of IM recruits in the strongest periods of MfS expansion is also unmistakably linked to the "tonnage ideology" (*Tonnenideologie*) of the planned economy, the driving force not only behind East Germany's economy but its State Security too. The aim was to achieve the highest production volume possible during a given planning period without regard for quality. In this respect, Fitzpatrick's analogy to the economy can be applied to an analysis of the IM network in yet another sense. The district offices, departments, divisions, and individual employees could simply not afford in the long run to recruit and command fewer IMs than their neighboring units or office mates. Particularly in phases of rapid expansion, in the wake of 17 June, for instance, or in the first half of the 1970s, an "unhealthy atmosphere of competition" took over in which those in positions of authority measured "plan fulfillment for recruitment almost exclusively in terms of quantitative indicators," as the minister Mielke criticized at an internal conference in 1975.[14] MfS leaders themselves contributed not a little to this attitude, with their excessive regulations and their annual and quarterly plans, in which service units had to stipulate how many unofficial collaborators they would recruit in each area. These were linked with curious "job profiles," which were supposed to outline the desired qualities of each IM.

In practice, the exact opposite occurred. Case officers strove by hook or by crook to create a certain buffer to compensate for plan deficits. The job descriptions were kept as vague as possible or secretly tailored to an existing candidate. Some IMs who had little information to offer but were especially willing to cooperate would be used to beef up the prescribed number of meetings. Weak reports were padded with general information until an adequate replacement could be found. Though the MfS did have internal control mechanisms to prevent fictitious recruiting and other abuses, the same skepticism is called for here as with the reports of the State Planning Commission, whose job it was to document the outstanding progress of the socialist economy. However invasive in a totalitarian sense the IM network might have seemed in the reports, and however visibly proud some former case officers may still be today of their ability to recruit under difficult circumstances, this flipside of the planned economy—unrealistically high performance expectations and the resulting tendency to fudge the numbers in order to meet these targets—should not be overlooked with regard to these recruiting practices.

The political profile of IMs is not surprising against this backdrop. Initial data on the makeup of the unofficial network show considerable overlaps with loyal system supporters. The complaint that there was a lack of informers in spheres of society far from the center of power (and therefore of particular interest to the secret police) was a constant companion of IM work in the 1950s. According to a spot check in 1962, the share of SED members in the regional administration of Neubrandenburg was 40 to 50 percent. Despite all the warnings to only recruit SED members in exceptional cases, in the 1970s and 1980s they made up no less than one-third of IMs. Stasi recruiters had better chances among these individuals, and they knew it too.

These findings can be supplemented by data on the much-talked-about "juvenile" IMs. Did these fanatic young hotspurs really exist, who supposedly joined the Stasi as children and would turn in their own parents if they complained at home about the supply situation or thought out loud about fleeing to the West? Age analyses show that about 10 percent of IMs were "juveniles" of up to twenty-five years.

Most of them had been recruited as eighteen- or nineteen-year-olds during military service or afterward as university students.

In the case of army recruits, the responsible Main Department I/ Administration 2000 had an easy job, as recruiting was relatively effortless under the pressure of military discipline. Yet these contacts often broke off once these individuals were discharged from service. In the case of university students, career perspectives apparently played an important role. A common practice was to recruit full-time FDJ functionaries as "social collaborators for security." Young people in the narrow sense, i.e., under eighteen years of age, made up a very tiny percentage of IMs. In the regional administration of Rostock, for instance, there were 68 unofficial collaborators and 5 social collaborators for security in this age group in 1988—less than 1 percent of the IMs there (not including IMKs). Some of these students and apprentices were candidates for full-time MfS service, receiving IM assignments on a trial basis or being hired for longer periods of service in the National People's Army.

All in all the findings for the MfS bear out those for Nazism and Stalinism. Hannah Arendt's gloomy diagnosis of the complete atomization of society under totalitarianism did not pan out; close family ties turned out, on the whole, to be exceptionally resistant social institutions in the face of external attempts to penetrate them. Famous cases such as dissident Vera Wollenberger, whose husband Knud spied on her intensively under the code name "Donald," were actually quite rare.

Spontaneous denunciations did play a certain role in the early years of persecution. Thus according to internal assessments, about 30 to 50 percent of operational cases opened in 1955 could be traced back to such tip-offs, whereas IMs only prompted 20 percent of them. The rest were presumably the result of independent investigations by full-time MfS employees, especially the product of extorted confessions during interrogations and of tip-offs by their Soviet "friends." These tip-offs, though, seemed not to come from the population at large for the most part. A report from the regional administration of Neubrandenburg comments apologetically:

> The work of the Ministry for State Security was greatly impeded during this period by the mistrust of people who associated the MfS with the Gestapo or the SD [Security Service]. The mistrust shown for the power apparatus of Fascism has been transferred to the MfS.[15]

This conclusion with regard to the Gestapo and Security Service is more than questionable for the reasons outlined above, but it does at least accurately portray the basic situation faced by the MfS. There is reason to believe that a large share of the denunciations came instead from the SED party apparatus and its secondary organizations, which was much more deeply embedded locally than the MfS at this point in time. As of 1968 these persons came under the new category of "social collaborators for security" (GMS). According to the respective guideline, the most eligible individuals had distinguished themselves by their "potentially proven solidarity with the security organs" as the expression of a "developed mass vigilance."[16] Their functions (investigative assignments in occupational, residential and recreational spheres) in reality often overlapped with the MfS's official cooperation with the police, state administration, and party apparatus. Only to a limited degree did these informers fit the image of the classic IM, because being visible in public as loyal servants of the state they were quite restricted in their ability to infiltrate supposed "hostile" circles.

The MfS played down the GMSs' importance in the last IM guidelines of 1979 on account of their limited effectiveness, and merely spoke of a "valuable addition to the operational basis."[17] But there were still around 33,000 GMSs in 1988, almost a fifth of the overall pool of IMs, due to the ease of recruiting these loyal (*staatsbewusst*) East German citizens.

Such structural findings and insights into everyday practices confirm the specific function of the IM network as an answer to the narrow social base of the SED state. Thus with a view to the entire IM network, the spectacular cases of IMs in the opposition movement were the exception rather than the rule, one reflected in the special category of IM with "enemy contact" (IMB).

Motives: Ideology, Personal Gain, and Fear

Despite the varied takes nowadays, the justifications of erstwhile unofficial collaborators are often in agreement with the files and the assessments of their former case officers in one particular point. Though it might be hard to explain it in retrospect, they assert, the main motive for their secret ties to State Security was to be found in their political conviction—their belief in the inherent goodness of the socialist idea and in the legitimacy of protecting against the covert operations of enemy forces, as well as their desire to communicate a better understanding of those under surveillance (the church, etc.) and thereby do something for international and domestic "peace." These justifications are sometimes conveyed in a pugnacious and enthusiastic tone, with reference to the suffering and struggles of their antifascist forebears or as a natural profession of allegiance in the world of a paternalistic welfare dictatorship. The respective service regulations, according to which appealing to the candidate's basic "conviction" was the "most important and chief manner of recruiting,"[18] provided the cues that case officers, too, were all too eager to follow when filling out their standardized forms, signaling as they did the unofficial collaborators' high level of commitment, reliability, and ideological solidarity with their defense and security organ as representatives of the working people.

If erstwhile informers and case officers have to deal nowadays with the misfortunes of the spied-upon and put up with the public leafing through their once-secret reports, it nonetheless seems more negligible if one claims it was all for a good cause. A closer inspection reveals, however, that these rationalizations only partly hold up against the historical evidence now available. In fact, there were complex clusters of motives with highly varied causes that greatly resemble those found in other fields of investigation in the historical research on denunciation.

Of course ideological motives played a role. The above-average share of functionaries and SED members serving as IMs is evidence enough. In practice the boundaries were fluid with the so-called "partners of operational cooperation" (*Partner des operativen Zusammenwirkens—POZW*): police officers, employees in the state apparatus, factory managers, and so on, from whom State Security "officially" demanded information or assistance. These individuals were generally notorious for being dyed-in-the-wool system representatives, or at least opportunistic and cynical careerists. This group included former full-time MfS employees who officially had to resign from the service for disciplinary reasons or due to "negative" Western contacts in the family and who were now being kept on a leash, unofficially. But intellectuals, too, and other people who credited the system with having a positive, idealistic core, were approachable on this level.

At the same time, State Security could also rely on a broad range of nonideological motives in its IM work (as shown by individual case studies as well as by internal MfS investigations): from the prospect of concrete personal gain or recognition from one's case officer to the particular fascination of sharing in the exercise of secret power. In an internal survey of unofficial collaborators conducted by the MfS regional administration of Potsdam in 1967, 60 percent indicated that their main motivation was the "awareness of social necessity" (*Erkennen des gesellschaftlichen Erfordernisses*) and 49 percent the "experience of moral duty and constraints of conscience" (*sittliches Pflichterleben und Gewissenszwang*)—in other words, "reputable" ideological motives in the broadest sense. But openly pragmatic and utilitarian considerations played a substantial role as well: 27 percent cited "personal gain" (*persönliche Vorteile*) as a reason for their IM activities, 40 percent "practical life objectives" (*lebenspraktische Zielsetzungen*), and 12 percent said it was an "end in itself" (*Selbstzweck*), such as the desire for adventure and the allure of secrecy.[19]

There is no mistaking the classic patterns of denunciation here. Competition, a lack of recognition at the workplace, or—as in the following case—revenge for the humiliations inflicted by a superior often provided the necessary incentive:

> It was evident during the contact meeting that the candidate had little good to say about First Sergeant J. He signified that J. had tried now and then to foist off unpleasant tasks on the IM candidate. J. is already counting the months until his transfer to the reserves. He often boasts that he only has 2 years and 4 months left to serve. . . . He thinks it will be a quiet posting, where he can earn good money.[20]

At the middle levels of the state and economic hierarchies, motives of security and proofs of loyalty played a particular role. As a study of engineers and technicians in the electronics industry showed, these "susceptible social climbers" often used IM work to compensate for their not being Party members or to buy the status of "travel cadre" (permission to travel to the West) by writing reports. Informers in this situation would frequently justify themselves by claiming that they wanted to use this "special channel" to override an ignorant plan bureaucracy and push through better conditions of production at their factory or in their development department.

Pragmatic considerations were also paramount in another, quite special area: the "management" of prostitutes by State Security. Although prostitution was officially prohibited in the GDR, the Stasi took advantage of this illegal scene to sound out Western businessmen (at the Leipzig trade fair, for instance) or to take compromising photos. The women themselves were primarily interested in securing material privileges, but were permanently under the threat of punishment.

It was only a small step from safeguarding against potential disadvantages or the withdrawal of privileges to more direct forms of pressure. This was particularly effective in the case of a special group, the so-called cell informers. These were prisoners who were expected to pump their cellmates for information or influence them psychologically, e.g., make them ready to talk. In exchange they were granted special privileges or given the prospect of a sentence reduction. The extreme institutional setting of prison made cell informers incomparably more vulnerable to pressure from State Security.

Pressure played a certain role for other unofficial collaborators as well. In the 1967 Potsdam survey mentioned above, 23 percent indicated that the experience of pressure and coercion was one of the main motives for recruitment, whereas another 22 percent cited it as a secondary motive—albeit in a survey conducted by the Stasi itself, which could hardly have been eager to hear such answers. This may have been an echo of the 1950s, when blackmail was a common and accepted practice of extracting information. Then again, we can assume that the number of unknown cases of recruitment under open or subtle threats was considerable in later years. Any contact in the West, for instance, could easily be construed as a covert contact to enemy secret services and used as an effective basis of blackmail. Fear of an eerily secret apparatus certainly played a significant role as well, especially if someone approached by the Stasi refused to offer the services requested, as the recollections of former IMs make clear.

On the Black Art of Bending

Compared to the randomness of spontaneous denunciations, the systematic initiation and cementing of the unofficial contact between case officer and informer allowed for a certain amount of flexibility. Establishing and handling the initial contact with the potential recruit required all the operational skills an MfS employee could muster. It was important, to start with, to find a way to circumvent or play down the offensive and odious aspects of work as a "snoop." The actual objective and the desire to pump as much intimate information from an IM as possible, often about his friends and close acquaintances, therefore took a backseat at first. The IM was first thoroughly scouted out to learn about his strengths and weaknesses and discover any "common" interests. This might mean solving church thefts in the case of a church employee, the observation of skinheads in the case of anarchist punks, or assistance in remedying the chaos of a planned economy or procuring scarce primary products in the case of technicians or economists. The content of this first conversation was not what mattered; the important thing was establishing contact, conveying a sense of partnership and dispelling any doubts or scruples. This distinction between the "way" and "goal" in the recruiting process was the key to overcoming frequent reservations. The result was a unique mixture of trust and dependence on the part of the IM. An intense emotional relationship could develop, especially in the case of mentally unstable individuals with strong emotional needs. Gradually the range of questions could be expanded and the focus shifted to include originally taboo topics of conversation. The operational employees called this process the "bending" (*Krümmen*) of an IM, a description at once fitting and brutal. The aim was the "full and unequivocal identification" of the IM with his case officer and the MfS. This meant encouraging "valuable motives," deepening mutual trust, creating a sense of achievement, and eliminating any "misgivings in the case of conflicts of duty and conscience."[21] The initiation process aimed little by little to help an IM overcome his inhibitions about providing information on people, saying negative things about others, touching on politically sensitive topics, and reporting on his or her close circle of acquaintances, so that in the end an IM was even prepared to reveal intimate details about close friends and family members.

A cadet described this handling method in his 1989 thesis at the MfS university, using the example of unofficial collaborator "Karin." During their initial exchange about the "basic operational concern," the case officer supposedly complied with some of her suggestions in order to motivate her as an "acknowledged partner in dialogue" and not as a "guided instrument" (*geführtes Werkzeug*). In this manner "Karin" was able, after a number of years, to largely develop her own approaches. She was able to abandon her initially avowed taboos and report, for instance, on her own parents. The "strewing" of negative information about certain role models "proved exceptionally effective" in getting IM "Karin" to "back off" from them inwardly.[22]

Without a doubt, this IM-handling method was among the most elaborate products of German "Chekism," as far as we can judge without really being able to conduct comparative studies with the work of informers in other secret services. The systematic selection of candidates and the elaborate preparation process during IM recruitment as opposed to trusting in the loyal and zealous "national comrade," and the intensive process of "relationship work" with its far-reaching effects on the psyche of the IM as opposed to the randomness of spontaneous tip-offs are both indicative of a professionality saturated with experience and which exhausted to the maximum extent possible the potential of its informers.

The MfS was miles away from such operational finesse and methodicalness until well into the 1960s. Instead of molding unofficial collaborators into what they wanted them to be, they first had to "educate" their mostly inexperienced and extremely young case officers. The latter were inhibited when faced with older, more educated candidates and IMs, and felt they were not being taken seriously. This was a major drawback given the numerous representatives of the traditional bourgeois elite in the state administration and economy. MfS employees frequently went months or years without a meeting with nominally recruited informers, or reacted to recalcitrant IMs by putting them under pressure, which ultimately provided an additional incentive for fleeing to the West. In other instances, case officers did little in the way of controlling and handling their agents and struck up private relationships with unofficial collaborators. The situation improved, from an MfS perspective, after the erection of the Berlin Wall. Case officers received more thorough training and, with all roads to the West now cut off, could generally count on a candidate bowing to what seemed like necessity. Despite all the strategies of intellectual "refinement," the use of pressure, intimidation, and dependencies continued to play a permanent role in recruiting IMs. What's more, as of the 1970s State Security had to place progressively more emphasis on communicating its concept of the enemy so as to counteract the effects of mental and spiritual demilitarization under the banner of détente. In reality, the dwindling force of utopia and ideology led to a decline in the significance of "higher" political motives.

The potential motives for covert cooperation with State Security examined here—and which could certainly be developed further—are naturally inappropriate for making more generalized moral judgments. Whether or not there were plausible reasons for entering into a secret liaison can only be discussed in a concrete, case-by-case manner, the first to rightly have their say being those who were deceived and betrayed—and who sometimes faced grievous consequences. Cheap pronouncements to the effect of "Let him who is without sin . . ." tantamount to a general pardon are just as inappropriate here as a blanket condemnation for being despicable "perpetrators."

In weighing this issue one thing should not be forgotten, though: for all the objective and subjective pressure to sign on as an IM, it was, in fact, possible to refuse. The most proven method was simply to tell other people about it. By having his cover blown—*Dekonspiration* or "deconspiracy," as it was called by the Stasi—the IM became worthless and contact was automatically terminated. This was a well-known tactic in the dissident and church scenes, and was expressly recommended too. Others tried to wheedle their way out with a variety of seemingly harmless excuses, without earning themselves the reputation of being an opponent of the system. It was not easy to be so self-assertive; it was a step often accompanied by intense feelings of anxiety and the fear of possible reprisals. But the number of re-fuseniks shows that an inner aversion to spying indeed had its place in the moral economy of the population. They were sometimes even loyal SED comrades who found the services requested of them repugnant. The exact number is impossible to determine. Those who refused directly would also include the ones whose case officers came to the conclusion that recruiting them was hopeless. According to MfS data, about one-third of all IM recruiting attempts in the 1970s were aborted. But this is just a rough estimate, because many attempts never reached a formal stage. Moreover, many IMs broke off relations with their case officer at a later point in time, either purposely blowing their cover or explicitly refusing to cooperate any longer. By 1986, the number of discharges exceeded that of new recruits. The rate of refusals, IM "dishonesty," and deconspiracy now accounted for 30 to 40 percent of all terminated IM contacts. In 1988, for example, the Stasi lost about 3 percent of its IM force for these reasons. Added to this were those who did not dare to openly refuse but who more or less did so tacitly—by failing to show up at their meetings or by not providing any useful information, in the silent hope of eventually being left alone.

All the talk of unofficial collaborators being the "main weapon of the MfS" certainly had its justification. Even taking into account the tendency to Potemkin-like statistical façades and the exaggerated descriptions of the will to cooperate as "close solidarity with the working people," it is still apparent that the Ministry for State Security got what it could out of its IM network, given the population's limited loyalty to the system. It operated with perfidious precision and positively Prussian meticulousness. The damage done to social relations was correspondingly disastrous, and will probably still take years to rectify.

Chapter 4

Blanket Surveillance?

State Security in East German Society

A Newfangled Form of Preventive Social Steering?

How long was the arm of the Stasi and to what end did the ministry use it? The basic hypothesis, discussed above in connection with personnel development, was formulated by Klaus-Dietmar Henke:

> The MfS, greatly expanded since the 1970s, was indeed all-encompassing [*flächendeckend*], at least in the Honecker era, and could be deployed in manipulative ways. Presumably it was even capable of partly substituting state steering functions in key areas. A most likely indispensable special authority for administrative coherence, the tasks of State Security included, apart from repression, the stabilization of an increasingly poorly functioning polity. An irony of "dialectics" or the cunning of history—the secret apparatus stabilized and destabilized at once. . . .
> What was historically new and characteristic about the State Security Service of the GDR was not primarily its methods of espionage, investigation, and repression, but its comprehensive covert steering and manipulation function, not only in important areas of state and society but also down to the level of primary groups and even personal relationships—undoubtedly a new and refined element of the exercise of total power [*Herrschaftsausübung*].[1]

Three questions have to be answered to get a clearer picture of this situation: How well was the MfS structurally prepared for its mission of blanket surveillance? How broadly and extensively did it penetrate society? And to what extent did the MfS assume other functions beyond its tasks of repression?

Territorial and Sectoral Structure: Regional Administrations, District Offices, Factory Units, Lines

State Security, from its very beginnings, was designed to be all-encompassing. The systematic buildup of local administrative offices had already begun with the reorganization of K-5 into the Administrations for the Protection of the National Economy. Thus the Ministry for State Security had territorial structures across the country as early as 1950: the five state administrations for state security, the Administration of Greater Berlin, and the administrative offices in the more than one hundred districts. The autonomy of states, districts, and local authorities had been largely eliminated by the early 1950s, so that the lower levels were subject to the ministry's authority and directives. The territorial and administrative reform of 1952 replaced the states or provinces (*Länder*) with 14 regions (*Bezirke*) and 217 municipal and rural districts (*Stadt- und Landkreise*)—meaning State Security had to more than double its number of offices. Since an employee substructure had to first be created, there were only 192 district offices to start with, some of which had to administer two districts at once. Separate district offices for the regional capitals of Leipzig, Chemnitz (Karl-Marx-Stadt), Dresden, Halle, Magdeburg, and Rostock were set up in 1954. This network, extending from the Isle of Rügen in the Baltic Sea to Bad Brambach in the Vogtland region of southern Saxony, had an average of fourteen employees (from director to cleaning crew) per district office at first. The figures ranged from 44 employees in Zittau (Saxony), to 7 or 8 employees in the district offices of sparsely populated Mecklenburg. Just how weak these structures were could be seen on 17 June 1953, when Stasi men found themselves more or less helpless in the face of the sieges and storms of protesters. The real backbone of the Stasi's "operational" work back then—and in a certain sense until 1989—was the much larger regional administrations, with their more differentiated specialist branches.

The state party's will to spy on its own people is even expressed in this territorial structure. Alternative structural principles such as the Offices for the Protection of the Constitution in the Federal Republic, organized according to potential threats like "left-wing extremism," "right-wing extremism," or "counterespionage," and without a local network,[2] were apparently never discussed. This would have contradicted the Soviet system that was supposed to serve as a model. Each regional administration and district office was essentially "responsible for protecting social development and guaranteeing state security"[3] in their entire territory. Though the regional administrations and district offices grew less rapidly than Stasi headquarters, their staffs continued to grow from 1952 on. In later years, at a time when Berlin was forced to economize, the district offices showed the most rapid growth rates, increasing their staff by 20 percent between 1982 and 1989, for their tasks steadily mounted with the concomitant increase in Western contacts, security checks, and applications to emigrate, as well as the growth of the opposition movement. Many employees of the apparatus therefore felt like the last overburdened link in a chain. Hence in 1988 Erich Mielke complained at an internal conference about "certain views that the district offices are increasingly burdened with tasks that actually have nothing to do with work on the enemy, . . . that the limits of operational capacity at the district offices have been reached or already exceeded, and that the district offices are supposedly moving farther away from their 'actual Chekist assignments.'"[4] Moreover, in their efforts to deal with increasing malfunctions in the state and economy, many state directors supposedly viewed the district offices as implicit "consultation partners"[5] well beyond issues of security and order. The district office of Jena, for example, had 97 employees in 1989; the unofficial network comprised 396 unofficial collaborators, 245 social collaborators for security, and 22 contact persons. Almost half of the 22 "operational cases" (OVs) and 106 "operational person controls" (OPKs) there were directed against applicants for emigration (*Ausreiseantragsteller*). Jena, moreover, was a center of the opposition movement. The Stasi likewise conducted 70 so-called "complex controls" at industrial enterprises and on farms, at Friedrich Schiller University, and at local academic institutes in order to improve the protection of secrets and maintain order and security, not to mention carrying out countless security checks on individuals.

The counterpart of the MfS's territorial structure was the "line principle," according to which certain specialist branches of the Stasi apparatus—called "lines" in MfS jargon—were assigned to virtually all domains of social life in the GDR. At headquarters, each of these lines had a main department (or part of one), and each regional administration had a corresponding department or division. Securing the national economy, for instance, was the responsibility of Main Administration XVIII (called Main Department III until 1964) and of the respective Department XVIII in each region. The portfolio of the Ministry of the Interior, including the People's Police, belonged to

Line VII, whereas the civilian state apparatus, public health system, youth, churches, and some other areas were the purview of Line XX. The district offices were not rigorously organized on the line principle but usually had corresponding divisions or individual employees, depending on local needs. All East German citizens had a district office responsible for them, according to their place of residence, and the line principle overlapped with this.

Added to this were lines that were not defined by security areas but by "lines of enemy attack," i.e., the defense against secret-service espionage or the struggle against the "political underground" (PUT). These two definitions of line work were variously combined in the service-unit structure of the MfS. Thus one of the largest and most important service branches of the MfS, Main Department II, was responsible for all cases of counterespionage against Western intelligence services but also had a number of security areas in the sense described above, such as the Western journalists accredited in the GDR since the early 1970s (Department II/13), the foreign embassies in East Berlin (Departments II/11 and 15), the East German Foreign Ministry (Department II/14), as well as the foreigners living in the GDR (Working Group for Foreign Nationals). Conversely, Line XX included the internal security domains mentioned above (e.g., Department XX/1, state apparatus/bloc parties), but also the branches for fighting "political-ideological diversion" and "political underground activities" (PID/PUT, Department XX/5 and 9), which were considered lines of enemy attack.

These three approaches—territorial surveillance, security areas, fighting the enemy in a targeted manner—overlapped with one another. Inevitable rivalries developed, along with a certain hierarchy regarding who was responsible for the surveillance and, if need be, repressive measures against a specific person or group of persons. The more severe cases naturally went "to the line" in the upper reaches of the apparatus, whereas routine observation was left to the districts. Nothing was to elude State Security with these working principles. To the average citizen, on the other hand, it scarcely mattered which of the three approaches the authorities used to train their sights on him; he could not perceive or see through them anyway, but certainly suffered the consequences—sometimes palpable, sometimes hidden.

Security Areas

Despite these comprehensive provisions, there were considerable differences in the Stasi's penetration of different social spheres at different times. For all its desire to control, it still needed to set priorities, either because parts of the state, economy, or society were considered particularly important for national security—that is to say, SED rule—or because supposed or actual enemies of the state were more abundant at certain locations. This is why the MfS generally tried to prioritize its efforts according to a third working principle (alongside the territorial and line principles): the "focal-point principle." According to the definitions offered by the *Dictionary of Political-Operational Work* from the early 1980s, the focal-point principle served to "concentrate operational forces and means, including available working hours . . . , on the key political-operational tasks and/or on the key factories and institutions [*Objekte*], areas, territories, groups of people, and individuals to be secured preventively."[6]

A focal point (*Schwerpunkt*) was defined as "a factory or institution [*Objekt*], area, territory, or group of people that is critical for solving important tasks of social development and state security and where a particularly high effectiveness of political-operational work must be achieved through the concentration of operational forces and means for the precautionary prevention, detection, and combating of enemy attacks and other negative manifestations."[7]

To be sure, this principle got out of hand over the years. The talk of "concentration" and "particularly high effectiveness," and the reminder appended to this that the focal points were to be kept "relatively narrow" and aims defined so as to be "accountable" (*abrechenbar*)—all of this was a reaction to the fact that a vast chain of "focal points" had accumulated by this point in time. The louder the "focal-point principle" was propagated at internal conferences and in Stasi directives, the more clear it became that it was basically not working as a lever for streamlining MfS forces and the critical appraisal of tasks. In the competition for resources among MfS service units and between ministries in general, the world was full of "focal points" demanding absolute "vigilance."

The most important sphere of surveillance was the other armed forces, which never lost their central importance as armed executive state powers in the minds of SED leaders. Already in the 1950s there was a high ratio of IMs in this area. The MfS put former Wehrmacht generals and officers who were now serving in the National People's Army (NVA) under especially close surveillance and did its best to recruit them as unofficial collaborators. They were considered a serious potential threat by the Stasi, "tainted" as they were by "Western contacts" and thought to be politically unreliable. According to the head of Main Department I, Karl Kleinjung, State Security managed to recruit one informer for every ten soldiers shortly after the NVA's founding in 1956, a statistical ratio that decreased later on with the expansion of the army and the introduction of compulsory military service. The optimal ratio in later years was set at one informer per twenty army recruits. In reality the ratio was rather varied. Main Department I/Administration 2000 placed a high number of IMs in border troops. Recruiting success among "construction soldiers" (Bausoldaten)—the East German civilian alternative to compulsory military service—was much, much lower, by contrast, although (and because) these conscientious objectors naturally represented a "legal concentration of hostile-negative forces"[8] in need of particular surveillance from the point of view of the MfS. Cooperation with higher-ranking officers was therefore more intense in the construction units. All in all, Main Department I had at least between 2,300 and 2,500 employees in the 1980s and more than 12,000 IMs (91 percent of them IMSs). With a total force of 215,000 in the NVA and border troops, that makes for roughly one informer for every twenty soldiers or less.[9] There was a strong cooperative relationship too, MfS border reconnaissance working closely with frontier troops and NVA Military Reconnaissance being closely allied to Main Department I by dint of its officers on special assignment and unofficial collaborators. There was a high ratio of IMs among the generals as well, all the way up to Colonel-General Fritz Streletz, chief of the Main Staff and deputy minister for national defense. His commitment even corresponded to the Stasi's link in the military chain of command in East Germany, for as of 1971 he was secretary of the National Defense Council, whose command the MfS was subordinate to. Not until 1981, when Streletz rose to the SED Central Committee, were his IM ties formally severed, thereby putting an end to this conflict.

The degree of penetration and entanglement was even higher in the People's Police, with 10 to 20 percent of its staff working as IMs. Here, in particular, surveillance and cooperation were almost inextricably linked. The most extreme case of this was K-1, a covertly operating branch of the criminal police, about 20 percent of whose staff were unofficial collaborators, as well as a range of officers on special assignment who occupied important positions. In a less politically sensitive area like the uniformed police in the region of Schwerin, about 12 percent of law officers had unofficial ties to the MfS apart from their official obligation to cooperate, whereas in the Prenzlau district office of the People's Police the figure was 16 percent. Although in rare moments of contemplation even the minister for state security had to ask himself if they needed an apparatus "to keep tabs on the People's

Police" instead of "solving security tasks with the help of the People's Police in such a way that it lightens our workload,"[10] this area of surveillance was one of the enduring focal points of the MfS.

The Stasi's interests were traditionally strong in the area of the economy too, even if the ratio of informers was considerably lower here. In the 1950s this primarily concerned securing and safeguarding "people's" (i.e., state-owned) property against the claims of previous owners, protecting factories, e.g., against sabotage, and, after 17 June, writing situation reports about the mood of factory workers. But the actual rise of State Security's economic line came in the 1960s, when the SED tried to increase efficiency through economic reforms. The MfS countered the decentralization of decision-making powers by building up an additional control network. As early as 1957 there were directives to set up special factory units in the two chemical combines of Buna and Leuna, as well as operational groups at 55 other plants. Mielke once again picked up this broad approach in 1966 when he began to build up a system of security officers in all important economic sectors and enterprises. Furthermore, 83 additional operational groups and seven factory units were set up in the ensuing years (though two of them, at the oil-processing plants of Böhlen and Schwedt, were later dissolved).

In 1969 the MfS expanded its network of security officers to include all sectors of the economy. In "central economy-directing organs," such as plan commissions and industry ministries, as well as important combines, factories, and other facilities, MfS officers on special assignment (OibE) acted as security officers; in the other factories they were signed on as unofficial collaborators or "social collaborators for security." In 1976, Main Administration XVIII (not including the regional administrations) had 93 OibEs; in 1989 it had 115. At the top of this network was the Working Group for Organization and Inspection in the Council of Ministers, comprising 25 OibEs and led by MfS officer Harry Möbis as of 1968. The MfS was likewise firmly established in the State Planning Commission and the Ministry of Finances. According to MfS doctrine, the security officers had a wide range of tasks. They were expected to contribute to plan fulfillment, monitor foreign business contacts in the West, uncover abuses and mismanagement, along with resolving production shortfalls and industrial accidents.

Stasi economic surveillance was further expanded in the 1970s and 1980s. There were two reasons for this. First of all, the GDR was transforming its foreign trade (especially with the West) from being a stopgap to a key growth factor. Integration with the world market and its most important Western trading partner, the Federal Republic, increased in line with its political opening to the West. To State Security this posed a variety of security risks. From 1965 on, economic managers and State Security assembled a permanent staff of travel cadre to handle economic contacts, which the MfS scrutinized and monitored intensely. Investigations have shown that in 1984 about one-third to one-half of the travel cadre employed at the chemical combines of Buna, Leuna, and Bitterfeld were working as unofficial collaborators, compared to only 5 percent at VEB Carl Zeiss Jena. The travel-cadre IMs were not only supposed to keep tabs on each other but were also expected to carry out espionage assignments in the West, if possible. In 1983–84, Line XVIII screened about 20,000 travel-cadre candidates. About 6,500 of these requests for a "license to travel in the West" were turned down by MfS security experts, who considered the risk too high that the candidate would not return or would establish contacts with an enemy secret service. Similar security checks existed for all important leadership positions and in sensitive areas such as research and development. It was not only the universal fear of enemy influences that lurked behind this surveillance strategy but tangible economic interests as well. The economically vital "strategy of replication" (Nacherfindungsstrategie) through illegal imports of embargoed goods and technological espionage was to be secured by the MfS and the circle of initiates kept under control. Thus, for example, the highly ambitious microelectronics program with which the GDR attempted to "keep pace in the race against time in the development of productive forces" (Erich Honecker)[11] in the 1980s was essentially based on such illegal transfers.

Second, its shared responsibility for "securing production and facilities" became an ever greater burden the more that production stoppages became due to the disastrous wear and tear of investment goods. The original task of State Security was to uncover acts of sabotage and other "enemy influences," but this other role took on a life of its own in the 1970s. A year after power supplies in the GDR collapsed in the winter of 1970–71, the then director of Main Department XVIII, Rudi Mittag (who later became Mielke's deputy), came to the conclusion that these losses in the energy economy were not caused by sabotage but were solely the result of technical deficiencies. But State Security was on the ball. The situation escalated in the 1980s, by which time many East German factories and production facilities, some of which dated back to the 1930s or the First World War, were hopelessly worn out. State Security meticulously documented this decline. In 1984 it counted eight major stoppages with losses of over a million marks and total losses of 15 million, nineteen cases in 1986 with 134 million marks in losses, and eight cases in April 1987 alone with losses of 508 million marks. It found no attacks by dissidents or enemy agents.

Apart from securing foreign trade and investigating and preventing stoppages at production facilities, State Security continued to monitor and document the mood in factories. After the bitter experiences of the early years, though, there was hardly any political agitation on the shop floor. In 1980–81, the Stasi was more concerned, for example, with listening in on industrial workers to detect any potential sympathy with the Polish independent trade-union movement Solidarity. It came to the reassuring conclusion that potential agitators were generally convinced that any strikes in the GDR would be "nipped in the bud."[12]

It frequently had to sound out reactions to supply crises or bottlenecks in energy production, or to report on the influence of "political-ideological diversion," when apprentices living in dormitories, for example, openly listened to RIAS and tuned into Western television or showed an interest in the "pacifist-clerical" views of church-affiliated independent peace groups in view of their impending military service. East German factories never became the focal point of political conflicts again after 1953, not even during the final showdown of 1989. Instead, a massive task in the 1980s, in factories as well, was the futile attempt to stem the flow of applications to emigrate, in this case among highly qualified—and sorely needed—engineers, technicians, and other specialists.

In the 1970s, the economic line of the MfS had about 11,000 unofficial collaborators working at Berlin headquarters and the regional level.[13] Added to this were the economic IMs at the district and factory level, whose estimated number was comparable. Individual combines offer a more detailed picture. The ratio of IMs to employees at factory units was not more than the East German average of about 1 percent. At VEB Chemische Werke Buna, for example, there were 204 IMs to 31,000 employees in 1982–83, at VEB Leuna-Werke "Walter Ulbricht" there were 306 to 32,000 employees, and at VEB Chemiekombinat Bitterfeld 173 to just under 20,000. The ratios at other factory units were comparable. The MfS achieved a higher ratio at the "Fritz Heckert" machine-tool combine in Karl-Marx-Stadt. In 1983 there were 390 IMs there to 27,400 employees, presumably due to the high share of exports (about 80 percent of production) and the attendant foreign contacts.

Special attention was given to armaments-related lines of production. A unique position was occupied by the Soviet, later (as of 1953)

Soviet-German joint-stock company Wismut, which mined uranium ore for the Soviet nuclear-weapons program. From 1951 to 1982 the MfS ran a site administration for this company equivalent to a regional administration and with 600 full-time employees at final count. From 1955 to 1962 an independent department monitored the heavily developing aircraft and armaments industries, especially with a view to the "bourgeois" engineers working there. With the end of aircraft production, the remains of this department were incorporated into the Main Department for Securing the National Economy. The model of intense surveillance being tested back then would be used again later on. Thus in the early 1980s at the Carl Zeiss Jena combine, the MfS used a Soviet-backed program to develop homing heads for sea-based missiles as an opportunity to covertly penetrate all parts of the plant involved in the project. All relevant Zeiss employees were security-vetted; many failed the screening and had to withdraw from the project. Last but not least, armaments espionage, the procurement of embargoed goods, and attendant security strategies played an important role here. Alongside special focal points such as armaments and foreign trade, the MfS heavily monitored the management level of factories, as well as engineers and technicians. The lower levels of the factory hierarchy, all the way down to the highly symbolic "workers" at the grassroots, were less infiltrated, on the other hand.

Precise analyses of Stasi infiltration have yet to be made for many other areas of society, such as the civil apparatus, educational system, or mass organizations. The health system, by contrast, is an example of a well-researched sector with an average level of secret-police and secret-service infiltration. State Security's main concern there was to come to grips with the high number of doctors and medical personnel fleeing to the West from the 1950s. Of course the number of escapes rapidly dwindled after the Wall was built, but many doctors still tried to make it to the West, either through illegal escape networks or, from 1975 on, applications to emigrate. IM recruiting had little success among the medical intelligentsia, one of the most stable and traditional bourgeois milieus in the GDR. Only with a new generation of "socialist" doctors did the situation improve, but even here there were discrepancies. The higher apparatus, with the Ministry for Health at the top, became a trusted cooperation partner. There was an intense official and unofficial exchange with leading functionaries such as longtime minister Ludwig Mecklinger (SED) and several main department heads. The respective department head in the SED Central Committee had also cooperated with the MfS unofficially before assuming his Party office. Contact with medical directors and senior physicians at clinics was likewise so close that it was often hard to distinguish between official and unofficial communication, whereby State Security always endeavored to make sure its IMs did not reveal their connection to the Stasi.

Contacts were considerably less firmly established, however, among actual doctors and other medical staff. Thus, for example, in 1981, at the medical training college of Berlin-Buch there were only 3 unofficial collaborators out of 1,400 nursing students and a teaching staff of 60—and this, even though "it was considered necessary to monitor the love lives of several hundred young women" due to frequent Western contacts.[14] Erich Mielke himself had complained in 1975 that the health sector (alongside higher education and technical training colleges, as well as the surprisingly Party-loyal public-education sector) had been infiltrated too little by the secret service: "There are entire areas of the public health sector, important hospitals, educational facilities, seminar groups, etc. where our unofficial collaborators are not firmly anchored."[15]

The MfS had similar problems recruiting a base among young people, at least beyond the official Free German Youth apparatus. Adolescent nonconformism, rebellious attitudes, and especially the passion for Western beat music, rock, and eventually punk—forms of youth culture initially tolerated and later repressed—had kept State Security on edge since the early 1960s. The minister's first "youth-specific" instructions, in which he railed against "mobs, groups of hooligans, clubs, gangs, and other negative groups," were issued during these years.[16] In the 1970s and 1980s the waves of subculture had reached the GDR and struck a chord among many young people: the antiauthoritarian hippies and punks, the apolitical Goths (*Grufties*), and right-wing radical skinheads, which the MfS deemed the "most extreme anti-Communist elements we have ever had among our youth."[17]

Just as the SED fanatically clung to its cult of youth with its state-sponsored FDJ despite the rampant Westernization of lifestyles, State Security, too, tried hard to work with adolescents. But the pickings were slim. Loyal FDJ members from "positive" parental homes had little or no contact to the respective scenes or themselves "fell prey" to these subcultures. The Stasi could only penetrate more tightly knit groups through the use of pressure and blackmail, "prying out" (*herausbrechen*) young people under the threat of prosecution. The information gained was correspondingly weak. IM work with young people was marked, on the whole, by "disinterest, deconspiracy, and lack of discipline."[18] For all the emotional and spiritual havoc wreaked by the "conspicuously inconspicuous" gentlemen who suddenly showed up and requested an audience with the school principal, making inquiries and sometimes concrete threats, State Security faced the same kind of problems as their Party comrades in schools and youth organizations. In other words, dealing with East German youths was no smooth sailing. Their willingness to adapt to the status quo had apparently dwindled so much by the 1980s that the Stasi had considerable trouble recruiting any new staff for full-time service.

The real focal points of surveillance in society apart from the directly or indirectly dissident-laden milieus are easy to make out. First of all, State Security deeply penetrated all sectors having anything to do with the physical executive powers of the state: the military, armaments industry, border protection, and police. Power, after all, was primarily armed power, and care had to be taken that it did not wind up in the wrong hands. Second, the presence of State Security in the upper echelons of the GDR—the sphere of functional elites and the nomenklatura—was virtually all-encompassing as well. Here, too, it was not really the strong potential of resistance that was behind this intensity of surveillance but the idea of preventive security in the corridors of socially relevant positions of power. It was certainly congenial to the MfS that in these circles of greater and lesser functionaries the understanding for such security interests and the willingness to cooperate unofficially were quite pronounced, potential scruples having largely been stunted.

There was, however, a major exception to these tendencies: the actual locus of power of the GDR, the SED Party apparatus and its executive bodies, was off-limits to State Security and its secret-service infiltration. This prohibition was a consequence of its subordination to the "vanguard" Party and was expressly affirmed in 1954—after the supposed consolidation and newly gained independence of the State Security apparatus under Zaisser—by the Security Commission of the SED Central Committee. The ruling formally relieved unofficial collaborators of their duties upon appointment to the Central Committee or a full-time Party position, effectively excluding intense "official" contacts. Exceptions to the surveillance ban had to be approved by the chairman of the SED Security Commission, as of 1960 the National Defense Council—which is to say, Walter Ulbicht until 1971 and Erich Honecker thereafter. Honecker made use of this, too, in inner-Party conflicts, such as the case of Politbüro member Herbert Häber, who fell from favor in 1985, was put under surveillance by State Security, and forcefully admitted to a psychiatric hospital.

This internal prohibition in the midst of otherwise heavy surveillance seems not to have harmed the MfS in any systematic way. In this respect as well, the talk of a "state within a state" is misleading. There were of course borderline cases where the insatiable curiosity of the minister and his desire to always be one up, if need be by means of intrigues and cajolery, infringed upon this iron rule. One way of doing this was through the bodyguards and servants supplied to the Politbüro compound in Wandlitz by the MfS's Main Department for Personal Security. While providing an all-round "service" to top functionaries and their families, they inevitably exercised a certain amount of social control as well. This sometimes resulted in close personal relationships, for example, when a Politbüro member paved the way for his son to make a career in the MfS or when his daughter married a bodyguard. In extreme cases this all-round care could of course be used to monitor the movements of individuals—which is exactly what happened to Walter Ulbricht, of all people, when he fought to maintain his status and reputation after his fall. It is not clear if Mielke was conspiring with the new SED head in doing so. Such information, at any rate, certainly worked to Honecker's advantage.

Little is known about the practice of surveillance in the lower levels of industry and administration beyond the meager statistical data. Of course unofficial collaborators and other cooperative forces in management and staff positions played a role here, for the eye and arm of cadre instructors or security officers extended down to the shop floor. Nevertheless, the level of surveillance at the grassroots of East German society was less intense than in the "arcane" corridors of power, so long as no one made themselves conspicuous by dint of a loose tongue, an application to emigrate, or the inadvertent mention of plans to escape. This was apparently a result of the monopoly party putting less and less pressure on the "ruling class" to conform to its scheme of things; if no direct political confrontation ensued, the Party was more or less helpless and powerless against frequent changes of employment, a Western orientation, and other such phenomena.

Manipulation and Steering

What did the Stasi do with its considerable presence, especially at strategically vital points? Did it act as a kind of "lubricant" to help overcome ingrained system deficits or as a "midwife" for adequate problem analysis? This question can best be answered at present concerning the economic sphere. For one thing, this was an area that State Security had deeply penetrated and in which it had a heavy potential influence. For another, the acute symptoms of system crises in the 1980s offered reason enough for (belated) intervention, whether through direct problem-solving on the ground or through an unvarnished critical analysis of causes in its reports to the Party leadership.

State Security intervened in economic affairs ever since its founding—to be sure not for economic, but for secret-police motives. These actions did not serve to increase economic efficiency but were a means of securing power, from the expropriations of the early 1950s and combating "bourgeois specialists" with their relics of "company ideology" (*Konzernideologie*, i.e., corporate identity) to radical anticontact policies, which in the 1980s led to a series of staff replacements among microelectronics specialists due to connections to the West or to a permanent loss of motivation.

At the same time, State Security gave the economy a leg up by acting as an information service. The Science and Technology Sector of the HVA, Main Department XVIII, and the Working Group on the Area of Commercial Coordination made a major contribution to balancing out the structural innovation deficits of the East German economy through technological espionage and the illegal foreign-trade business of the Area of Commercial Coordination in the Ministry for Foreign Trade, as well as to overcoming the balance-of-payments crisis by procuring hard currency. All that was really new here was the effort expended and the methodicalness with which economic espionage and the circumventing of export bans were conducted.

Finally, State Security fulfilled an important function with its information gathering. It served as a kind of "ersatz public sphere," providing SED decision-makers at all levels of the hierarchy with situation and mood reports. Similar reporting channels existed in the SED, the FDGB trade union federation, and the administration, but the Stasi was potentially better equipped for providing more realistic reports: it had a broader base of information by virtue of its covert procurement channels and could report with the detachment of a secret observer. The state, Party, and trade-union apparatuses, by contrast, made themselves accountable by reporting on their successes and failures, which naturally encouraged window dressing. A direct comparison reveals, however, that the differences in reporting were less pronounced than one might think. MfS officers, too, were under a certain pressure to deliver positive results, and generally didn't dare to take the critical facts presented in their reports and offer an analysis of the underlying causes, which would have implied a criticism of Party leadership. State Security was by no means out of the picture with the general disappearance of supposed or actual enemy activities in factories. But instead of acknowledging its relative uselessness and assuming new and original tasks, or accumulating competence as a special kind of supervisor that the other analytical bodies were lacking, it limited itself to providing a kind of "parallel information." Hans-Hermann Hertle and Franz-Otto Gilles come to the following conclusion in their analysis of the MfS in the largest chemical combines of the GDR:

> The "proven" conspiratorial instruments were largely ineffective in trying to reduce the deplorable, structurally conditioned state of affairs in the East German economy. The unofficial information gained for the most part through the work of IMs all too frequently duplicated the information already available at the political level. Thus many an industrial minister rubbed his eyes in astonishment when he found on his desk the same well-known confidential reports he had received from his department a few weeks before concerning deficiencies in his area of responsibility, only this time on MfS letterhead and labeled "top secret."[19]

This applied not only to the devastating effects of failing to invest in local production facilities but to the entire economic development of the GDR. The respective calculations were not done by the Stasi itself but had to be procured through unofficial collaborators. Thus while "rereporting" the crisis scenarios pointed out by the ministries and the State Planning Commission, it did not dare to criticize the actual decision-making center of economic policy, the SED Central Committee, with its economic secretary Günter Mittag and general secretary Honecker. The only documented attack on Mittag and Schalck by employees of Main Department XVIII, citing their radical export strategy as the reason for the GDR's impending insolvency, was blocked in 1980 by a savagely threatening Erich Mielke, who declared it "hostile to the Party." Referring to the Five-Year Plan of 1986 to 1990, he once again defined the tasks—and, with it, the taboos—of the MfS as follows:

> The trouble-free and consistent implementation of the resolutions of the Eleventh Party Congress of the SED on the further realization of economic strategy and on continuing the course of the main task in its unity of economic and social policy is to be maximally supported by the political-operational or specialist work of all service units of the MfS even under the persistent and complicated conditions of foreign policy and foreign trade. What matters most is to broadly and reliably protect this policy from any enemy attacks and other hostile disruptive activities.[20]

And this is exactly what State Security did—however much the officers in charge might have gritted their teeth, distressed about the deterioration of factories and machines they encountered there.

Without a doubt the MfS got deeply involved in the economy on account of its security doctrine and the increasing "potential threat" deriving from integration with the West, but there are no indications that it assumed any kind of distinctly original, productive steering function in the 1980s or earlier. In the maze of homogenized institutions, it doubled or multiplied the responsibilities of the People's Police, factory fire brigades, industrial-hygiene inspections, state building inspectors, etc., of combine managements, industrial ministries, and the State Planning Commission—all of which tried to patch up the gaping holes in their respective areas through appeals, disciplining, and a good deal of improvisation, but in doing so merely opened new holes elsewhere.

Since the MfS did this with its own very particular sense of power and its "extraordinary" capabilities, it was viewed as a kind of a lifeline by many individuals in positions of authority, such as ministers, managers of state-run enterprises, engineers, hospital directors, and so on. Who, if not the omnipresent and omnipotent State Security, was to help them get their hands on urgently needed roof tiles for decrepit buildings or spare parts for idle production lines, and who else was able to use its information channels to signal the alarm and pass on candid reports to those at the top in order to bring about a change of course?

The all-round competency of the Party was essentially duplicating itself in these yearnings for a secret steering and corrective authority, without, of course, State Security being in a position to make decisions itself or being able and willing to compensate for the Party's weaknesses. Just as the agenda of the Politbüro read like the "calendar of a disorganized manager,"[21] so State Security gradually adopted the role of a "maid of all work," which always had something to report to the Politbüro and—from the viewpoint of the functionaries and factory managers—was expected to do precisely this. The same thing happened at the level of the SED regional and district secretariats and their first secretaries, whose endeavors to get the obvious system flaws in their territory under control with a combination of improvisation and idealism were likewise accompanied by meetings with the regional and district chiefs of State Security and their weekly, sometimes daily reports.

State Security was not able or willing to meet these expectations. In theoretical terms, it only functioned in one respect as an authority for conveying specific rationality criteria in the undercomplex "institutional order"[22] of the GDR—namely, as custodians of security and order. The systemically underrepresented logic of other spheres such as the economy or the legal system occupied a subordinate position in the minds of the Chekists.

State Security, in other words, by no means suffocated under the mass of its own information but was in fact able to process it until the very end. What it lacked was the will and the mental equipment to undertake a critical analysis of the underlying causes of the deficits and problems it uncovered in East German society, beyond the mere formulation of additional security needs. In this respect it remained a loyal servant of the Party leadership, which had fixed on a ruinous course over the long term. To make matters worse, the general secretary—by his own account—gauged the significance of Stasi reports by the extent to which they matched his own opinions, dismissing bad news on principle then remarking critically that he could read that in the Western press.

State Security therefore had a special, more policy-making manipulative function only in fields where the Party abstained from direct interference from the outset—in church policy, for example, or where it no longer followed through over time, in the alternative literary scene of the 1980s, for instance.

Unlike other areas of society, the churches did not follow the principles of democratic centralism and were therefore not amenable to direct orders. This lent them their unique function as a social space for expressing opinions. Thus, the "Firm" was all the more important as a means to fill this gap with the work of its unofficial collaborators. State Security's efforts and scope of action here were a direct result of the SED's withdrawal from this sphere.

There has been much debate in recent years about the character and effectiveness of this conspiratorial aid policy. As Walter Schilling, one of the founders of church-based "open youth work," concluded in his analysis of Stasi influence on the Protestant Church of Thuringia, in the two decades after 1969 almost 8 percent of the clergy were eventually listed as IMs. Added to this were many laypeople. State Security was therefore not any less well-informed about internal church affairs, especially at the leadership level, than it was in any other field where official reports were available. It undoubtedly had an influence on the church in Thuringia but did not steer it in any far-reaching way:

The MfS curbed and repressed, intensified existing conflicts, reinforced the need for harmony and not getting into too much trouble, and certainly exploited the concerns of a church in an atheist state as well as the purely theological concern of defending its "true" teachings.[23]

State Security was undoubtedly a weighty factor in the network of negotiations between Party offices and state institutions, church leaders, synods, parish community, and opposition groups, but by far not the only one responsible for the churches' slip-ups in their "balancing act ... between risky confrontation and risk-free conformity."[24] The manipulative lever of secret Stasi instruments as a means to push through democratic centralism on the sly would therefore remain an "unrealized utopia"[25]—as is evident, in particular, in the importance of the church as a safe haven for the growing activities of the opposition movement in the 1980s.

A similar tendency towards a manipulative function can be seen, albeit less extensively, in the subcultural literary scene of the 1980s. The height of persecution of writers, the forced expatriation of Wolf Biermann in 1976, and the subsequent exodus of many well-known writers and artists was followed by the SED's attempts to find less sensational forms of discipline and its acceptance, for the most part, of a "temporary autonomous zone"[26] with a variety of small independent samizdat publications. It eschewed drastic measures as far as possible in an effort to avoid bad press. It succeeded, however, in building up agents of influence like Sascha Anderson and Rainer Schedlinski as leading underground avant-gardists who endeavored to push the scene towards a depoliticized aesthetic and to torpedo publication in the West by means of obstructionist tactics and by giving early warnings to their case officers. Key figures in the literary scene were to be "decentralized," e.g., with artist's grants for Mongolia or Yemen. They were fairly successful in doing so, even though their influence and the development of the art scene in general were not reducible to their IM activities.

This new role of State Security beyond the realm of straightforward repression, as the extension of a policy that could no longer resort to drastic measures, is sometimes construed as an especially artful form of informal rule—that is to say, as yet another intensification of totalitarian rule by means of more refined methods.[27] This line of thought overlooks the fact that the successive withdrawal from direct intervention is quite obviously a symptom of weakness rather than strength, because the political costs of losing face would have been too high otherwise. This was evident not least of all when State Security did make arrests, as in the case of authors Lutz Rathenow and Frank-Wolf Matthies in 1980. The same rules applied here as they did to the burgeoning political opposition movement in the last decade of the GDR's existence, of which more below.

Reports from the Republic—
State Security as an Ersatz Public Sphere

The talk about the MfS being a surrogate or "ersatz" public sphere has another dimension beyond its feedback on functional problems in the economy or potential areas of unrest such as the church. It raises the question about the importance, for SED leaders, of secret reports from the grassroots level. Though Ulbicht and Honecker were not dependent upon approval at the polls, given the dictatorial one-party system of the GDR, they still, for the sake of the system's functionality, had to keep an eye on mood swings and the potential for unrest in the population. Besides which, they sought legitimacy without elections. They were eager to find validation for a course of their own making, and which they deemed conducive to the welfare of the people. They received this validation by way of public and internal Party reporting, at thoroughly staged mass rallies on May Day and on the "Birthday of the Republic," 7 October, or at encounters with the people at factory inspections or dedication ceremonies for new apartments. The MfS played a role in this context, with regular reports on the "reaction of the people" to resolutions of the Party leadership, to public events such as the Kennedy assassination, or to acute supply shortages.

MfS reports assumed a special role in the ensemble of information flows. As with all other channels, they too propagated the Marxist-Leninist view of the world, convinced of the historical mission of the SED and the "inevitable" (*gesetzmässig*) congruence of the Party leadership with the objective will of the working class and, with that, the majority of the people. At the same time it was the Stasi's job to recognize potential sources of unrest and enemy influence and to weigh the potential threat. It was therefore clear that, unlike the reports in *Neues Deutschland* and many internal reports by Party secretaries, Stasi reports could not be limited to good news. An evaluation officer put it like this in 1988: "The Party wants to hear from us what other organs cannot report or what they often don't want to report—this supposedly happens too—or what is wrong in the reports of other organs."[28] MfS evaluation officers did follow the ritual "social class theater"[29] and always began by emphasizing that the people approved of the general Party line. But the ratios of praise to criticism, as well as the tone of reporting could vary, allowing the seasoned reader to get a differentiated picture of what really preoccupied East German citizens and what really mattered to them most personally.

Mood reports of this sort had a long tradition. They were introduced as daily "reports from the front" in the cold civil war against the GDR's own population after the uprising of June 1953, and were transformed into a regular series of reports on specific topics in the late 1950s. The reports on "reactions from the population" varied in number depending on the occasion, with fifteen reports a year being typical. Party leaders had an ambivalent attitude towards these reports. They were indispensable as a gauge of popular appeal and approval, but all too negative reports, of course, ran the risk of rubbing top functionaries the wrong way, undermining their self-image. This resulted in a series of restrictions. When criticism of Ulbicht had become too great in 1957–58, the first secretary gave State Security a dressing-down for "legally spreading enemy hate propaganda,"[30] and markedly restricted the pool of recipients, so that only the most narrow circle would receive the reports from then on. The restrictions were later relaxed in the 1960s, when empirical sociology, and with it a certain openness in observing society, experienced a boom in the GDR. This corresponded with a manifest professionalization of the information system within the MfS.[31]

Mielke opted for a targeted use of information just prior to ousting Ulbricht. Whereas the enfeebled dictator only received reports of secondary importance, the rising Erich Honecker, Willi Stoph, and Werner Lamberz were provided with detailed reports in rapid succession about Brandt's visit to Erfurt and, above all, the acute economic crisis in the fall and winter of 1970–71. To be sure, circumstances quickly changed once Honecker ascended to power. Issues of supply became taboo for a while. Following a report about the East Germans' enthusiasm for Willy Brandt and his election victory in November 1972, the Central Evaluation and Information Group (ZAIG) under the leadership of the strategically important Werner Irmler had to cut off all reports to the first secretary and his closest cohorts about the "reactions of the population," compiling them from then on only for the minister and his deputies.[32] It seems that Mielke sometimes put sensitive information in his oral reports to Honecker or spread it discreetly among other Politbüro members or Soviet officials. But it would take seventeen years until the Party leadership stood up and took note of this source of information again. Only in September 1989 did the Politbüro decide (in the absence of an ailing Honecker) to commission three comprehensive reports from Mielke about the situation in the GDR with respect to three groups: the population at large, SED members, and those applying for emigration.[33]

MfS reports are interesting from today's perspective because they were based on statements from the "small public sphere"—those moods and opinions, in other words, that Stasi employees and informers picked up among their coworkers and neighbors at club meetings or waiting in line at the store. The collection work was done by the so-called evaluation and information groups (AIGs) at the district offices, right up to the Central Evaluation and Information Group, which reported straight to Mielke. The reports were repeatedly filtered on their way through the hierarchy. Thus the reports at the district offices were much more straightforward than those that reached the minister. Even in the "quiet" 1970s, the talk in village pubs was not infrequently "hard on the limit of slandering the state."[34] All the same, exchanges at the local level did percolate up to the center of power in cases of nationwide significance—in 1977, for instance, when the SED massively cut back coffee imports for a brief period of time due to increasing world-market prices and introduced a coffee substitute, a mixture of roasted grains and real coffee beans. This new blend under the brand name "Kaffee-Mix" soon acquired the popular sobriquet "Erich's Crowning" (in reference to the famous West German brand Jacobs Krönung, literally "Jacob's Crowning"). The Party leadership quickly intervened and frantically raised even more hard-currency loans in order to stabilize East German coffee supplies, 25 percent of which were provided by care packages from family and friends in West Germany anyway.[35]

There were a number of recurring themes in the reports. Huge events such as the collectivization of agriculture in 1960, the suppression of the Prague Spring in 1968, or the Party congresses of the SED and CPSU were accompanied by a rapid succession of reports. The effects of "enemy" activities among East German youths, in church circles, or at universities and technical colleges figured in as well. Moreover, occasional walkouts into the 1960s were closely watched by State Security. In one respect, the key issues concerned everything that had to do with inter-German affairs, from frontier-crossing agreements for Berlin as of 1963, and negotiations in the wake of the new Ostpolitik, to visiting and travel regulations. On the other hand, the supply situation and the promises of SED social policy were a constant focus of reports as well—a topic that East German citizens could express their opinions on relatively freely. The unofficial system of privileges and the inequality of the "Intershop" hard-currency economy (i.e., special state-run stores selling Western goods for Western currency) were frequently the subject of popular grievances. These two topics made for an explosive mixture in the final years of the GDR. Breakdown rates for machines and vehicles of up to 60 percent and the general decline in production and supplies heightened an already dramatic situation, which "constantly gave rise to ... vehement and heated, sometimes aggressive disputes," a report from late 1988 said.[36] Added to this were the pictures painted by hundreds of thousands of East Germans returning from trips to the Federal Republic, which Honecker had allowed in the run-up to his visit to Bonn in 1987: they "glamorize the range of goods in many ways since returning, in their conversations with friends or coworkers," as well as praising the overall standard of living in the West, evaluation officers helplessly bemoaned in June 1987.[37] The third topic was the lack of a public sphere itself. An open exchange about problems was something not only average citizens wanted, but many journalists as well, and Gorbachev's "glasnost" was just what they were looking for. The first reports, just a few weeks after the Soviet Party leader took office, already talked about the "breath of fresh air," and in 1986 they spoke enthusiastically about his "heartfelt, open, and casual manner"—qualities that no other Soviet or East German party boss had ever been able to pride himself on.[38]

The MfS, in others words, certainly didn't "choke" on its information system. Rather, it produced a straightforward analysis of the situation, which, tainted as it was by its ideological viewpoint and limited in terms of content, was actually quite detailed, essentially reproducing what was being said in the semipublic sphere, on the street, in bars, and at the workplace. Neither the downfall of the SED nor German reunification, the two major themes of the autumn revolution, played a significant role, however. These two topics were evidently so taboo and criminalized that no one even dared to talk about them, at least not openly. Or perhaps normal East Germans just didn't bother to think about them, given their enormous unlikelihood.

A public sphere beyond the Party's self-staging, a serious discourse with independent protagonists, and an influence on political decision-making processes did not exist in state-socialist systems. MfS reporting did nothing to change this either, being curtailed by Party leaders whenever it stepped outside the bounds of SED thinking and no longer reaching the Politbüro in most instances as of 1972. Not even as a one-way street was the flow of information effective. This notwithstanding, MfS reports were revealing in two different ways. First, they showed that a "small," spontaneous, and local public sphere beyond the immediate personal sphere did indeed exist—albeit without much response from the media, apart from the occasional Western report. Second, they showed that a differentiated picture of the range of opinions and their transformation over time was obtainable after all, if the strict taboos were not blanked out. Götz Aly came to the conclusion for comparable reports in Nazi Germany that it would be more appropriate to talk about an "unpublic opinion," about "processes of collective understanding which took place osmotically in the subcutaneous layers of society."[39] This is without a doubt correct. And yet it is still possible to make out trends of enthusiasm, approval, tolerance, and rejection in the—extremely different—mass bases of both regimes, as well as the respective taboo zones.

Big Brother? The Presence of the MfS in Daily Life

Was East German society "poisoned to the core" by spying and surveillance? Were the people in this country "totally controlled"? Did they vegetate in an "Auschwitz of the soul," as Stefan Wolle postulates in his fast-paced survey of Honecker's GDR?[40] If so, how did they manage to develop the culture of political jokes he so vividly portrays, the "rumors and urban legends," a veritable coffeehouse culture qua "surrogate public sphere" in university towns, their spirited approach to life?

There is no denying that State Security could get a comprehensive picture of any East German citizen it pleased. It perfected the classic tools of secret-police surveillance. It systematically monitored letters and packages, telephone calls and telegrams, and especially cross-border mail and telecommunications. In East Berlin alone it listened in on 20,000 telephone calls in 1989. These surveillance techniques could be complemented by bugs and hidden cameras or observation teams in the case of sufficient evidence against or growing interest in an individual. State Security also had an extremely broad range of sources from which to procure information: petitioning agencies, state insurance companies, banks and savings institutions, hospitals, registration offices for venereal disease, libraries, and, of course, judicial authorities and offices of the interior, i.e., state prosecutor's offices, departments of the interior of the district and regional councils, and, especially, the People's Police. In Stasi jargon, these institutions were called "partners of operational cooperation" (POZW).

The MfS could even demand support from these institutions through official or unofficial channels. One individual, for instance, was summoned to a routine medical checkup to "tie him up" (*binden*) while the MfS was installing a bug in his apartment. Many of these institutions, such as Party groups or FDJ basic organizations, cadre departments or factory managements, not only served as accomplices but performed a considerable amount of "disciplining" themselves before State Security ever got involved.

The most important partner here was the People's Police. The system of beat patrol officers (ABVs), in particular, was an important grassroots instrument for conducting investigations in residential and recreational areas. The ABVs were each responsible for 3,000 to 4,000 inhabitants—several city blocks or a handful of villages. They went on patrol, had calling hours, and maintained contact with (ideally ten to thirty) volunteer helpers, house administrators (*Hausgemeinschaftslei-tungen*), and other local residents. On top of this, they, too, were expected to handle secret informers, albeit in a less formal and elaborate way than the MfS. Even if by the 1970s and 1980s the ABV system ultimately boiled down to the desire of a patriarchal and authoritarian state for a petty-bourgeois brand of "order and security," it was still an important information-gathering resource for State Security. An ABV, for example, had to put together for future reference a character study of anyone applying to emigrate. The "secret" colleagues from the MfS were not necessarily popular among these officials. They often acted in an arrogant manner, demanding total obedience but rarely playing with open cards themselves. Still, the cooperation worked.

In the case of IMs, too, things are not as obvious as they seem at first. For one thing, an IM was not just an IM. The label concealed an exceptionally wide variety of activities and behaviors. Historical studies of "everyday life and mentalities" have shown that no East German citizen recruited this way was "merely" an IM, but that IM work was an additional, secret role among others: a department head, an engineer or economist in a factory, who might very well touch upon his own interests and predilections when talking to his case officer. In the village of Dabel, in Mecklenburg, for instance, historian Jan Palmowski identified 46 IMs, 10 of whom had been put on the local pastor. And yet the files are full of complaints by Stasi officers about the unwillingness of locals to say anything incriminating about their neighbors.[41] Thus, the "bending" of an IM was by no means always successful, as the barriers to reporting on one's family and friends often proved insurmountable.

Spying within families tended to be the exception, in other words. And the child IMs so often brought to bear were even more of a rarity. What we have learned to date about spying and denunciations would seem to indicate that—as with Sheila Fitzpatrick's findings about the Soviet Union of the 1930s—the family as a shelter and basic community tended to be strengthened rather than weakened when pressured by the system.

IM deployment was most effective in the secondary environment of East German citizens, i.e., informing at the workplace or in study groups, on neighbors in the building or at the summer cottage, on sports club teammates, etc. The threshold of inhibition to report here was lower, and the opportunities for sounding people out under a fictitious identity ("legend") were greater. Unlike in the primary private domain of family and friends, the typical double life cultivated by many East German citizens, with its private and its official face, was harder to disentangle here: the system's claims to loyalty and denouncing someone for personal reasons were often quite compatible.

From today's perspective it is also important to note that roles could change in the course of one's life, as the biographies of prominent dissidents such as Robert Havemann and Wolfgang Templin have shown. Thus it is not uncommon nowadays that many people applying to see their files had once pledged to work as IMs but were under surveillance themselves either before or after their being recruited.[42] The categories begin to lose their contours when a microhistorical approach is taken. The many "contact persons" handled by the MfS but not formally and officially recruited, as well as other East German citizens the Stasi occasionally talked to seem more important, whereas the category of unofficial collaborators suddenly loses its usefulness.[43] Though this might not affect a clear moral judgment in individual cases, it does change the way we look at East German society as a whole.

A second dimension can be added to this. The question of the MfS in society has to take into account more than its mere presence, whose real dimensions only became clear in retrospect; it must likewise consider contemporary notions about the potential threat the Stasi posed and its embeddedness in everyday life, as well as the influence these notions had on people's overall behavior. Behind the changing sociopsychological role of the MfS as a myth was an ensemble of experiences, impressions, and traditions. We can distinguish—very roughly—between two phases here. As American historian Andrew Port elaborated in his microhistorical study on the Thuringian town of Saalfeld, two factors played a crucial role in the first two decades of the GDR's existence. First, the suppression of the June uprising in 1953—and, in the case of Saalfeld, a local revolt in 1951—left a deep and lasting impression on East Germans. The lesson they learned was that the regime would defend its position resolutely.[44] Second, tens of thousands of East Germans had suffered through internment in Soviet special camps and persecution in the immediate postwar years, both of which were taboo topics in GDR society.[45] It was the experience of massive violence, in other words, that hung menacingly over daily life. Actual Stasi presence in the 1950s and 1960s in a district town like Saalfeld and at the factories located nearby, such as the "Maxhütte" steel and rolling mill in Unterwellenborn, was still miles away from the invasiveness of the 1970s and 1980s. The village of Dabel, mentioned above, provides a similar picture. The Stasi sought in vain there, well into the 1960s, for the person responsible for subversive graffiti, in one instance scrawled with tar on the house of the local policeman. The investigators were convinced that local villagers knew who was behind it but failed to apprehend the culprit. In the perception of the locals, the MfS (in contrast to, say, local SED members) was something external to village life: dark sedans and men in leather coats who turned up to conduct investigations then disappeared again.

The specific way the Stasi made itself felt in daily life would change with time, analogous to the functional change the MfS underwent in general. The younger generations had not personally experienced the harsh waves of repression of the 1950s. Rather, they tended to associate the MfS with certain signals sent out by a broad but hidden presence, "like an itchy undershirt."[46] The findings of microhistorical research are complex and the topic still rather hard to investigate, because small communities in general practice an entirely unique form of communal living and in a country like the GDR followed their own agenda even if they went through the motions of party-state rituals. State Security was always treated and perceived as an external factor in village life, even though the files do show that local system representatives, like the mayor, heads of social organizations, or civics teachers, were often working for it officially or unofficially. Many of those active in local heritage work, for example, claimed that they were not particularly intimidated by the possibility of surveillance—an ambivalent statement, as it shows that the thought of observation and its associated dangers was at least subconsciously present.[47]

The many whispered jokes, rumors, and ironic connotations, as well as double levels of communication in general, show that ordinary East Germans were not exclusively guided by their fear of the invisible "Firm" but did allow themselves certain behaviors and carved out certain spaces where the Stasi wouldn't be listening in or threatening them with sanctions—though sometimes they were wrong, a lesson painfully learned. Complaints about supply shortages—with no direct political connotations—were frequent. The ever-present murmur of dissatisfaction and the culture of grumbling considerably increased in the waning years of the GDR. Thus, for example, in 1989, at a public electoral meeting prior to the last local elections, some elderly inhabitants of Leipzig recalled that "before the war" the trade-fair city had received its guests looking neat and tidy, and that now it was shamefully dirty and dilapidated.

The sociopsychological balance sheet of Stasi presence and of life in general under or in a dictatorship is therefore confusing as well as divided. It produced a mentality of subservience, especially in the (politically and socially) intermediate spheres of the East German population, which frequently became involved in entanglements of this sort. The critical theory of the "authoritarian character" has pathologized this subservience into a sickness that needs to be healed, Hans-Joachim Maaz and Joachim Gauck being two of the main proponents of this idea.[48] In terms of social history, this phenomenon can be construed, rather, as a continuation of older German traditions stemming from a political culture that developed under the conditions of a predemocratic social order.[49]

To be sure, in the course of East German history, other spheres took shape in which a different tone and attitude was possible. Once an individual decided against having high expectations in terms of career opportunities and social advancement, a kind of inner freedom emerged which even the eavesdropping Stasi accepted so long as the boundaries of political protest and collective action were not transgressed. There came to be a "division of the social world into an immediate personal sphere amenable to individual influence and the arcane one of SED rule."[50] In sum, we can conclude that the MfS intruded ever more and with ever greater effort into all areas of life while at the same time losing its bite, failing by a long shot to suppress all deviant forms of behavior. In this perspective, the exorbitant expansion of the apparatus and its potential of surveillance was not so much a direct expression of the totalitarian claim to social engineering inherited from the mobilization phase of the Communist regime, but rather a misguided redirection of activity to compensate for the fizzling out of such schemes.

Getting back to sociopsychology, the constant reproduction of subservience had its flip side in the strong and persistent reserve which the majority of the population felt towards the internal opposition, and even towards the victims of State Security in the narrow sense, e.g., political persecutees upon their release from prison.[51] Protest was therefore not only a provocation of the authorities but was also a challenge to one's own personal brand of conformity and could easily lead to defensive reactions. It is doubtful that Communist dissidents such as Biermann and Havemann were really expressing what the East German population felt. There was a palpable sense of alienation from the long-haired, bearded activists of the opposition movement with their Western, "alternative" style of dress—except, of course, among a growing youth scene gathered around the churches. Unlike in Poland, at any rate, there was no broad and sustained social base for the actions of the East German opposition. This reservedness did not break down until the summer of 1989, with the avalanche of refugees escaping through Hungary—and returned again with the fall of the Wall on 9 November 1989, when the majority of citizens in the GDR no longer wanted anything to do with their own brand of democratic socialism.

Chapter 5

RESISTANCE—OPPOSITION—PERSECUTION

Emigration and Unrest in Half a Country

State Security was active in many fields but never lost sight of its founding cause and main purpose: detecting and fighting any kind of resistance or rebellion against the SED regime. The opposition in the GDR was always strongly affected by the existence of two German states. A variety of contacts and interactions of both an affirmative and inhibitive nature evolved between the GDR and the Federal Republic. Sociologist Albert O. Hirschman developed a model to explain the two basic options East Germans had if they no longer agreed with the system and found their lives within it intolerable: exit and voice. Unlike Poland, Hungary, or Czechoslovakia, the citizens of East Germany had better prospects of leaving the country one way or another with neighboring West Germany right next-door. About three million of them did so before the erection of the Berlin Wall. Thereafter the number significantly dwindled, but still an uninterrupted flow of about a thousand East Germans a year was willing to brave the considerable risks and flee to the West. As of the mid-1970s, the so-called "application for permanent emigration" (*Antrag auf ständige Ausreise*) gained in importance, creating an outlet for potential unrest. Apart from exit there was the second option of voice—that is to say, various forms of oppositional behavior from within the country.

There was a complex interplay between these two paths. Both variants were distinctly evident in the 1950s, but the high level of emigration weakened the potential for resistance within the system over the short term. The result was a politically induced "cleansing" of the population within the framework of two German states: Communists went to the East, whereas democrats and anti-Communists headed West.

Emigration to the West was severely curbed after the Wall went up, though it never ebbed entirely. By no means did this lead to a stronger opposition, however. Emigration in the 1970s and 1980s, in particular of the many demoralized activists of the internal opposition movement, resulted in a permanent bleeding of resources, with devastating consequences, whereas the rapid growth of the emigration movement in the final throes of the German Democratic Republic apparently served as the most important trigger for the internal opposition and mass demonstrations on the domestic front.

Apart from emigration, the internal opposition movement was linked to West Germany in numerous other ways, both positive and negative. On the one hand, the SED and MfS directly associated all manner of deviant behavior with Western influences, because in their view socialist society had eliminated the objective basis for dissent. According to this logic, anyone active in the opposition, in defiance of this "scientific" claim, was inevitably being steered by the West German foe. This doctrine put the internal opposition in a paradoxical situation in which they developed an even stronger need to dissociate themselves from the West in order to free themselves of this general suspicion. On the other hand, fellow opposition members who had emigrated as of the 1970s and correspondents from the Western media accredited in the GDR helped the opposition movement reach wide sections of the population via radio and television. There were frequent and heated debates among dissidents and in "dialogue" with the powers-that-be about whether or not a specific issue should be disseminated internally in the GDR, i.e., with little effect because of censorship, or through Western media channels, where it could be discussed more openly.

There was emigration from other Communist countries as well, from Hungary and Czechoslovakia to Austria, for example. But emigrants from East to West Germany tended to integrate and assimilate themselves more fully—apart from a handful of dogged dissidents such as Jürgen Fuchs and Roland Jahn, who made it their mission in life to continue supporting the opposition from abroad. While it is true that even assimilated West German citizens with Eastern origins never abandoned their roots entirely and reactivated their ties in 1989, as in the case of foreign minister Hans-Dietrich Genscher, such persons could no longer be directly mobilized for the internal opposition movement in the East. Their "reconnections," if anything, served to swell the number of applications to emigrate in the 1980s.

From this brief look at the basic setup it is apparent that further distinctions are necessary to do justice to the wide range of dissident behaviors with their varied aims and forms. Researching the resistance to National Socialism has taught us this already. The diversified terminology developed in this scholarship has been applied to the GDR as well, producing such distinctions as resistance, opposition, dissidence, and immunity, or even more finely differentiated terms. A spectrum like this eschews black-and-white labels in favor of a more nuanced approach, allowing for the partial loyalties and antagonisms that were typical of East German society in the 1970s and 1980s. In an in-depth analysis, the range of attitudes towards the ruling system would consist of an aversive half, from militant system hostility to disgruntled loyalty, and a sympathetic half, from partially well-meaning acceptance to "150 percent" participation in the exercise of power.

The "peripheries" of this spectrum have been examined relatively well: open hostility on the one side, active system loyalty out of conviction or opportunism on the other. The attitudes in the wide-ranging "center," though, are hard to put down to one side or the other. They allow for all manner of speculation about the "real" inner stance of "normal" East German citizens, who belonged neither to the active class of system supporters nor to the hard core of dissident subculture. The hodgepodge of articulate and silent attitudes, of consent and the potential for resistance, the juxtaposition of public and private behavior all require more investigation.

Resistance (*Widerstand*) is understood here as a fundamental opposition to the system. Its aim was the elimination of SED rule and, with it, in effect, the GDR altogether, combined with the restoration of a bourgeois social order and/or parliamentary democracy. This type of behavior was particularly strong in the 1950s. It included organized defense efforts in connection with organizations like the Eastern bureaus of the West German parties, the Investigating Committee of Free Jurists, the Combat Group Against Inhumanity, and similar institutions. Most of these groups had Western notions of democracy in mind. In the early years there were even militant forces in the anti-Communist resistance that sought revenge for the defeat of Nazi Germany. These included the clientele of former functionaries of the Nazi regime which the early Federal Republic tried to integrate, e.g., in the initially American-backed League of German Youth (BDJ). There has been no systematic investigation to date into whether such a potential group of resistance-prone Nazi activists existed in the GDR as well.

The term opposition (*Opposition*) or political protest is used to refer to organized resistance against larger or smaller parts or aspects of the system of rule that did not aim to eliminate the system as such. It included, for example, the demand for a greater diversity of opinions or criticism of the militarization of social life.

A variation of opposition is dissidence (*Dissidenz*). This refers to the deviant positions of declared Communists, usually formulated within the ranks of the Party and generally invoking the Marxist classics and their doctrines as distinct from the Communist system in practice.

Finally, there is a fourth form of behavior referred to as immunity (*Resistenz*), which is used to designate relatively unorganized, usually individual acts of noncompliance, e.g., refusal to join the FDJ, or self-willed forms of behavior in opposition to the system's claim to shape society. This kind of behavior often fed on certain social milieus that continued to exist in whole or in part despite the "cultural revolutionary" transformation that attempted to blot them out. The ones most frequently cited are the bourgeois and Christian traditions. It would be interesting to investigate, though, if proletarian traditions, more specifically their youth subcultures, figured in here as well.

The last category is extremely hard to delineate. The problem is not only one of definition but is also quite concrete in nature: though the SED may have upheld its claim to totality until the very end, by the 1970s it effectively no longer insisted on its enforcement, contenting itself instead with compliance or consensual agreements largely limited to the public sphere. The "invitation to schizophrenia" that resulted from this creates problems of classification. This form of resistance, or nonconformism, is the most interesting, however, extending as it did into a wide variety of daily behaviors and constituting a characteristic feature of totalitarian systems. Immunity was naturally coupled with a more or less disgruntled loyalty and acceptance of the status quo in other areas of society.

A differentiated take like this or an even more nuanced approach to the varied forms of politically deviant behavior provides a more accurate perspective on the dissident potential among East German citizens, without underestimating their margins of maneuver or, conversely, fashioning large swaths of the population into resistance fighters.

From the Berlin Wall to CSCE

With the building of the Berlin Wall, the fate of fundamental resistance to the GDR was sealed once and for all. The collectivization of agriculture had broken the last great social potential for revolt. The classic organizations of resistance such as the Eastern offices of the West German parties, the Investigating Committee of Free Jurists, and the Combat Group Against Inhumanity had likewise lost their bases under the intense persecution of the 1950s. This also went for secondary schools and universities, where time and again, and for a relatively long time, groups of "bourgeois" youths protested against discrimination and SED rule in the form of political pamphlets, etc.

The sealing of the border to the West cut off contacts to Western organizations and—perhaps more importantly—buried the option, most likely present in the minds of many individuals until then, of heading West in the event of a serious confrontation with state authorities. At the same time, the "secret founding day of the GDR," 13 August 1961, and the feeble or, rather, nonexistent reaction of the West must have elicited resignation on the part of those who still had hopes of SED rule ending soon and the two German states being reunited. The considerable size of this group of people is evident from the many protests in the days and weeks after the border was sealed and the harsh wave of arrests carried out by State Security.

The potential for political and social resistance was, of course, not done away with entirely, but the option of active protest had largely become a lost cause. Western efforts to aid the escape of East Germans resulted in a number of spectacular operations in the first months and years after the Wall went up, such as the building of tunnels between West and East Berlin, damaging in a lasting way the image of the GDR. Fundamental resistance in the GDR was limited to rare individual acts such as lathe operator Josef Kneifel's bomb attack on the Soviet tank monument in Karl-Marx-Stadt, intended as a protest against the Soviet invasion of Afghanistan. All in all, however, the construction of the Berlin Wall and the wave of arrests that followed effectively broke the resistance of the population.

What remained was a hard-to-quantify potential for resistance. Many individuals who probably would have gone West eventually had the border remained open were now suddenly faced with a new reality that they had to come to terms with somehow. The SED leadership abandoned its unyielding course in a matter of months, proclaiming its new mantra of the "socialist human community." By the same token, the introduction of compulsory military service in January 1962 created a new area of conflict, which developed into a permanent focal point of political protest and conscientious objection in the form of the "construction solider" movement and, later, the demand for a Social Peace Service (*Sozialer Friedensdienst*—SoFD).

From the 1960s to the mid-1970s, there were two essential socio-moral milieus which turned out to be sources of resistance and deviant behavior. One of them was the remnants of the traditional bourgeoisie, e.g., university professors and doctors. The church was also an important factor here (mostly Protestant, to a lesser extent Catholic). How the church was to deal with its special role—the question, for example, of belonging to the all-German League of Protestant Churches (EKD) or the concept of a "church in socialism"—was a constant point of contention within the church itself as well as between the church and the state. Yet despite internal and external conflicts, the church remained the most stable expression of potential resistance in East German society against the totalitarian claims of the ruling party, serving as a shelter against the atomization of social life—without the church itself ever having to consider itself part of the political opposition.

The second important source of deviant behavior was the intellectual and artistic dissidence. With Ulbricht's harsh repression of rival forces in the Party leadership and the sentencing of Communist dissidents Wolfgang Harich and Walter Janka, as well as writers such as Erich Loest, to long terms in prison, Party-internal dissidence had indeed largely run dry. But alternating trends between a loosening of the culture-political reins and dogmatism succeeded, after the construction of the Wall, in producing a number of prominent figures who, though not engaged in system opposition as such, nevertheless articulated their own positions in the framework of the socialist system. The two most lasting and important representatives of this movement were professor of chemistry Robert Havemann, who, expelled from the SED in 1964 for his unorthodox views and dismissed from Humboldt University in Berlin, was celebrated into the 1980s as the nestor of Communist dissidents, and his friend, the poet and singer Wolf Biermann, who was banned from performing in 1965 in connection with the notorious "clean-sweep" plenary of the Central Committee and could subsequently only publish his books and records in the West. Moreover, there was a large group of writers, directors, actors, and other creative artists—*Kulturschaffende,* or "creators of culture," to use the East German term—who endeavored to reflect critically and publicly on reality and its taboos in the GDR: Stefan Heym, Ulrich Plenzdorf, Reiner Kunze, and a host of others. Many of them defined themselves as socialists and Marxists and even welcomed the building of the Wall to relieve the pressure on an embattled political system. Yet the hope of being able to talk more openly "among themselves" ultimately turned out to be an illusion. Anyone venturing out too far risked being accused of playing into the hands of the class enemy.

In the population at large, young people in particular were a constant source of unrest. Their "tough guy" defiance and hooliganesque behavior (earning them the nickname *Halbstarke* or "half-strongs"), their passion for beat and rock music and a wild life, though not political in the strict sense, repeatedly collided with the "wholesome" and "disciplined" virtues of FDJ role models. The SED failed to cope with these waves of subculture throughout the whole of its existence, and tried to keep them in check through a fragile mixture of coercion and more or less spurious compromises.

A new generation of dissidents experienced its first formative conflicts in the confrontation between this youthful zeitgeist and the educational system's demands for loyalty—when being admitted to secondary school or the university, for example—and especially in the form of compulsory military service, the traditional "school of the nation" for young males, introduced in the GDR in 1962. Being disqualified from attending the *Gymnasium,* the path to higher education in Germany, expulsion from university for having long hair or an "unsocialist" lifestyle, or refusing military service were often the first steps along the way to becoming part of the opposition. To be sure, only a small percentage ended up on the dissident track on account of such experiences. But these circles gradually developed into the nucleus of a "new" opposition in the 1970s and 1980s, beginning, for example, in 1964 with the formation under church pressure of so-called "construction-soldier units," whose members refused to take up arms for reasons of conscience. This new generation first came to the fore politically in the protests against the suppression of the Prague Spring in 1968. Three-quarters of the almost 1,200 individuals arrested and prosecuted for these "criminal offenses" were thirty years of age or younger, and almost all of them (84 percent) were "workers"—whatever this label meant for an embarrassed SED.[1] All in all, the protests of 1968 were bigger than those after the Wall was built. Mood reports from the SED and MfS revealed that a majority of older East German citizens also rejected the Soviet invasion, but that given their experiences of 1953, 1956, and 1961 they were hardly surprised and therefore barely protested against it. The MfS concluded contentedly: "There was no serious discord, disturbances, or incidents involving larger segments of the population or specific population groups that could have potentially escalated into political actions against the GDR and the measures taken by the five Warsaw Pact signatory states."[2]

The "New" Opposition

The first protagonists of a "new" opposition emerged in 1968. The Ministry for State Security was quick to notice this development. Only about a quarter of the protests were ever cleared up, and most of the "culprits" had never before been on the Stasi's radar as "hostile-negative" forces. Unlike Poland and Hungary, and especially Czechoslovakia, where the efforts of the opposition to establish a democratic-socialist "Third Way" were crushed along with the Prague Spring, dissidents in the GDR still attached great importance to the double message of the reform-Communist experiment: that the Soviet Union would tolerate no reform, but that such an initiative on the part of the ruling Communist party was at least the historical "possibility."

This "nonsynchronicity" with the East European opposition was partly the result of intellectual cross-connections with the New Left in the West and its main theorists, Adorno, Marcuse, Fanon, and Bloch, whose antiauthoritarian and utopian ideas offered perspectives for criticizing real socialism too. The last, and at the same time most elaborate and respected work to emerge from this tradition came from the pen of the charismatic maverick Rudolf Bahro. Published in 1977 by the press of the West German trade union federation under the title *The Alternative: A Critique of Actually Existing Socialism*,[3] it resulted in its author being sentenced to eight years in prison for "conveying intelligence" (*Nachrichtenübermittlung*) to a foreign power and "betrayal of [state] secrets" (*Geheimnisverrat*). Naturally, his idea of "human emancipation"[4] was naturally little known in the East German opposition, whereas the book had a lasting impact on the image of Soviet Communism among New Leftists in West Germany. A strong wave of solidarity arose among Trotskyites such as Ernest Mandel and independent antiauthoritarians the likes of student protest leader Rudi Dutschke, but even the federal chairman of the Young Socialists, the Hanover lawyer and later chancellor of reunified Germany, Gerhard Schröder, was among those to express their support for Bahro. In October 1979 the SED released him from prison and banished him to West Germany.

Dissident Marxism in the East German opposition movement suffered a heavy blow with the deportation of Bahro and the expatriation of Wolf Biermann, though, admittedly, it never had much of a following among the mass of the people anyway. The next oppositional "tome," Rolf Henrich's *The Tutelary State: On the Failure of Real Existing Socialism*, published in April 1989—yet again in the West—would say goodbye once and for all to this tradition of leftist thought.

In the 1970s another opposition movement was brewing as well, which picked up these traditions of protest with their roots in Christianity and democratic socialism. With the closing down of free zones in youth clubs and the like, the movement began to gather under the roof of the Protestant Church, which, thanks to the commitment of many pastors and deacons and the movement's concept of "open youth work," opened its doors to this scene. It was never the intention of this opposition to engage in fundamental resistance to the system. Instead, it tried to articulate its criticism within a legal framework and with reference to the written law of the GDR, asserting its own concepts of living and breaking out of the standardized paths prescribed by real-socialist society. Its initial criticism was primarily aimed against the pressure to conform and the internal militarization of the GDR, e.g., when the SED introduced "socialist military training" (*sozialistische Wehrerziehung*) as a compulsory subject in East German schools in 1978. The arms race and environmental pollution were subsequent points of criticism.

As such, the opposition movement of the late 1970s and 1980s had a dual character. On the one hand, it took up themes that played a key role in the so-called "new social movements" of Western industrial societies. It was no coincidence then that the West German Greens were one of their closest allies. In this respect its criticism went beyond the East-West divide and avoided any affirmative stance towards the Western capitalist model. The extent of this can perhaps best be measured by the fact that even during the most heated phase in the fall of 1989 the new opposition groups were still concerned about exploitation in the Third World or were battling the destruction of MfS files because burning them would cause air pollution.

At the same time, however, by articulating these themes they conveyed the demand for the vested right to publicly discuss and participate in political decision-making processes. The protest against contaminated rivers was also a protest for the right to publicly talk about contaminated rivers and the ability to politically fight for their cleanup through democratic participation, and was ultimately a protest against all forms of repression which they and others suffered from for advocating such causes. In this respect the new opposition was increasingly and expressly committed to democracy, the rule of law, and personal liberty, and was thus opposed to dictatorship.

What these demands and aims did not have in mind was the wholesale adoption of Western models of liberal democracy. Politically the new opposition debated concepts of grassroots democracy, whereas socially and economically it tended to take the unredeemed promise of "people's property" (*Volkseigentum*) at face value rather than wanting to put the factories back into private hands. The radical expropriations of the early years and the fact that the expropriated generally went to the West meant that the restoration of presocialist property relations in the East was never a topic of the opposition prior to 1989.

To be sure, this was an unsettled question. When the question finally became acute in 1989–90, further discussion turned out to be superfluous. The factories and their emplyees demanded one thing above all else: a lot of money to make up for years of underinvestment and to implement a program of structural modernization—and this could only come from the West. The utopia of a just and ecologically sound "people's property" fell from the agenda so quickly that some of the erstwhile participants have no memory of it nowadays.

The organized and continually active core of the opposition was small. In May 1989, the MfS's Central Evaluation and Information Group counted 150 local groupings and 10 republic-wide networks. About 2,500 people were more or less active in these groups, 600 were considered leaders, and about 60 "incorrigible enemies of socialism."[5] In the early 1980s a considerably larger scene had developed in the background, in the environs of the Protestant Church and its open youth work. Thus, for example, in February 1982 about 5,000 people gathered for a peace forum at the Church of the Cross (Kreuzkirche) in Dresden, despite the many attempts to prevent it. In the weeks preceding it, the youth parish offices had passed out more than 100,000 patches reading "Swords into Plowshares" as a symbol of the peace movement. The patches were a common sight, especially on young people, before the state authorities intervened and essentially banned them in January 1982. Although the reach of such campaigns was visibly wide, the organized internal opposition itself was relatively small. This was thanks to Stasi repression, but also to the peculiar character of the opposition milieu, which failed to attract many people.

The Emigration Movement

More than 650,000 people left the GDR between 1961 and August 1989, despite the closing of its borders. This was less than the 3 million who had left before the Wall was built, but still a lot of people—much more than the number of people active in the opposition movement. The number of people fleeing to the West went down dramatically when the Wall went up. Nevertheless about 2,000 East German citizens were fleeing to the West each year by mid-1975. Thereafter the number sank to about 1,000 individuals a year by 1985. In the final years of the GDR the number of those leaving the country illegally shot up again to nearly 7,300 in 1988. The vast majority of these were East German citizens who never returned from their trips to the West which the state was now granting on a large scale.

The number of smugglings and outright cases of flight across the border went down, because a less risky way of leaving had appeared as of the mid-1970s: emigration with the official permission of East German authorities. Though the GDR basically considered these applications illegal—with a few notable exceptions, such as pensioners moving to the West or in the case of family reunifications—the number of applicants grew with the GDR's signing of the CSCE Final Act in 1975, finally spiraling out of control by 1984. More than 10,000 East Germans a year were now leaving their country for good in this manner. At the same time a backlog of applicants was building up which the SED and MfS were powerless against. Between the wave of approvals in 1984 and the crisis of 1989, more than 120,000 applications awaited processing.

Which of the aforementioned categories of deviant behavior do flight and emigration belong to? Applying to emigrate was in itself a sign of refusal and rejection of the system but ultimately not an act of resistance or opposition. Rather, it was a quiet act of evasion on the part of those who had had it with the East German state for any number of reasons. They tended to reject the GDR more radically than the internal opposition but posed less of a challenge to the system as such by dint of their individual initiative. GDR leaders used emigration or expatriation in large part as a kind of safety valve to weaken the internal opposition. The relationship between the opposition and those wanting to emigrate was therefore correspondingly tense. The fate of opposition groups as of 1990 shows that this strategy was successful to a certain extent, though the SED failed to capitalize on it.

Emigration has rightly not been credited to the resistance or opposition, but characterized instead as "resistance through withdrawal."[6] And yet the personal—and, in a sense, apolitical—option of emigrating was subject to a dialectic quite explosive for the SED. First of all, those wanting to emigrate came primarily from the social "center" and rarely from the dissident scene. As the most consistent form of noncompliance vis-à-vis the claims of the state, applications to emigrate were a serious signal from the silent majority. Moreover, the individual decision to emigrate was being transformed by the epidemic-like growth in the number of applicants, as well as by the experience that pressure on the authorities could be increased by making a concerted effort. Hence the emigration movement was born. When the Soviets abandoned their claim to hegemony in May 1989 and the borders of the Eastern bloc became porous, the emigration movement, and the many people who hadn't lodged an application, but who thought and felt like those who did, mutated into the driving force of implosion.

Change in Political Justice

Both forms of deviant political behavior—internal opposition and flight or emigration—obsessively preoccupied State Security. They were considered punishable offenses and were therefore persecuted with secret-police methods, not infrequently ending in prison sentences. The burden of repression was to remain as high as possible, but not at the cost of tarnishing the GDR's public image all too much, given the changing political situation.

The SED had shown—at the very latest with its active assistance in suppressing the Prague Spring in 1968—that it was by no means willing to embark on an experiment in democratically reforming communism. It saw its monopoly on power challenged by such a scenario and firmly reckoned with losing its grip on power in the case of reform that was driven by "imperialist influences." It did, however, adjust its course during the 1970s. Following its radical (and quite literal) policy of "demarcation" (Abgrenzung) from the West, it was now willing once again to integrate politically and economically with the Federal Republic, as well as with the capitalist world market.

The two types of "currency" the GDR accepted in exchange for a limited opening of its borders were international recognition, diplomatically and politically, as an equal member of the community of states, which the West had refused to grant it to date, and the flow of hard currency in the form of increased foreign trade, loans, and monetary payments from the Federal Republic. For all intents and purposes, its increased contacts and relations to the West beginning in the 1970s led to a creeping and irreversible Westernization of values, which the East German state was willing to accept or at least to tolerate in its citizens. The culture of daily life had always been strongly oriented to the Western standard of living anyway. The West German mark, moreover, had become the de facto second currency, with incomparably more purchasing power by way of the official Intershops and the black market. The Party's monopoly on information only lasted until the evening, when East Germans turned on their television sets. What's more, accredited Western journalists could now report directly from the GDR, potentially giving voice to nonconformist views. In the end, the East German leadership was even planning to provide cable television service to new housing developments in Dresden, the so-called "valley of the clueless," so they could pick up the coveted Western stations that were out of reach of their antennas.

The tasks and scope of the MfS went from an offensive form of repression, with the aim of pushing through Party rule, to a more defensive kind, aimed at preserving and safeguarding the existing structures of domination. This resulted in a double strategy of looking for more undercover or legally defendable courses of action while at the same time softening its practices of criminal prosecution overall. From the erection of the Berlin Wall until the late 1970s there was a constant albeit fluctuating drop in the number of investigations launched by the MfS with the goal, generally achieved, of a criminal conviction. Whereas the number of criminal proceedings averaged 3,200 a year in the 1950s, by the 1960s it was 2,350, and in the 1970s around 1,700. But even this figure, given the bleeding of the opposition milieu, bespeaks a strong repressive power, even against petty offenses. With the increase in applications to emigrate and the growing willingness of applicants to stress the point through concerted public campaigns or aggressive protest letters, the number of MfS investigations shot back up in the 1980s to more than 2,500 a year on average. It was not always up to the MfS to decide when proceedings would be opened, and in general there were stark fluctuations depending on the overall political climate. Thus the number of proceedings between 1972 and 1975 markedly declined in the short term due to inter-German negotiations and the CSCE conference, whereas they increased dramatically in 1984 with the surge in emigration as well as during the final crisis in 1988–89. Refugees caught at the border were also subject to legal proceedings. In practice State Security would take its targets into custody. Proceedings against persons unknown were a rarity, on the other hand. The so-called investigative organ of State Security, Line IX, conducted about 90,000 investigations throughout the forty years of its existence, a good 40,000 of them in the "quiet" 1960s and 1970s.[7] Half of these proceedings resulted from the "operational" work of the MfS itself—IM reports, surveillance, or the interrogation of other suspects—whereas the other half were cases taken over from the People's Police (e.g., when would-be emigrants protested with signs in front of the State Council and were arrested), as well as from the security services of the other socialist countries, usually after an attempted escape.

Most of the investigations were due to frontier or emigration "offenses" (attempts to speed up applications, etc.). First and foremost were the "illegal border crossings" (*ungesetzliche Grenzübertritte*) defined by Section 213 of the Criminal Code (StGB), which made up 40 to 50 percent of the Stasi's criminal proceedings annually. On top of this were the side effects of the emigration movement in the 1980s, especially from 1984 on. Anyone who protested to the state authorities about an application to emigrate being declined could potentially count on being charged with "impeding state and social activity" (*Beeinträchtigung staatlicher und gesellschaftlicher Tätigkeit*, Section 214); anyone turning to Western institutions or organizations for support in filing their application was guilty of an "illicit contact" (*ungesetzliche Verbindungsaufnahme*, Section 219); and anyone who demonstrated in favor of emigration, on town squares or outside government offices, by linking hands in a silent circle or chanting, was threatened with criminal proceedings due to "public degradation of state organs" (*öffentliche Herabwürdigung staatlicher Organe*, Section 220).

The number of investigation proceedings against the internal opposition was considerably fewer. Offenses such as "incitement to subversion" (*staatsfeindliche Hetze*, Section 106) or other acts of protest were pursued less and less by State Security in the form of criminal prosecution. There were still some waves of arrests, however, following the protests against Wolf Biermann's expatriation, for example, when a range of less prominent regime opponents, such as the writer and psychologist Jürgen Fuchs and the youth deacon Thomas Auerbach, were arrested and held in detention in Jena for months before being deported to the West. The more prominent initial signatories of the protest petition were put under massive pressure, but none of them was arrested. State Security later stopped short of arrests, often under orders from the highest authorities. Anyone in the internal opposition of the 1980s belonging to a well-established group, holding a church office, or in a position to attract the attention of the Western media was rarely in danger of being arrested or subject to criminal prosecution.

There were hardly any cases of classic spying (Sections 97 and 98) anymore. In 1978, for instance, the MfS tried 66 "spies" in court, of which only 22 were supposedly operating in the GDR in the employ of "imperialist" secret services, the others apparently being on trial for gathering or providing secrets to the West in connection with intended or actual escape. In the interest of legitimizing State Security as an organ of defense against Western secret services, such "secondary offenses" played a major role in many trials against aborted attempts to escape. There were a number of elastic clauses for this: for nonsecret information "treasonous communication" (*landesverräterische Nachrichtenübermittlung,* Section 99) and "working as an agent," i.e., espionage (*Agententätigkeit,* Section 100), or, a milder form, the above-mentioned "illicit contact" (Section 219) or "betrayal of secrets" (Section 245). These clauses essentially made any contact to the West punishable by law. As the Bahro case showed, this also applied to dissidents and writers publishing in the West.

With the Second Amendment of the Criminal Code in 1977, the SED defined a series of offenses in such a way that they were particularly well-suited for combating would-be emigrants. From then on it was the criminal offenses listed in the eighth chapter of the Criminal Code (crimes against the public order) that most often applied and which replaced the often similar articles of the first and second chapters (crimes against the sovereignty of the GDR, against peace, against humanity and human rights, or against the GDR), albeit with considerably more lenient punishments. Thus instead of "treasonous communication" (Section 99), with a potential punishment of two to twelve years without the possibility of parole, it was often "illicit contact" (Section 219) that applied, with a maximum sentence of five years or a monetary fine and the option of parole. The same went for paragraph 220 ("public degradation of state authorities"), with a maximum sentence of five years in prison, as opposed to paragraph 106 ("incitement to subversion"), with a maximum sentence of up to ten years in prison.

The sentences prescribed in the second chapter of the Criminal Code remained in force for the sake of maintaining a certain power of intimidation. With the Third Amendment of the Criminal Code in 1979, the SED made the relevant paragraphs public, in order to scare off would-be emigrants, as well as the emerging peace movement. The real turning point, however, came in 1984, when the GDR was confronted with a growing number of emigration applicants who had contacts with "enemy organizations" in the West, as well as with those who were occupying embassies, but at the same time found itself under enormous economic and financial pressure. Instead of a wave of proceedings for treason, the MfS laid down the line that it would primarily conduct investigations into offenses listed in the eighth chapter, with correspondingly lower sentences.

The number of convictions pursuant to chapters one and two of the Criminal Code declined in the long run from approximately 5,200 in 1961 to exactly 132 in 1988. In 1988, almost 75 percent of the sentences in the few convictions according to these chapters were still for more than two years. The mass offenses of the 1980s, such as attempts to flee the republic, impairment of state activities, public degradation, and so on, resulted in sentences of more than two years in no more than 10 to 15 percent of the cases. All in all, more than half of the MfS proceedings instituted in 1986, for example, ended with prison sentences of between one and two years.

Meanwhile the ransoming (*Freikauf*) of political prisoners by the Federal Republic, a practice begun in 1963, had developed into a cynical ritual during the final decade of the GDR. East German citizens tired of living in the GDR were jailed by State Security for plotting to emigrate, sentenced, and subsequently "bought free." Whatever may have motivated them to apply for emigration in the first place, their path through the "bone grinder" of interrogations and imprisonment most certainly transformed them into what the MfS had made them out to be from the start: implacable enemies of the GDR. The well-dosed sentences would seem to suggest that these prisoners were specially "manufactured" for the very purpose of raising hard currency, had their expulsion from the GDR not been so damaging to East German society. Over the years a total of 33,755 prisoners were sold to the Federal Republic in this manner.

All of these developments created certain expectations among would-be emigrants and dissidents as to which behavior would be punished with sanctions—expectations which, naturally, influenced their actions. There was no real juridification to speak of: East German citizens gained no legally enforceable guarantees. Following the opportunity principle, arbitrary severity was often replaced by a certain leniency that was just as arbitrary, without affecting the underlying threat of criminalization. Thus in 1988 dissidents such as Vera Wollenberger and Wolfgang Templin, who were arrested in connection with the Luxemburg-Liebknecht demonstration, could be credibly threatened with sentences of ten to twelve years in order to extort their consent to being deported. By the same token, however, the instrumentalization of judicial policy for the sake of the overriding interests of state leaders led to unwanted side effects even in the area of common crime. When Honecker announced the greatest general amnesty in the history of the GDR before his visit to West Germany in 1987, this supposedly generous gesture of goodwill emptied East German prisons but led to a massive spike in crime (only to fill up the prisons again).

All in all, there were nearly 110,000 political prisoners in the GDR from 1960 to 1989, serving sentences of varied duration. Apart from those persecuted by the MfS there were also cases in which the investigations were conducted by the People's Police. This was especially true for a good number of those attempting to flee the republic, as well as for more minor offenses according to chapter eight of the Criminal Code. The extent of the People's Police contribution to political persecution has not been adequately assessed to date, but the information on hand does indicate that no strict distinction was made between political and nonpolitical crimes, even disregarding the varied auxiliary services it performed for the MfS in the framework of their "political-operational cooperation."

Although prison terms were getting shorter and the use of physical violence during interrogations and detainment were now the exception rather than the rule, pretrial custody and incarceration were still the most brutal experience in confronting state authorities. Since the 1950s other methods had come to replace outright violence during interrogations. One of the key tactics was total isolation of the detainee for weeks or months. The interrogator would thus become the prisoner's only contact to the outside world—for example, with regard to the fate of one's spouse or children. This situation produced a strong psychological pressure to communicate with the interrogator, encouraging him to confess. An entire repertoire of interrogation techniques could be used as well: deep understanding and tokens of sympathy followed by a sudden harshness and threats, etc. Moreover, the MfS listened in on prisoners in their cells or interrupted their solitary confinement for targeted encounters with "cell informers" (ZIs). Solitary confinement and the demonstrative omnipotence of the MfS drove even those dissidents who were mentally prepared for the possibility of incarceration to the limits of their strength, especially when relief seemed so near—by making the desired confession, by agreeing to be deported to the West, by pledging to work as an informer. On top of breaking down an individual's powers of resistance through forms of "white torture" came arbitrariness and the degrading conditions of imprisonment. Despite the constant flow of political prisoners (and tales of their experiences) to the West through the practice of ransoming, the threat of a public backlash, and the subsequent tendency to treat prisoners decently, there was still the occasional sadistic prisoner guard, even in the 1980s.

A separate chapter in this regard was the Stasi's contingency plans for war or crisis situations, the German Chekists' way of paying their tribute to the "century of camps"[8] down to the very end. Every unit had continually updated index files with the names and addresses of all East Germans considered special security risks. In accordance with the "preventive complex" (as updated in late 1988), 2,955 persons were to be locked up in prison, 10,726 persons were to be put within twenty-four hours into specially constructed isolation camps with barbed wire and watch towers, and 72,258 persons were to be placed under intensified surveillance. Furthermore, 937 "unreliable" cadre in state leadership positions were to be removed from their posts. The Ministry of the Interior also planned to set up 35 camps for the internment of 26,000 foreigners and transit passengers, in accordance with international law.

In retrospect, such apocalyptic scenarios of ideological world civil war may seem anachronistic. But for the cohesion of MfS employees as "soldiers on the invisible front" they fulfilled an important function, effectively setting the parameters of their margin of maneuver. The belief that, in spite of all the political changes, when push comes to shove rebellious dissidents could be made to "cower in a furrow" like "bandits," as the MfS regional boss of Karl-Marx-Stadt, General Siegfried Gehlert, imagined it in August 1989, kept full-time Stasi employees together until the very end, even though the importance of harsh repression had diminished in their daily operational work. The mass arrests after the imposition of martial law in Poland in 1981 and, not least of all, the massacre at Tiananmen Square in Beijing in 1989 were a reminder that such scenarios were possible.

Finally, a special domain deserves to be mentioned in the context of political justice: the hunting down of Nazi criminals by State Security. For many years this issue was held up as proof of the "good," antifascist side of State Security. Over the course of decades, the MfS built up an enormous secret special archive for Nazi documents. It collected files found in the GDR and did extensive microfilming of files in Poland, Czechoslovakia, and other Eastern bloc states.

Only in the early 1960s did the MfS assume sole jurisdiction over the respective investigations and criminal procedures. Thousands of Germans had already been tried by Soviet or East German courts as Nazi or war criminals, the culmination of which was the Waldheim trials of 1950. It was a paradox of this initial phase that, although many of the countless number of people convicted were undoubtedly Nazi criminals, they were generally not condemned for the actual atrocities they committed but for the usual offenses of Stalinist justice, in summary procedures based on confessions extracted under torture or duress. What's more, almost all of these individuals imprisoned in the GDR or the Soviet Union were released in 1956 at the latest, through general amnesty, and could henceforth claim to have atoned for their crimes. From 1956 on, there were very few Nazis on trial. East German State Security, for its part, processed only 165 cases in formal investigations in the 40 years of its existence. Each of these resulted in long sentences or the death penalty. But behind this façade of consistent criminal prosecution was a highly instrumentalized game. Most of the publicized cases served as showcase trials with the primary aim of discrediting West German courts and their lack of will to prosecute such individuals. But sometimes there were shocking discoveries of former Nazis living in the GDR. The latter were quickly convicted and sentenced by East German courts to prevent them from testifying in West German proceedings. This strategy was only expedient, of course, in conjunction with the theory of the occasional "bad apple." If there was any risk of sustainable damage to the GDR's image, they were quick to hush up incriminating evidence, as in the case of a group of euthanasia doctors in Jena who had meanwhile achieved high academic honors in the GDR. Requests for legal counsel fell on deaf ears. At the same time, the MfS adopted a Soviet practice and put a considerable number of Nazi criminals to work as unofficial collaborators in both the East and West. This was a form of "making amends," in other words, blackmail. In fact, many case officers expressed their frequent admiration for the professional experiences of former Gestapo and Security Service men or recruited them on the basis of their common "anti-Zionist" convictions.

The full scale of Nazi perpetrators living in East Germany became clear in the 1970s, when the focus shifted from campaigns exclusively designed to malign the politics and judiciary of West Germany to the systematic evaluation of the mountains of files. The result was diametrically opposed to the notion of fascism commonly cultivated in East Germany, which solely highlighted the political and economic elite of the Third Reich and their subsequent social advancement in West Germany. It turned out that those "perfectly normal men" who committed mass murder in SS *Einsatzgruppen* and concentration camps were living by the hundreds, undisturbed, in the German Democratic Republic as well. All of them were put under surveillance, yet only a handful of them were convicted.

State Security as Executioner—
Resolved and Unresolved Deaths

Several institutions were to blame for deaths in the GDR due to political persecution. Soviet authorities played a big role in the 1950s, but "hard" options of repression such as kidnappings and assassinations were also part of the job for East German State Security alongside criminal prosecution. About 63,000 prisoners died in Soviet special camps between 1945 and 1950 on account of the disastrous conditions of detention. At least 1,963 death sentences were passed by Soviet military tribunals until 1955, 1,201 of which were carried out, if not more. This figure comprised 1,140 men and 61 women. In another 108 cases it is uncertain whether the sentence was actually carried out. In 616 cases the sentence was commuted to life in prison.

The anachronistic talk of revolutionary martial law or "short shrift," still proclaimed by Mielke in the 1980s, was no mere theory. To be sure, State Security rarely carried out such attacks, kept official death sentences secret, and thoroughly camouflaged its assassination attempts using all the tricks in the book. The assassinations targeted individuals whose activities touched a sore spot in the GDR: "traitors" (i.e., defectors) in the ranks SED functionaries, officers in frontier troops, the army, or the MfS itself, and, especially, escape agents and resistance activists working in the West against the GDR.

Official death sentences and executions handed down by courts were rare as of the 1960s. Of the 52 documented cases of death sentences for political offenses (state crimes, espionage, economic crimes) carried out in the Soviet Occupation Zone and the GDR, only ten occurred after 1961.[9] They were mainly for serious instances of espionage, especially in the armed forces. The last three death sentences carried out were against MfS officers Gert Trebeljahr and Werner Teske, as well as Winfried Baumann, a military intelligence officer in the National People's Army, each of whom had tried to defect to the West. Werner Teske's execution in Leipzig on 26 June 1981 by an "unexpected close-range shot in the back of the head" was the last in the GDR. Erich Honecker abolished the death penalty in 1987, before his official visit to Bonn.

These sentences against bearers of secrets were clearly intended as deterrence and revenge. State Security was trying to symbolically establish the impenetrability of its own apparatus and the army as "total" institutions. A Stasi officer defecting to the West would not be tolerated. The topic became explosive when HVA Lieutenant Werner Stiller defected to the Federal Intelligence Service in January 1979 and could neither be extradited to the GDR nor assassinated in the West, despite considerable efforts to do so and a bounty of 1 million marks.

There were still a number of kidnappings in the 1960s—the case of Heinz Brandt, for example, a longtime Communist and Auschwitz survivor who was dismissed from his post as a functionary in the SED regional leadership of Berlin in the aftermath of 17 June 1953 and escaped to the West in 1958. On 16 June 1961, just weeks before the

Berlin Wall went up, he was abducted by the MfS in West Berlin and sentenced in 1962 to thirteen years in prison for "aggravated espionage in coincidence with seditious propaganda and incitement of the first degree." Ulbricht pardoned him in 1964 in response to massive international protests, and released him to the West. The MfS subsequently avoided such high-profile kidnappings but did not shy away from assassinations, as reconstructed in a number of cases.

Bernd Moldenhauer, for example, an opponent of the East German regime, was murdered in 1980 by the MfS in West Berlin. Attacks of this sort are also documented for escape agent and former political prisoner Wolfgang Welsch. One such attempt occurred in 1981, when an IM he was "befriended" with tried to poison him and his family while on vacation together. All received medical help and were saved. Another case reconstructed in detail is the death of another former political prisoner, Michael Gartenschläger. After being ransomed in 1971, he too worked as an escape agent, and in April 1976 dismantled two of the notorious "SM 70" self-firing devices on the border. After a number of sensational press reports, he was caught in an ambush by a commando of MfS Main Department I on the night of 30 April 1976, and shot to death trying to dismantle another. Here, too, a Stasi employee "smuggled in" close to Gartenschläger provided the decisive tip-off.

Unresolved to date is the fatal car crash of professional soccer player Lutz Eigendorf on 5 March 1983. Eigendorf played for FC Dynamo, the MfS-sponsored soccer club in Berlin. In March 1979, just a few weeks after Stiller's defection, he too defected to the West, deserting his team after a friendly match against FC Kaiserslautern. He was henceforth placed under constant surveillance in Operational Case "Traitor" (OV "Verräter"). Evidence suggests that he then fell prey to Mielke's apparatus, which wanted to get revenge and set a warning example three days before a friendly match of FC Dynamo in Stuttgart. According to the murder theory, Eigendorf was the victim of an ill-fated mixture of circumstances: the unappeased resentment of State Security over its failed efforts to nab HVA defector Stiller; the prestige accorded to sports in the thinking of East German leaders; and the oppressive paternalism of the minister and soccer buff Erich Mielke towards his favorite team, the "Firm's" own soccer club Dynamo. Was Eigendorf merely vicarious satisfaction for the desire to take revenge on the "traitors" of an ungrateful new generation who sought their salvation in the glittering West?

There were also plans to assassinate members of the opposition. Never carried out, but quickly discovered in 1990, were plots by officers of Department XX in the regional administration of Berlin to kill dissidents Rainer Eppelmann and Ralf Hirsch by rigging their cars or through alcohol poisoning. The designs were an attempt by these officers to find a way out of the mounting tensions between the militant "Chekist" self-understanding of the MfS, which demanded an uncompromising stance on dissidents, and the politically imposed obstacles it faced, which effectively granted an increasing margin of maneuver to the opposition members working in groups and well known in the West for their critical engagement with the system. Of course these assassinations had to be conducted without any evidence of the Stasi's involvement, but it seems that these Berlin officers enjoyed the undisguised sympathy of their superiors. The plans were shelved when four state-security officers in Poland were dropped by political leaders in 1984 and sentenced to long prison terms after murdering priest Jerzy Popiełuszko. Apparently their colleagues in East Berlin began to doubt whether their own superiors would stand by them if it came to a head. It is impossible to reconstruct nowadays if additional plans of this sort were made or even carried out. Ehrhart Neubert, at any rate, an expert on the opposition, has pointed out a number of mysterious dissident deaths that leave room for speculation.

Among the Stasi's victims was Matthias Domaschk from the Junge Gemeinde of Jena-Stadtmitte, who was arrested on a train to Berlin, one day before the start of the Tenth SED Party Congress in 1981, and died under unclear circumstances on 12 April after thirteen hours of interrogations while in custody at the Gera regional administration. The official version of the story says that he hanged himself from a heating pipe after signing—under duress and constant interrogation—a declaration to work as an informer. It remains an open question whether the subsequent cover-up by the MfS officers involved, which continues into the present, was hushing up a murder or a suicide committed out of despair (and no less damaging to the GDR's reputation). Suicide and attempted suicide by political prisoners, it should be added, were not uncommon occurrences in State Security detention centers and the penal system overall, for that matter. There are a number of reports from the pre-1953 era about deaths resulting from torture. Poor prison conditions were also a cause of death, as many prisoners contracted fatal illnesses. There is no data on suicide and attempted suicide at Stasi detention centers. Nearly 500 suicides between 1953 and 1989 are documented for regular prisons, as well as for remand prisons of the People's Police. (This figure includes suicides by nonpolitical offenders.) The details of a number of additional cases seem to suggest hushed-up murders.

Those forced to commit such acts of despair should also be counted among the victims of East German socialism—even though they are generally overshadowed by the so-called "border violators" (*Grenz-verletzer*). The latter were generally East Germans trying to escape, but also some deserting Soviet soldiers, as well as West German intruders. Most of these deaths were the doing of East German border troops, as shown in the Gartenschläger incident, though it is not unlikely that the MfS had a hand in them as well. A precise count and clarification of the cause of death are missing in many instances, but the figures compiled by the August 13th Working Group at least give a rough indication of the magnitude involved. According to this organization, between 1949 and 1989 a total of 202 people died at the borders of Berlin, 331 at the Western frontier of the GDR, 181 while trying to escape via the Baltic Sea, and 51 at the Western frontiers of third countries (Hungary, Bulgaria, etc.), making a grand total of 765 individuals. Of these 326 were shot or killed by mines and self-firing devices, 208 drowned, 22 had fatal accidents or died, for example, from heart failure while fleeing or being arrested, and 13 committed suicide when faced with the prospect of failure. (The causes of death in the remaining cases are still unsolved.)[10]

Thus, whereas the Stasi increasingly relegated the use of violence to the realm of secrecy, only occasionally holding it up as a warning and cultivating it in internal discourse as a late echo of the Chekist tradition, as it were, killing at state borders continued unabated. Anyone trying to leave the country over the Wall, expanded metal fences, or the open sea was to be shot down by border guards if they failed to stop him otherwise. This demonstrative use of force was a vital precondition for the effectiveness of border fortifications and—in the broader sense—for the continued existence of the GDR. Which is why things worked in reverse here: it was the *rescinding* of the "shoot to kill" order in April 1989 that Honecker kept secret.[11]

Zersetzung or "Quiet Terror"

If the SED was not criminalizing its opponents as often or as harshly as it used to in the early years, its threat potential and power of intimidation were naturally sinking along with it. To compensate for this discrepancy between its claim to omnipotence and the inevitable loss of face in the event of a crackdown against internal opposition groups, State Security—as did the other Communist secret-police forces, incidentally—pushed the development of new methods to replace the standard criminal punishment of imprisonment and court verdicts. Thus the so-called techniques of *Zersetzung* were born. These working methods were first defined in detail in Guideline 1/76, "On the Development and Handling of Operational Cases."

The German word *Zersetzung* can be variously translated into English as corrosion, decomposition, breakdown, disintegration, annihilation, demoralization, undermining, or subversion. *Zersetzung* measures were aimed at opposition groups or individuals and used psychological manipulation on an individual or group basis in an effort to influence attitudes and convictions, with the ultimate aim of limiting or eliminating the effectiveness of dissidents. Guideline 1/76 lists a range of specific methods for "corroding" a target: discrediting his or her public image; orchestrating professional failures or problems in his or her social sphere; undermining convictions and sowing doubts about his or her personal perspectives; stirring up personal rivalries and mutual suspicions in groups; assigning a remote job; circulating compromising photos, letters, telegrams or similar material; spreading malicious rumors and fabricated indiscretions about Stasi activities, e.g., IM meetings with group members; or issuing unwarranted summons to state authorities to give the impression that the target is an IM.

All of these measures were to be conducted covertly so as to keep State Security off the map, unlike its intentional displays of power. These undercover activities could be combined with official measures, however, if it meant the difference between success and failure—temporary arrests, interrogations, and warnings, as well as psychological terror in the form of violence or threats. Groups of "hostile-negative forces" (*feindlich-negative Kräfte*) were to be fractured, crippled, and disrupted by these tricks, whereas individuals were to be isolated and all their energies absorbed by dealing with personal problems.

If the conventional methods of State Security aimed at rounding off their "operational cases" (*operative Vorgänge*—OV) with conclusive evidence of punishable offenses so as to pass the case on to Main Department IX, where a formal investigation would be launched, *Zersetzung*, according to Guideline 1/76, was intended to have "relatively independent closure," especially in cases where, despite hard evidence, the "respective Operational Case should not be concluded with criminal prosecution for political and political-operational reasons in the interest of achieving a higher social utility."[12]

Training material on the "rational and socially effective handling of cases" put together in 1977 cited four key target groups in the GDR: groups of people applying for emigration, hostile groups of critical artists, "reactionary clerical circles," and politically undesirable Christians, as well as "negative" groups of adolescents. Added to this were contact persons and supporters abroad, i.e., escape organizations, human-rights groups, or émigré dissidents. *Zersetzung* was mainly the business of Line XX, or in the case of emigration a range of district offices. The actual terminology and practice of *Zersetzung* were not an invention of the 1970s. The term was used as far back as the Weimar Republic for the mutual infiltration of political organizations or the Reichswehr with the aim of weakening and crippling them from the inside out. State Security (and probably many other secret services) resorted to similar tricks to wreak as much havoc as possible on enemy forces abroad—in the political landscape of West Berlin, for instance, so as to intervene in its own interests. New to the Honecker era was that State Security systematically applied this method in the GDR's own domestic sphere. The aforementioned training manual from 1977 put it like this:

> Applying criminal law to privileged persons such as diplomats and correspondents, as well as the citizens of nonsocialist foreign countries can, in the case of certain offenses (Sections 106 and 107 of the StGB), lead to considerable foreign-policy strains and conflicts which run counter to, disturb, or obstruct the Party and government's policy of détente. Criminal prosecution measures . . . against citizens of the GDR with good national or international repute and connections can harm rather than help the domestic- or foreign-policy interests of the GDR. Here, too, it can be better to act "silently" and prevent enemy activity conspiratorially.[13]

This effectively limited the Stasi's scope of action, but it did its best to outmaneuver this restriction. In contrast to the many years of applied experience, the training manual explained: "Persons active in a hostile way and who have an ideologically corroding [*zersetzend*] influence on citizens of the GDR are—if forced into inactivity and free—much less dangerous than 'martyrs' in prison."[14] This wording reveals quite clearly the Janus-faced nature of *Zersetzung* strategies: more refined methods of repression were no longer visible as Stasi activities and could not be denounced so easily. If totally effective, the victim would not even notice he was being influenced at all. At the same, however, State Security was forced to forego the deterrent effects of more harsh repression.

It is no coincidence that the first major plans for *Zersetzung* in the 1970s were devised in the Berlin regional administration and at Main Department XX of MfS headquarters. Wolf Biermann, for instance, before being expatriated in 1976, was to be neutralized by destroying all of his romantic relationships. Even minors were to be "smuggled in" close to him (*herangeschleust*) in order to prosecute and compromise him. The MfS later used similar operations to harass leading dissidents Ulrike and Gerd Poppe. The Stasi endeavored to escalate the conflicts in their relationship—which it recorded up-close in their bugged apartment—by having an unofficial collaborator woo her as a lover. Dissident pastor Rainer Eppelmann reported similar advances by female visitors allegedly seeking his spiritual guidance. Both operations were ineffective.

The world of sexuality in general seemed to fire the imagination of the Chekists. A voyeuristic gaze into the intimate sphere of their victims was accompanied by the rather conspicuous efforts of some IMs to present their case officers with lewd and dirty material—evidently a reaction to the projected and imaginary image of the clean and orderly East German citizen. Thus pornographic photo collages and fabricated accusations of marital infidelities by pastors were the order of the day.

State Security also liked to play with the widespread and uneasy feeling among dissident circles that they were being intensely spied upon. It frequently tried to blacken the reputation of activists by spreading rumors that they worked as informers. Extensive plans are documented, for example, for measures against Wolfgang Templin, a founding member of the Initiative for Peace and Human Rights (Initiative Frieden und Menschenrechte), established in 1985. One of the leading figures of a more aggressive brand of opposition that endeavored to break out of the church sphere, Templin was made out as a Stasi-steered "agent provocateur" in front of his companions. The Stasi captain assigned to the case noted in February 1987:

> 5.1. It shall be organized by the state administration that facts and clues are made public which are suited to making persons in the political underground come to the "realization" that Templin is being supported from influential quarters.
> This will be based on the fact that Templin received a spacious four-room apartment, installed a self-contained central-heating system with no financial contribution of his own and had the wiring in his entire apartment overhauled, without the respective state organs (Council of the Municipal District of Pankow), well knowing that Templin is an enemy of the GDR, being able to do anything about it.[15]

After this the actual unofficial collaborators around Templin were supposed to spread and stir up rumors to the greatest extent possible.

If this succeeded, point 5.5 of the planned operation was to come into effect:

> One person shall be selected from Templin's field of acquaintances and summoned to a fictitious recruiting talk. To "win the willingness" of this person, ... the employees conducting the talk will "disclose" strictly internal PU [political underground] information whose source is exclusively identified as Templin.[16]

Even if State Security was not successful in discrediting actual dissidents in the eyes of their allies in such a manner, the rumors created mutual mistrust and absorbed a lot of energy.

In the case of Templin, resourceful MfS officers resorted to simple terror tactics as well. For weeks and months on end, they placed ads in his name and had goods delivered to him. In February 1986, for example, he received 110 lbs. of parakeet food, 66 lbs. of finch food, and 110 lbs. of "Bello" brand dog biscuits. For weeks and months, deliverymen and prospective buyers kept him and his family in a constant state of suspense. The Templins had to send back cars and stereo systems, live chickens, tropical fish, cats and dogs, and tens of thousands of condoms, as well as fend off people selling used cars, whom the Stasi had offered exorbitant sums in Templin's name. The phone and doorbell would ring nonstop, especially on the weekend, and sometimes a disappointed trading partner, having traveled for miles in the hope of making a sale, would threaten to get rough when the pastor turned him away. The nightmare only came to an end in the run-up to the Eleventh SED Party Congress, when the Stasi learned that Templin and the Initiative for Peace and Human Rights were about to leak to Western journalists what was going on.

Similar things happened to Jürgen Fuchs in West Berlin, who had been deported from the GDR in 1977. He was awakened in the middle of the night by locksmiths, was heaped with deliveries of pornographic materials, subjected to telephone terror, etc. But the embittered struggle against him went beyond these "quiet forms of terror." State Security went so far as to have explosives detonated outside his home, apparently to intimidate him. His mother-in-law, who had stayed behind in the GDR, took her own life after interrogation by the Stasi. Whereas in Templin's case it was soon obvious who was behind these stunts, it was harder in the case of Fuchs, since no one in West Berlin could believe that the MfS would go to such lengths to harass an exiled dissident.

In the case of leading dissidents, these products of "criminal energy of a special kind"[17] were ultimately ineffective—at least none of them willingly gave up the cause or were systematically isolated by their fellow activists. We have no way of knowing how many less prominent critics of the regime and would-be emigrants State Security tried to "corrode" with such measures and to what extent it succeeded in doing so. It was possible, at any rate, to run a certain "standard program" without much effort and effectively make rebellious citizens preoccupied with themselves, e.g., by refusing to provide them with adequate work or spreading slanderous rumors.

Elaborate *Zersetzung* measures were presumably used on internal opposition groups, as well as on groups of emigration applicants. The more active a "hostile-negative" person was and the more protected from prosecution by the Western media and church, the more extensive the measures taken against him. Less elaborate standard measures were probably used in most operational cases—between 1985 and 1988, the MfS carried out an average of 4,500 to 5,000 operational cases per year—and most likely formed a part of the 20,000 operational person controls carried out annually. This roughly corresponds in scope to the number of unofficial collaborators with "enemy contact," of which there were nearly 4,000 in 1988–89. These and other data have led expert Sonja Süss to conclude that "in the 1970s, all told probably a four- to five-digit number of people were subject to *Zersetzung* in group contexts" and "no more than a three-digit number of individuals (with especially high intensity)."[18]

The opposition scene—this much is clear—was considerably burdened by the consequences of covert operations. The countless unofficial collaborators with enemy contact transformed it into an arena of obstruction. The spectrum was broad: intentionally chaotic behavior at discussions, the constant calling to mind of risks, fostering rivalries within the group, diverting attention to secondary areas of conflict. While it is true that the IMs' margin of maneuver was limited in these groups, as they had to be careful not to be too conspicuously destructive, their numbers were sometimes so abundant that the "genuine" dissidents often got nowhere. This is certainly one reason, apart from numerous other internal obstacles, why the many local opposition groups never managed to band together into a unified movement across the country. The transregional network Concretely for Peace (Konkret für den Frieden) suffered considerably from the fact that the will to decisive action against human-rights violations and the lack of democracy were constantly being blocked by timid compromises in its programmatic declarations or by straying into other topics such as the exploitation of the Third World. In the Initiative for Peace and Human Rights, for example, unofficial collaborator Monika Haeger

(IMB "Karin Lenz") was expressly charged with introducing the "specific interests of women in the fight for guaranteeing human rights, using these additional problems to water down or stall the preparations" for a human-rights seminar.[19]

In the fight against applications to emigrate, the hope of relieving pressure through a safety-valve strategy turned out, by 1984, to be a disastrous miscalculation. For every East German citizen they permitted to leave, two new applicants would soon appear. Thus the SED began to "diversify" its strategies against would-be emigrants. It began to differentiate between two groups in order to maintain a window of influence. The more "stubborn" and "hostile-negative" applicants were fought with the usual severity but were often, and paradoxically, allowed to go West after months or years of struggle, e.g., before a "major social event" so as not to be an embarrassment to state leaders. Even in the case of arrests, those prosecuted for public protests, or caught trying to escape, repression tended to amount to nothing. The almost routine procedure of conviction, imprisonment, and ransoming to the Federal Republic put Stasi interrogators in an absurd situation. They were basically acting as "emigration consultants."

In the case of other applicants, however, the SED showed the obliging side of its paternalism. If the would-be emigrants complained about concrete injustices—waiting in vain to be allocated a suitable apartment, for instance—it showed itself ready to remedy them. With these "efforts to win back" its citizens (*Rückgewinnungsbemühungen*), State Security backed off from its overall repressive thrust and took on a real social-steering function in cooperation with other authorities. The aim here was not only to understand the exact motives behind these applications, but when it doubt to lend a helping hand. To be sure, the strategy failed miserably. There was no measurable increase in applications being withdrawn, whereas the number of new applications continued to grow.

In hindsight, it is rather astonishing how much energy and perfidious personal passion was invested by young, academically trained specialists at the Berlin regional administration in conducting their "operational combinations" against opposition groups in the capital, and this with an amazing level of perfection. In this respect, the notions of "refinement," of "quiet" forms of repression,[20] and of "gentle [*sanft*] totalitarianism"[21] are, in fact, warranted as a way to capture these extreme techniques of persecution.

On the other hand, it is hard to overlook the fact that repression in the 1980s was less severe than in the 1950s, let alone in comparison to Soviet Stalinism or National Socialism. Direct killings or long camp and prison sentences, in particular, were only used as methods of persecution under very specific conditions, even though, for instance, group-building in the late 1970s could have easily been criminalized as "anticonstitutional assembly" (*verfassungsfeindlicher Zusammenschluss*) according to Section 107 of the StGB. The paragraphs, with their severe threats of punishment, were still valid, and State Security itself put much store in collecting relevant "evidence" in order to keep this option on the table. But it never came to that.

Eschewing criminal prosecution in favor of other methods of "battling the enemy" (*Feindbekämpfung*) was ultimately a symptom of the SED state's weakness. The Party leadership and MfS bosses long tried to conceal this gradual process of enfeeblement—with all the more radical outbursts of rage against the "bandits," "scoundrels," and "sad sacks" apprehended on a fairly regular basis by a geriatric Mielke in the 1980s; with verbose remarks about the necessity of a "policy of dialogue" and foreign-policy triumphs; and not least of all with a vocabulary of perfectioning: of enhanced "methodicalness" (*Planmässigkeit*), "scientificness" (*Wissenschaftlichkeit*), and a "still universal [*allseitig*] use" of forces, which filled the instruction manuals and speeches of internal training courses and conferences. That the belief in their own legitimacy had long since wasted away underneath this rigid armor of Chekist rhetoric would become apparent in 1989.

Chapter 6

WOLF AND CO.

MfS Operations Abroad

Myths and Sources

The foreign intelligence operations of the GDR are surrounded by a special mystique. Strictly speaking, the most important respective unit, the Main Administration for Reconnaissance (HVA), was only formally part of the Ministry for State Security, or so its employees argue in retrospect. What's more, it was an intelligence service of the kind any state would maintain for its own protection and benefit, whether capitalist or Communist, democracy or dictatorship. If there was anything unique about it compared to other intelligence services, they go on, it was its particular effectiveness and the quality of its work—and, of course, the noble aim of stabilizing peace in the East-West conflict and thereby contributing to the success of its own system. Thus the MfS called the agents it sent out into the world "enlighteners" (*Aufklärer*, also translatable as "reconnaissance men") and "scouts of peace" (*Kundschafter des Friedens*). In the personal ranking of Heribert Hellenbroich, the former president of the Federal Intelligence Service and the Federal Office for the Protection of the Constitution (BfV), West Germany's foreign and domestic intelligence agencies, respectively, the HVA took fourth place behind Israel's Mossad, the CIA, and the KGB—ahead of the venerable British and French secret services and his own West German agency. Most notably, he credited East German espionage with the "nearly perfect use of the particularities of a divided country for the purposes of espionage" and its "very good commanding officers."[1]

The elite image of MfS foreign espionage was thanks, above all, to its longtime head, Deputy Minister for State Security and Colonel-General Markus Wolf. Until being identified by defector Werner Stiller in 1979, he was known in the West as the "man without a face," a legendary and exceptionally gifted spymaster. He was the only man in the leading ranks of the MfS to hail from the artistic circles of the Party intelligentsia. Wolf was born in 1923 in Hechingen, in the province of Hohenzollern. His father was the Communist writer and physician Friedrich Wolf, his brother the film director and president of the East German Academy of Arts, Konrad Wolf. Wolf was thought to have intimate ties to the Soviet Communist Party and the KGB thanks to his formative years spent in the Soviet Union of the 1930s and 1940s. This chapter of his life distinguished him from the demonstrably proletarian Mielke and his generals. Retiring from active duty in 1986, Markus Wolf knew how to capitalize on this mystique to portray himself as a critical intellectual and would-be bel esprit.

There is something true and something false about this image of an "elite reconnaissance," markedly different from "ordinary counter-intelligence" in terms of its role and responsibilities, going down undefeated, as it were, with the rest of the GDR.[2] The balance sheet was indeed impressive. Top agents in the Federal Chancellery, the Federal Intelligence Service, the Office for the Protection of the Constitution, NATO headquarters, as well as practically every ministry in Bonn and every party headquarters, along with a high level of professional expertise in the international competition of intelligence services show that the GDR did in fact achieve and help set the "world class" standards it ambitiously aspired to in this field. The conditions and consequences of this superlative standard will be discussed in greater detail below.

Absolutely false, on the other hand, is the claim that its operations were strictly separate from the other MfS branches. The self-understanding of its staff as Chekists and professional revolutionaries, as well as its inclusion in the intra-ministry division of labor militate against this. The HVA, too, was involved in persecuting East German citizens to the extent that it was able. Of course it had different priorities than, say, Main Department XX, but its unofficial collaborators in the West were eager to help out whenever they could by providing information. Especially in the 1980s, foreign intelligence was increasingly involved in the effort to spy out real or imagined Western contacts of the internal opposition and the emigration movement—always with the aim of proving the existence of secret-service connections, such as the supposed recruiting of dissident Bärbel Bohley as an agent of the Federal Intelligence Service or the alleged steering by intelligence agencies of Roland Jahn, who was working in West Berlin for the East German opposition. The reconnoitering of "plans, intentions, agencies, means, and methods of the CIA and BND, the secret services of other imperialist and nonsocialist states, the centers of political-ideological diversion and other centers of diversion . . . against the socialist community of states" was fourth on the list of the nine "information focal points" of the HVA. This included not only classic counterespionage in the offensive sense of spying on the other side's intelligence services (*Gegenspionage*), but also counterespionage in the defensive sense of collecting information about supposed centers of political-ideological subversion and their "enemy activities" against the GDR (*Spionageabwehr*).[3] Military policy, armaments production, and the general policies of the West toward the socialist camp occupied places one to three, and five to eight on the list of focal points were Western commitments in crisis areas, the cooperation of enemy states among themselves, the domestic policy, research, and technology in these countries, as well the security of its own IM network.

Just as implausible is the self-fashioning of these *Aufklärer* into straightforward intelligence men, who plied their trade with an ethic above and beyond the international norm. "Wetwork," the secret-service jargon for operations where blood is spilled and violence is used, was part of the standard repertoire of East German foreign espionage at least in the early years—though, granted, its agents were never sent out with ice picks, like the murderers of Leon Trotsky under orders of Soviet state security. It is no coincidence that Markus Wolf was finally convicted of forcible abduction (whereas the Federal Constitutional Court of Germany ruled in 1995 that the actual espionage carried out under his watch was not punishable by law as long as it was conducted on East German soil).

It was not only HVA's apologists, however, who thought East German spies and agents to be particularly effective and omnipresent. Its fiercest detractors shared this view. As with the first revelations of the IM network inside the GDR, the fall of the Wall gave way to wild speculations about MfS operations in the West and abroad. Nightmare scenarios began to proliferate in government circles in Bonn when, in 1993, the first details were leaked from the "Rosenholz" files, which, secretly obtained by the CIA, contained the real names of MfS agents working in the West. A host of "experts" outdid each other in the media with their claims about the number of unofficial collaborators in the Federal Republic. Thus the public imagined tens of thousands of agents of influence occupying key positions in the state, parties, and organizations in the Federal Republic, steering the fate of the country in the interests of the SED. By the 1960s at the latest, they claimed, State Security had, for example, gained a controlling influence over all major political protest movements, such as the students' movement, anti-Vietnam protests, and the peace movement. All in all, the Federal Republic had allegedly become an "infiltrated republic" in which the "Stasi . . . was ever-present."[4] Not only did State Security operate in a highly efficient manner, they claimed; on top of it all it availed itself of the crumbling anti-Communist consensus of the Federal Republic ever since the late 1960s:

> It is clearly evident that "change through rapprochement," the programmatic maxim that served to underpin the social-liberal coalition's Ostpolitik, was also and particularly effective the other way around: the dichotomy between dictatorship and democracy was blurred, the moral bar against communist-party rule was lowered or abolished entirely, the immunity to a system based on violence and repression vanished in the spirit of "détente."[5]

There is no room here for a general discussion of the costs and benefits of the policy of détente, but we can assess the extent and limits of secret-service influence. Did the Main Administration for Reconnaissance and the other MfS units operating in the West merely have their "sights set on Bonn,"[6] as the last head of the HVA, Werner Grossmann, suggested, or did they have Bonn "in their grip"? And to what extent has this covert network of informers and agents of influence been uncovered at all, allowing us to come to any conclusions?

The historical investigation of secret-service operations and their effects is subject to one general caveat: "We do not know how much we do not know," was the conclusion of British secret-service historian Christopher Andrew.[7] Thanks to the opening of the files, this does not apply to the MfS for the most part, but the situation is more complicated in the case of the HVA, its most important espionage unit. We only have an inkling of how much we could know if the HVA had not been allowed to disband itself in 1990 and hence destroy its files with the tacit approval of the citizens' committees and the Central Round Table. The possibilities of analyzing operational cases, IM files, etc., are unfortunately very limited. On the other hand, there are numerous remnants from the HVA, as well as from other service units, which at least allow us to piece together an outline of the overall picture.

Compared to international standards, HVA researchers have a good deal more authentic and, especially, unfiltered material at their disposal. Information on sources and methods generally protected by secret services are at least partly accessible to them. To be sure, this information is usually not consistent enough to enable a conclusive verdict, which opens the door to speculation and projection, especially with regard to concrete instances of putative espionage. The problem is complicated by the lack of access to the records of enemy secret services. The mysterious behavior of many a Stasi spy, for example, could perhaps be explained by his being a double agent.

The situation has meanwhile improved with the availability of two important resources: considerable parts of the central HVA personal index file (F16/F22), last updated in 1988 and referred to under the code name "Rosenholz," as well as a series of databases from the System of Reconnaissance Information Research (SIRA), offering an overview of incoming and outgoing information at the HVA, filed by registration number, code name, etc. SIRA contains 484,881 entries and basically covers the period from 1969 on. The combination of Rosenholz and SIRA enables new investigations of individuals, and has even provided clues to more than a thousand files with an HVA connection that, contrary to previous expectations, still exist in other MfS archives. Moreover, about 60 percent of the HVA reports drawn up for Party leaders, the military, and other offices have been preserved. (From the period from 1969 to 1979 alone there are more than 5,000 such reports.) None of this, however, can replace the core files that have presumably been lost for good, i.e., the actual working files on agents and their targets.

But the knowledge that is available to us at least allows us to elaborate on the general scope, main priorities, and preferred methods of MfS foreign espionage. It is evident as well that considerable parts of the espionage network have meanwhile been exposed, leading to numerous criminal investigations and convictions in cases where the statute of limitations on "work as a secret-service agent" does not apply. According to Joachim Lampe, the federal attorney in charge of these cases, "all agents handled by the primary . . . espionage outfits of the MfS [have been] unmasked," with the exception of some of the economic spies and handling agents from the Science and Technology Sector of the HVA, Main Department XVIII, and the related Area of Commercial Coordination in the Ministry of Foreign Trade.[8]

On the Structure of MfS Operations Abroad

The GDR was perhaps a small country, but in the Cold War it figured as an object of high politics, as an actor with the status of a veritable middle power. Located in the heart of Europe and bound up with the German Question, it invariably played a key role in the system conflict between East and West. Though perhaps not as weighty as the issue of nuclear confrontation, in the historical discipline of Cold War studies the GDR is more than just another country study in the East-West conflict.

At last count there were about 9,000 to 10,000 full-time MfS employees involved in activities outside the GDR. The largest complex here was the Main Administration for Reconnaissance, including the subordinate branches (Department XV) in the regional administrations for state security, with 4,744 employees (as of 31 October 1989, not including full-time unofficial collaborators), as well as individual employees at the district offices, all told about 100 to 200 people. Added to this was the radio intelligence and radio counterintelligence unit (Main Department III) with 2,361 employees. The other units mentioned above or the parts of them concerned with foreign affairs (Main Departments I, II, XVIII, XXII, as well as the respective rearward units for personnel, finances, etc.) had about as many full-time employees in total.[9]

Thus in international comparison, the MfS had somewhat more staff than the West German Federal Intelligence Service, with 7,500 employees in 1989, but was considerably larger than its British and French counterparts, whose official staff numbers were 2,300 for the British MI6 and about 4,000 for the French SGDN and DGSE. Even compared to other Eastern bloc states, these personnel outlays were unusually high. The only apparatuses that were bigger were those of the globally active superpowers. The KGB's First Main Directorate supposedly had around 12,000 employees at last count, whereas the CIA had about 20,000 employees after the massive expansion under President Ronald Reagan. On top of this were special units such as military espionage or satellite and interception espionage, known in secret-service jargon as imagery intelligence (IMINT) and signals intelligence (SIGINT). In the age of nuclear confrontation, these sources of information were of exceptional importance. The U.S. National Security Agency (NSA) alone supposedly had about 40,000 worldwide employees working to this end in the 1980s. The Military Intelligence Service of the NVA had about 1,200 employees by contrast. The historical development points to a continual expansion of foreign espionage. Forces were limited in the early days of the 1950s: in 1958 the HVA had 481 employees (plus about 100 to 200 at regional offices). From 1972 to 1982 the GDR doubled the staff of the HVA from 1,425 to 2,973, continually expanding to the aforementioned figure of 4,744 by 1989.[10] A particular spike in staffing came in 1976, with more than 600 additional HVA employees. This was presumably linked to the establishment, shortly before, of East German embassies in the Western world which were outfitted with so-called "legal residencies" (*Legalresidenturen*), i.e., covert secret-service agents among the embassy staff, as well as with security forces.[11]

Unlike the globally active secret services of the nuclear states and superpowers, the work of the HVA was against the Federal Republic, a task which was covered by three big procurement departments focused on the West German state apparatus (Department I), on political parties and organizations (Department II), and on military installations (Department IV).[12] To be sure, the other focal points were expanded in the 1970s. A separate unit, Department XII, was set up in 1971 for the procurement of information about NATO and the European Community. In 1989 it had about 60 employees. In 1973 a separate Department XI for North America (including military espionage against U.S. troops in Europe) was added, which had about 80 full-time employees in the end.

The main task of all of these departments was the procurement of information by means of human intelligence (HUMINT), in other words, with the help of secret agents. In 1988, according to the Rosenholz files, the HVA handled 1,553 such unofficial collaborators with West German citizenship.[13] Added to this was a hard to quantify but most likely considerably smaller number of Western agents of other nationalities. These figures are not as reliable as genuine MfS documents with a traceable transmission history. Having gone through the hands of the West German Federal Office for the Protection of the Constitution, the CIA, and before that—according to the official story—the KGB and its successor organizations, they should therefore be treated with caution. Cross-checks with other materials, however, indicate that the numbers essentially do reflect the real extent of the HVA network in the Federal Republic. In other words, the ratio of Stasi agents in West Germany to the number of IMs in the GDR itself was a little less than one to a hundred. According to estimates (based on investigations of the German attorney general, among others), the counterintelligence units (counterespionage, terror defense, combating political underground activities) and reconnaissance division of the National People's Army had about as many Western IMs, meaning there were probably just over 3,000 unofficial collaborators working in the Federal Republic in 1988.

Of the 1,553 HVA agents, 449 were so-called "site sources" (*Objektquellen*) who supplied information directly from the target institutions. An additional 133 IMs gathered their information indirectly as "pumping sources" (*Abschöpfquellen*), i.e., through personal contacts to the "bearers of secrets" in question. There were also 66 IMs for special tasks. Unlike the other IMs, their main purpose was not primarily to procure information but to serve as "agents of influence," working, for example, on behalf of the MfS as journalists to initiate and steer disinformation campaigns against politicians. These three groups, comprising about 650 people, were the real heart of the network. They were assigned to the state, parties and organizations, the economy and the military, higher education, and the media, and ensured a correspondingly broad flow of information. Added to this were 166 "perspective IMs" (*Perspektiv-IM*) who did not yet occupy interesting positions but were likely to end up there in the course of their careers. Not part of the unofficial State Security network but nevertheless part of the overall system of HVA information procurement were the "contact persons" in the Federal Republic. These were citizens of West Germany who were "pumped" (*abgeschöpft*) by full-time or unofficial collaborators without their knowing about the latter's secret-service connections, or who were to be induced covertly to act in the interests of the GDR. Rosenholz identifies 376 such contact persons for late 1988. This method was frequently used on politicians. Thus, for example, Bundestag member Horst Peter (SPD) and deputy in the Berlin House of Representatives Uwe Lehmann-Brauns (CDU) were listed as contact persons without their knowledge.

This form of espionage could only work with an elaborate staff infrastructure. In 1988, 32 MfS officers disguised as West German citizens (so-called "residents") and 26 controller IMs assigned tasks to their sources and discussed security questions with them; 231 couriers, radio operators, smugglers, etc. delivered messages or organized secret meetings; 275 recruiters and 41 investigators kept their eyes peeled for new spy candidates, established contact with them, and procured information through them; and, finally, there were 134 assistants working for the residents or security IMs. The assistants were often the wives of sources or residents who (contrary to practices in the GDR) were usually involved in these clandestine activities. This was also true of agent couples from the GDR smuggled into the Federal Republic. Not included in these figures but likewise an important pillar in the practical work of foreign espionage were the HVA IMs in the GDR, of which there were an estimated 7,000 to 10,000 in 1988.

Another point of reference is offered by the partial database of SIRA, with about 4,500 different "sources" listed by Evaluation Department VII in the area of political and military espionage for the period from 1969 to 1987. Apart from unofficial collaborators, however, the sources could also include other MfS units, foreign "brother organs," or full-time Stasi employees who had procured information themselves, e.g., by "pumping" unwitting conversation partners as "contact persons." Radio intelligence (Main Department III) alone stored their discoveries in several thousand SIRA entries under code names such as "Friedrich" or "Lupine." Apart from direct IM work, the "legally covered residencies" (*legal abgedeckte Residenturen*—LAR) at diplomatic missions were also an important source. Thus, for instance, one of the last HVA deputy chiefs, Ralf-Peter Devaux, had been director of the residency in the Permanent Mission (Ständige Vertretung) of the GDR in Bonn from 1977 to 1981. In his official capacity as first secretary of the mission he took part in talks with Federal Chancellor Schmidt and wrote reports about them. Moreover, several informers could be listed as a single source (with a common registration number) or, vice versa, the information of one important agent could be distributed among several code names in order to make it harder to trace. In other words, the figure of 4,500 SIRA sources is merely a vague indication of the actual extent of the HVA network.

This overview of the available data makes clear that the HUMINT network was expanding considerably in the 1970s and in some respects even reached its peak. The HVA had been building up "perspective agents" since the 1950s and 1960s, some of whom had now managed to work their way into sensitive areas. The HVA's work became increasingly difficult in the 1980s, however, not in terms of working with "site sources" but recruiting new agents. According to HVA employees, enlisting sources under the banner of the GDR was virtually impossible by that point in time, so that they attempted to recruit under false colors—a difficult task—or otherwise had to content themselves with "pumping" contact persons.[14] An HVA department head complained at a meeting in 1986:

> In the past, the pioneers of reconnaissance, scouts, as well as officers, created a range of good to excellent starting positions which to this day have continued to develop into top positions. We are still, we must admit quite matter-of-factly, living off their achievements. . . . How much

harder it hits us, then, that we as a department in the third year after the so-called transition [the coming to power of Kohl's government] have still not achieved to a satisfactory degree the necessary break-through in creating operationally significant positions in the camp of the governing parties.[15]

Nothing would happen to alter this headwind in the remaining four years. In this respect, the end of East German socialism cast a long shadow even on the GDR's thriving foreign espionage.

Political Espionage and "Active Measures"

SPD politician Horst Ehmke, director of the Federal Chancellery under Willy Brandt, once declared that the three top priorities of the West German Federal Intelligence Service were "GDR, GDR, GDR." This fixation on the other Germany also applied the other way around, particularly with regard to political espionage. This can be seen at all levels: in the programmatic regulations, the division of departments, the distribution of the IM network, and last but not least the reporting to state and Party leaders. The "rest of the world," on the other hand, was only of moderate interest to the political espionage of the MfS. Even in those operational departments not defined by target country, the activities of the Federal Republic were usually top priority. Department IX ran external counterintelligence (*Gegenspionage* and *äussere Spionageabwehr*), primarily against the Federal Intelligence Service, the Offices for the Protection of the Constitution, and the Military Counterintelligence Service (MAD). Department X was concerned with "active measures," i.e., disinformation campaigns, in the political landscape of the Federal Republic.

This concentration of forces gave the Main Administration for Reconnaissance a rather dense network of spies in politics and the state apparatus of the Federal Republic. Of the sources at target sites (O sources), 85 each were placed in politics and administration. Division 1 of Department I, responsible for the Federal Chancellery, the Office of the Federal President, the Press and Information Office of the Federal Government, and the Bonn Security Group of the Federal Criminal Police Office, had 5 O sources, for example, including a secretary in the economic department of the Federal Chancellery, a journalist, and a former employee of the German Institute for International and Security Affairs (SWP) in Ebenhausen (subordinate to the Federal Chancellery). The HVA had six O sources active against the Foreign Office in Bonn, including foreign ministry officials Klaus von Raussendorff and Dr. Hagen Blau. Similar numbers were assigned to the other more important federal ministries and political parties.

Its spying on the SPD was revealed in the Guillaume affair. The site sources in 1988 included former Social Democratic member of the Bundestag Paul Gerhard Flämig (registered as an IM since 1967) and several state parliament members, such as Bodo Thomas ("Hans") in Berlin and Ruth Polte ("Blumenfeld") in Hamburg, as well as a range of party employees and other staff members, among others Henning Nase, the personal adviser to social-policy expert Rudolf Dressler. The HVA had another Bundestag member on its list of informers until 1966 in the person of Josef Braun. The former KPD member had joined the SPD on Communist Party orders after the war and was handled as an agent by the SED's own reconnaissance service, then later taken on in the HVA. From around 1968 until his death in 1987, Bonn SPD chairman Rudolf Maerker likewise provided a wealth of information from inside the party. A total of 1,281 documents are listed in SIRA under his code name, "Max."

Along with a number of subordinate employees, the agent network in the CDU in 1988 comprised longtime top agent Hans-Adolf Kanter (code name "Fichtel"), who likewise had about pieces of 1,200 information units to his credit in SIRA. Kanter had joined the Rhineland-Palatinate "Young Union" in 1949 on behalf of SED party reconnaissance and was active ever since on the side of the young aspiring politician Helmut Kohl. As of 1974 he worked in Bonn as a lobbyist of the Flick concern. This provided him with close contacts to leading circles in politics and the economy, and gave him deep insights into the campaign contributions later made public during the Flick affair. He also rented a house to the architect of the New Ostpolitik, Egon Bahr, which, according to Markus Wolf's memoirs, was equipped with bugging devices. This enabled the MfS to eavesdrop on Bahr's domestic conversations with high-ranking negotiating partners from East and West. Kanter lost many of his best political contacts, however, as a result of the Flick affair of 1981 and was largely dropped as a source for the HVA after the near exposure of his East Berlin courier in 1983. Among the earliest top sources in the CDU was Bundestag member Karlfranz Schmidt-Wittmack, who absconded from the GDR in 1954. Of historical fame thanks to information provided by Schmidt-Wittmack was representative Julius Steiner, who took a bribe in the vote of no confidence against Willy Brandt in April 1972.

The HVA was active in the small parties as well. There were five site sources in the FDP at last count, among them such high-ranking spies as Hannsheinz Porst, who, exposed and convicted in 1969, had multifarious contacts to party leaders, especially as a party financer, as well as Bundestag and European Parliament member William Borm, who was never exposed during his lifetime. Borm was incarcerated in the GDR in 1950 and enlisted as a spy before his release in the late 1950s. Markus Wolf later handled the agent personally.

The MfS had several sources with the Greens as well in 1988, including Berlin Bundestag member Dirk Schneider, who had earned the derisive nickname "Permanent Mission" because of his overly GDR-friendly stance in the Greens' *Deutschlandpolitik*, European Parliament member Brigitte Heinrich, as well as two party staffers, Doris and George Pumphrey.

Apart from politicians with their support staff and advisers, secretaries too played an important role in all of the areas mentioned above. The MfS used the so-called "Romeo" method, seeking out single women and assigning carefully chosen MfS agents to make advances toward them. This went so far as enacting fictitious marriages and other such bogus events. It was often only after their exposure that these women would realize what was going on, that their supposed lovers had merely been using them. They sometimes did not have the faintest idea, when recruited "under false colors," that their orders came from the GDR. With the exposure of several such secretaries in the 1970s, this method eventually became less common.

A separate branch for disinformation campaigns, so-called "active measures" (*aktive Massnahmen*), directly subordinate to HVA chief Wolf, was greatly expanded in the 1960s. Department X actively supported the SED in its campaigns to unmask alleged or actual former Nazis occupying high-profile positions in public life in the Federal Republic. To this end it made considerable efforts (in cooperation with Department IX/11, the MfS investigative body responsible for Nazi issues) to collect and present relevant archive material and witnesses. Failing to do so, they manipulated the materials to seemingly substantiate their claims or make them more effective.

Thus, for example, from 1966 on, the SED denounced Federal President Heinrich Lübke as a "concentration camp builder" on account of his once having been a building supervisor at an aircraft factory in Neu-Stassfurt, where he worked on the construction of barracks that were later used to house concentration-camp inmates. He had also employed concentration-camp inmates to build workers' barracks at the Peenemünde rocket-testing center. To maximize its propaganda value, the disinformation experts assigned to the case "supplemented" these authentic documents with a new cover sheet explicitly referring to "concentration camp" buildings.

A criminal investigation against Lübke was dismissed after a thorough examination by Frankfurt's chief public prosecutor, Fritz Bauer, for the "lack of any suspicion of crime," but the GDR pressed on with its campaign to discredit the beleaguered and overworked Lübke with ever new information from the files. The SED and MfS knew how to capitalize on these frictions in West German politics: striking a debilitated figure in the highest public office, highlighting once again the (in this case rather limited) complicity of a high-ranking West German politician in Nazi affairs, and finding willing partners in the form of West German journalists who wanted to help a social-liberal coalition to power in the atmosphere of transformation in the post-Adenauer era.

Military Espionage

Military espionage had a vital importance on both sides of the Cold War during the arms race and the eventual nuclear stalemate between the superpowers and their respective blocs. Secret-service reconnaissance was to act as an early-warning system for all enemy war plans. This applied first and foremost to any first-strike nuclear attack, but to conventional attacks as well, especially in Central Europe. As a member of the Warsaw Pact, East Germany's military espionage primarily served as an information provider for Soviet military leaders. All relevant reports went straight from its procurement departments to the KGB, and were likewise passed on to analysts in the HVA. The latter's summary reports then went back to KGB representatives in Berlin-Karlshorst, as well as to various East German recipients.

These close working relations were reflected in the guidelines to agent work that were periodically compiled. In the procurement priority lists of 1959 to 1968, the military centers of the Federal Republic, the United States, and NATO took second place—in 1959 behind securing the GDR and the socialist camp from subversive imperialist attacks, and in 1968 behind the *political* centers of the enemy and their plans against the GDR in the areas of foreign, domestic, and economic policy.[16] Though actual procurement was still primarily focused on the Federal Republic, the priorities would later change. This shift was presumably based on the newly formulated espionage doctrine of the KGB of the mid-1970s, which aimed at minimizing the risk of a surprise nuclear attack by NATO, while addressing the alleged rise of "extremely aggressive circles" in the United States, the Federal Republic, and Japan. The key new risks were Western attempts to divide the Eastern bloc as well as the qualitative leap in military electronics. The HVA was now mainly supposed to gather information on military policy as well as on arms research and production in NATO and the United States. In political espionage as well, the United States and NATO were the top priority.[17] When Soviet leaders sounded the alarm in the early 1980s, having thought they discerned an imminent nuclear first strike by the U.S. government under President Ronald Reagan in the form of NATO exercises ("Able Archer"), they upped the responsibilities of East German military espionage. Soviet head of state and party leader Brezhnev ordered Operation RYAN, with a long catalog of intelligence-gathering indicators for detecting preparations for an attack. The HVA subsequently set up its own special situation room and delivered monthly reports on its findings in this area. Soviet demands put the GDR under extreme pressure to recruit the greatest possible number of informers. From 1983/84 to 1989 the West German Military Counterintelligence Service registered about 1,500 recruiting attempts in the Bundeswehr.

The HVA profited here from the deployment of West German delegates to the Western alliances, among them, as of 1977, probably the most prominent Eastern spy at NATO headquarters, Rainer Rupp, code name "Topas." Military installations of the Federal Republic likewise offered potential information of broad, alliance-wide importance. The U.S. troops stationed in West Berlin and West Germany were a potential point of attack as well, whereas in the United States itself the MfS had little in the way of highly developed espionage activities, apart from the standard legal residencies in Washington and the United Nations office of the GDR in New York.

HVA Department IV (military) and Department XII (NATO) were active in these areas, as well as the Reconnaissance Administration of the National People's Army, which for its part worked closely with MfS Main Department I. While the HVA concentrated on general military policy, the focus of the Reconnaissance Administration of the NVA was to reconnoiter the Bundeswehr down to its lowest formations. In 1988, Department IV (military espionage) had 74 West German citizens working as unofficial collaborators or contact persons, 22 of them directly on location. Department XII (NATO / European Community) had 72 IMs and contact persons, 12 of them on location.

At the evaluation level, the share of military information in the 1970s and 1980s—several hundred reports a year—remained constant at around 30 percent of the overall volume of HVA information. In this way the NVA and—via the KGB—Soviet military leaders had a steady stream of detailed reports about enemy armed forces. In a number of cases the GDR even passed on its knowledge to other the Warsaw Pact partners. Apart from key information from NATO quarters, these recipients obtained a wealth of reports from inside the Bundeswehr, providing a detailed picture right down to individual units. The East was well informed about the fighting power and weaknesses of West German troops, as well as about new weapon developments and long-term military planning. In the event of war with the Bundeswehr, the armies of the Warsaw Pact would have clearly faced a familiar foe and profited militarily from their detailed tactical and operational knowledge.

NATO reporting was considerably more focused on strategic questions, the political stances of member states, possible points of difference, and similar politically relevant issues. In the military domain in the narrow sense, there was a series of reports—presumably highly informative for East European armies—about technical innovations, experiences with maneuvers and exercises, but also the basic expectations underlying NATO operational planning with respect to the attack plans of the Warsaw Pact or the threshold for deploying tactical or strategic nuclear weapons.

The tone and content of these reports are surprisingly matter-of-fact, in sharp contrast to other MfS reports, and provide a nuanced account of Western positions. Thus, for instance, the war scenarios adopted by the West for planning purposes and which regularly posited the Warsaw Pact as an aggressor were in most cases left wholly uncommented. Though exercise scenarios of the 1970s did contain references to a Western first-use policy employing tactical nuclear weapons to stave off an attack by the Warsaw Pact in Central Europe, there is not a single mention of attack or first-strike plans of the West, contrary to the official Soviet military doctrine of that era. These reports basically conformed for the most part with the official positions of Western defense doctrine, in bold relief to the alleged threat held up by the East as legitimation for the Soviet Union's armament efforts.

The situation is not so clear for the height of the arms race in the early 1980s. Rainer Rupp, the most important informer from NATO headquarters, paradoxically assumes even today that the United States, since achieving nuclear stalemate in the late 1960s, was continually pursuing a nuclear first-strike option, especially under Reagan. The HVA's U.S. expert, Klaus Eichner, agrees. Rupp's reports—at least according to these accounts—might indeed have confirmed Moscow's fears and heightened the need for a corresponding preventive strategy. Rupp's and Eichner's higher-ups, HVA chiefs Markus Wolf and

Werner Grossmann, on the other hand, claim that the information they provided allayed Moscow's fears of attack. The notion of "espionage for peace" has been reduced to absurdity here, as identical information could apparently be interpreted in opposite ways, both for and against an arms buildup.

Economic and Technological Espionage

The Main Administration for Reconnaissance had a highly developed unofficial network in the area of economic, scientific, and technological espionage. A separate Science and Technology Sector (SWT), created in 1971, was responsible for it. The sector had its own evaluation department (Department V) and three procurement departments (Departments XIII, XIV, and XV). Compared to political espionage, the number of active spies was exceptionally high here. Of the 334 IMs and contact persons, 240 were on active assignment. There was evidently less need for logistic safeguards here than in more protected areas such as government and administration.

Economic espionage played a significant role in the GDR. It developed over the years into an essential productive force in some parts of the East German economy, intended to help overcome innovative weaknesses and growing lags in technological development. To this end, the Science and Technology Sector closely cooperated with the respective ministries of industry and the foreign-trade sector. Apart from the direct industrial espionage of the HVA, this branch also supported the legal or illegal procurement of goods through the Area of Commercial Coordination (BKK, or more colloquially KoKo) in the Ministry of Foreign Trade, which in turn cooperated with Main Department XVIII and the MfS Working Group on the Area of Commercial Coordination.

The focus of economic espionage corresponded to the current problem areas in the domestic economy and the prevailing course of SED economic policy. Thus, for example, in the 1960s procedures for manufacturing synthetic fibers were one focal point. The fabric "Präsent 20," for example, developed for the twentieth anniversary of the GDR, was supposedly the result of knowledge "procured" (i.e., stolen) from the laboratories of Western chemical companies—the feat of subsequent SWT director Major-General Heinrich Weiberg, a chemist by training. Efforts of the HVA to boost domestic production of polyurethane on the basis of knowledge acquired though espionage ultimately foundered on plan bureaucracy, even though the MfS had gone so far as to present head of state Walter Ulbricht with a couch made out of the material for his birthday in the hope of making the project more palatable.

Bottlenecks in the energy economy and the scarcity of natural resources in the GDR were the top priority in the 1980s, the Soviet Union having raised the price of oil and cut back on its deliveries. At the top of the wish list of the "HVA's information focal points" were therefore "concepts, research projects, programs, and other projects to secure energy supplies, . . . to engage with questions of the rational use of energy and of lowering the specific energy use in production, transportation and consumption, and to develop new energy sources," followed by "solutions for the effective use of economically vital raw and other production materials," for "achieving a higher degree of processing primary raw materials—such as petroleum and coal—" and for the "use of ashy and saliferous lignite."[18] State-of-the-art technology and expertise in microelectronics, as well as biotechnology and genetic engineering in industry, food production, and pharmaceuticals were likewise in demand.

The GDR's ambitious microelectronics program, in particular, rested in large part on the procurers of the HVA's Science and Technology Sector and the embargo dealers in the Area of Commercial Coordination in the Ministry of Foreign Trade, the special domain of State Secretary and MfS Colonel on Special Assignment Alexander Schalck-Golodkowski. Both organizations were well positioned for this purpose. Many of their spies were unmasked as of 1990 in electronics companies the likes of Texas Instruments, Siemens, and Digital Equipment Corporation. But there had also been arrests after SWT lieutenant Werner Stiller's defection—engineer Gerhard Arnold, among others, who had been infiltrated into IBM and in Stiller's estimation was the secret "father of data processors in the GDR."[19]

KoKo traders also endeavored to get their hands on blueprints, models, and other equipment. In 1986–87, the Japanese company Toshiba, for example, secretly provided them with chip templates and was even planning to develop a chip especially for the GDR. The Japanese pulled back, however, when they came under fire from the United States for other embargo-related dealings with Warsaw Pact states. Their East German trading partners were ordered to destroy all of the materials supplied to them (which they only pretended to do, despite being under supervision).

In end effect, the computers produced in the GDR since the 1970s were essentially IBM replicas. The GDR's strategy to build up its own chip industry was a complete failure:

It simply did not have the technical know-how and equipment to do it. By the time the GDR had produced the 16- and 32-kilobit chips they were outdated, and capitalist countries were already on to the new generation. By 1989 the GDR was able to produce 90,000 256-kilobit chips, whereas Austria, a small country, had produced 50 million. By contrast, Japan was already mass producing one million megabit chips per month by April 1986.[20]

The "prototype" of a one megabit chip that Honecker presented to Gorbachev in 1988 as proof of the GDR's exemplary prowess was merely a mock-up from the West.

Varied economic and military interests played a role in arms espionage. Its aim was to scout out as precisely as possible the enemy's military technology. A spin-off of this was information relevant to its own (that is to say, primarily Soviet) weapons production, which figured into its export business and hence the GDR's hard-currency trade. The companies spied on most intensively included Messerschmitt-Bölkow-Blohm (MBB). One of the East German operatives deployed there was Dieter Feuerstein (IM "Petermann"), whose parents had gone to the Federal Republic as HVA spies in the 1950s. When their son began to show an interest in the West German Communist Party (DKP) as a student in school, they told him about their double lives and put him in touch with their handlers in 1973. The latter seized the opportunity and won him over for a long-term career as an agent. Though inclined to the humanities (his grandfather was none other than the Marxist philosopher Ernst Bloch), Feuerstein reoriented himself at the behest of the MfS. He studied aerospace engineering in West Berlin and began a career as an engineer, which eventually, in the mid-1980s, landed him in the research department of the defense contractor MBB. Here he had access to the construction plans of the Tornado and Jäger 90 fighter planes, as well as tanks and helicopters, and was able to deliver hundreds of pages of microfilm through "dead letter boxes" in trains to East Berlin. He regularly met with his instructor Uwe Albrecht (code name "Ronald") in Italy, Austria, and Germany, and at the end of each year with his case officer, Lieutenant Colonel Kurt Thiemann of HVA Department XV, in East Berlin. According to Western sources, Feuerstein tried to join up with the KGB in 1989–90, though the last head of the HVA, Werner Grossmann, takes this for a feint of West German counterintelligence, which was cooperating with a defector from the Science and Technology Sector. A transformed Soviet Union was no longer a "socialist partner" for Feuerstein, he claims, which is why the engineer rejected any such overtures to cooperate.[21] Feuerstein was arrested in 1990 and sentenced in 1992 to eight years in prison.

Counterintelligence

Forming a qualified opinion about the achievements and weaknesses of Eastern secret services undoubtedly requires getting a realistic picture of the activities of Western secret services working against the GDR and the efforts of the MfS to avert these activities. There are two obstacles to this, however. First, the sources available on the Western side are extremely sparse. The West German secret service continues to almost totally deny access to its files. The situation in the United States is somewhat better, thanks to the Freedom of Information Act and a special CIA program to declassify documents for historical research. Stasi files on the sources and methods of the BND and other secret services are still under lock and key to the extent that their disclosure could jeopardize the welfare of the nation, according to Section 37 of the Stasi Records Act (StUG). In short, the age of historical research into Western espionage against the GDR has yet to begin.

Second, Communist secret services generally assumed that every kind of critical activity had its origins in the subversive agitation (*Wühlarbeit*) of enemy secret services. It is no coincidence that the big Stalinist show trials aimed to get leading Communists to confess that they were working as fascist or imperialist spies. This tradition was continued by East German State Security, albeit in a milder form. Honecker's insistence, mentioned above, that they figure out Bärbel Bohley's BND registration number is proof positive of this. What's more, MfS generals are still convinced that the autumn revolution of 1989 was the work of Western intelligence agencies, even if it can't be proved at present. A realistic look at this field therefore has to clearly distinguish between "counterintelligence" in the sheer unlimited self-understanding of Communist security doctrine and counterintelligence in the conventional sense of the word. Neither of these obstacles, however, can obscure the fact that the Federal Republic and its allies did indeed spy against the GDR. Main Department II of the MfS was responsible for averting these activities.

With an open border until 1961, the battle of the secret services was somewhat akin to a slugfest. Given the relatively open possibilities of infiltration, the Western secret services were well present even in the higher positions of the East German state. This went for agents recruited, for example, in Allied POW camps and planted in strategic positions over time, as well as for East German citizens who viewed their work as an act of resistance. Among the agents working for the Gehlen Organization were Karli Bandelow, an employee in the State Secretariat for Motor Traffic and Road Engineering, arrested and executed in 1954; the personal secretary of East German Minister-President Otto Grotewohl, Elli Barczatis, until her arrest and subsequent execution in 1955; Deputy Minister-President Hermann Kastner (LDPD), who fled to the Federal Republic in 1956; and deputy director of East German military espionage, Siegfried Dombrowski, until 1958. The flow of refugees from the GDR, 456 former MfS employees among them, provided a steady stream of information as well.

In the context of the American policy of liberation towards the Eastern bloc, these agents were not only needed as suppliers of information, but as potential points of support in the case of a serious system crisis. But it turned out that these forces played an insignificant role in the case of crisis, such as the uprising of 17 June 1953, contrary to SED propaganda, and that ultimately the policy of liberation proved to be a dead end, as the United States shied away from (nuclear) war as a means of achieving this end. What's more, Soviet and East German counterintelligence inflicted some bitter defeats on Western intelligence services. The pressure caused by the waves of arrests slowly drained the potential for recruiting among the East German population. With that, the Western secret services (apart from the Federal Intelligence Service) lost their interest in the internal situation in the GDR and shifted their focus to reconnoitering the Soviet Army on East German soil.

Despite arrests by the MfS, part of its agent network was able to be retained even after the Wall was built. As it was no longer possible to enter and exit the country freely, the classic instruments of radio contacts, clandestine letters, dead letter boxes, etc. now had to be activated. The CIA, for example, had several well-placed sources in the 1960s among subaltern employees in the SED Central Committee, including telephonist Gertrud Liebing, who until her arrest in 1966 had listened in on talks between Politbüro members and other high functionaries. State Security, unlike Liebing herself, knew when arresting her that she was terminally ill with cancer and had just a few months to live. She was sentenced to twelve years in prison in December 1966 and died seven weeks later. Yet to be resolved is the question of which organization in the West was giving orders to sound technician Arno Heine, who from 1958 until his arrest in 1970 regularly supplied the latest tape recordings of meetings of the Central Committee and other executive bodies, by his own account several hundred reels. As a projectionist and television technician he also routinely passed through the offices and homes of top functionaries like Otto Grotewohl and Walter Ulbricht. Heine was sentenced to life in prison and died in 1980 in Bautzen II penitentiary. Severe cases of espionage like these were a field day for Mielke, who could boast about his exploits before the SED apparatus. He had a long list of tightened security precautions drawn up for Central Committee headquarters in 1970, and demanded the right to put the inner workings of the Central Committee apparatus itself under surveillance if needed. This had been denied to him before, because—as Central Committee department head Günter Glende confided to spy Arno Heine—the Central Committee felt that the MfS "only comes up to our chest."[22]

The MfS intensified its counterintelligence in the decade to follow with an unparalleled amount of resources. Main Department II was augmented from 214 to 988 employees between 1968 and 1982, first and foremost to keep the new diplomatic missions and journalists from the West under control, all of whom were generally suspected of working as foreign agents. There were now no longer any restrictions on postal and telephone controls. On the other hand, there were relatively few arrests and convictions being made. In 1973, for example, the MfS convicted thirty-three spies "in the employ of imperialist secret services" and opened up fifteen new preliminary proceedings. In 1980 there were fifteen convictions and thirteen new hearings. As far as we can tell, most of these were less spectacular cases of military espionage against the NVA and the Soviet Army. But Main Department II was increasingly shifting its counterintelligence activities to the West. In the early 1970s, for instance, it successfully established its "Residency Center" agent ring at the Military Counterintelligence Service and the State Office for the Protection of the Constitution in Lower Saxony.

The greatest defeat for East Germany's counterintelligence came in January 1979 with the defection of HVA lieutenant Werner Stiller. Contrary to the legend he later propagated in his autobiography, though, Stiller by no means worked for several years as a mole, supplying information to the Federal Intelligence Service in Pullach, but only made contact with it right before he fled. A minor copycat effect ensued with two other MfS officers, Gert Trebeljahr and Werner Teske, plotting to flee as well, both of whom were apprehended before they could carry out their plans. The two men were subsequently executed.

Essential for the success of counterintelligence was the Stasi's work against its direct adversaries in the Federal Republic. The KGB had an agent at the Federal Intelligence Service (and its precursor, the Gehlen Organization) in the person of Heinz Felfe, until his arrest in 1961. Felfe directed the counterintelligence division responsible for the Soviet Union. As of the 1970s there were two MfS agents there:

Captain Alfred Spuhler, active in operational procurement from the Eastern bloc, and Gabriele Gast, in the evaluation department for the USSR. From the early 1980s, senior government official Klaus Kuron reported to the East from the Federal Office for the Protection of the Constitution—from its counterintelligence division, of all places. He volunteered these services and betrayed most of the "reverse" (*umgedrehte*) East German spies he himself was handling while at the same time warning the HVA of imminent arrests. A lucky break for the HVA was the defection of group leader Hans-Joachim Tiedge, a senior employee of Kuron. The MfS succeeded in neutralizing many Western spies and double agents thanks to the information provided by Kuron, but wasn't able to arrest them without endangering its source. The defection of Tiedge was the perfect opportunity to carry out a wave of arrests, pinning the responsibility on Tiedge when it was actually Kuron's doing.

MfS Main Department II had a comparable site source at the Military Counterintelligence Service (MAD) in the person of its deputy head, Colonel Joachim Krase, from 1973 until his death in 1988. Having lost a considerable source when Krase passed away, the HVA endeavored to make thorough use of a "pumping" contact. Herbert Kloss, an editor at Deutsche Welle radio, had interested MAD leaders in a book project about their work. Krase had been one of the two official coauthors. The HVA apparently made the most of this contact: it updated its knowledge by having Kloss send manuscript drafts with intentional mistakes to MAD for verification, with the latter conscientiously correcting these factual errors and providing additional information in the process. At least as far as West German agents working against the GDR are concerned, there were therefore very few spies in the 1970s and 1980s who could work for long in the GDR without being detected. The situation was perhaps more favorable for other Western secret services, but their work with "live sources" on the territory of the GDR had limits of a more practical nature. There was something true about a joke that appeared around that time in the BND's in-house newspaper: "A command post director asks his employee how many internal sources he's recruited this year. The employee answers, 'None.' The director thoughtfully shakes his head and says: 'None is a lot for internal sources.'"[23]

And yet Western espionage was by no means empty-handed. Targeted counterintelligence work and disclosures by unofficial collaborators and East German functionaries abroad allowed them to penetrate the enemy camp. Thus, by the early 1980s at the latest, the BND and BfV were more or less aware of the MfS's involvement with Schalck-

Golodkowski's business empire and his activities in the embargo and arms business. Some of the MfS couriers, too, who supplied DKP headquarters in Düsseldorf with cash injections from East Berlin were double agents as well, and gave officers from the Cologne Office for the Protection of the Constitution a look at their coffers.

HVA military espionage came to the conclusion that Western knowledge of the NVA and the Warsaw Pact was on the whole accurate and detailed. And new opportunities were opening up in other areas. There were several reasons for this. For one thing, the secret services made full use of the growing potential of technological espionage, fitting the areas around Soviet military bases with satellite-aided electronic sensors, for instance. Many a risky observation mission could be avoided in this manner. This method was supplemented by reconnaissance services of the three Western allies' military liaison missions in the GDR, which thanks to their diplomatic immunity were able to tour the countryside by car, securing a dense flow of information about the Soviet Army's West Group stationed there. (The Soviet missions in the Federal Republic were doing the same thing.)

Another abundant source for the Federal Intelligence Service was the informal interviewing of East German citizens who had visited West Germany or left the GDR. This was essentially the old method of "prisoner interviews" used by the Wehrmacht's Foreign Armies East Department in the Second World War and by the Gehlen Organization in the postwar years. The growing number of travelers and Easterners settling in the West made this source increasingly important. Moreover, the BND succeeded in intercepting the directional radio links for the telephone lines of the SED apparatus. Former BND president Hans-Georg Wieck still brags today that this was how, in the late 1980s, his organization learned about a supposed 500,000 applications to emigrate, from which they extrapolated the figure of 1.5 million. Though the BND had undoubtedly stumbled upon one of the most urgent problems faced by SED leaders, its estimate was exaggerated: in 1988–89 there were 120,000 such applications.[24]

Partisans on the Invisible Front:
The Sabotage and Terror Squads

The military tasks of the Ministry for State Security not only included spying out the enemy's war plans but had an offensive component as well: preparations for its own military operations. This was essentially a carry-over from the Soviet struggle against the German occupation during World War II. The nascent GDR of the early 1950s, after all, was thoroughly in the hands of former partisans. In 1953, one of the oldest and most experienced Communist resistance fighters, Joseph Gutsche, began building up an MfS department "for special duty" (*zur besonderen Verwendung*—z.b.V.), which planned bombings in the Federal Republic and carried them out in a number of documented cases. In 1957, another former partisan and Soviet secret agent, Gustav Röbelen, began building up Administration 15 (Verwaltung 15) in the National People's Army, likewise for the purpose of planning acts of sabotage and terror and establishing a corresponding logistics and personnel network in the Federal Republic. A number of former resistance fighters were gathered in the leading positions of this apparatus, some of whom had had trouble adjusting to the extravagant security bureaucracy and preferred the kind of work they did in former days.

The branch, however, was thoroughly professionalized by the MfS in the early 1960s, in cooperation with the KGB. Hence the practitioners of a romantic notion of partisan work had to give up their game. Röbelen was replaced by Ernst Haberland, a former prisoner in Buchenwald and one-time Western resident of SED party reconnaissance, who immediately set to work reestablishing the training methods of Administration 15. In 1962, however, Mielke succeeded in incorporating the unit into his ministry, a move apparently long in planning. At the time of the takeover, the outfit (apart from its 150 full-time employees) had 265 East German citizens who had completed or were still in training. The MfS also took over the camps for the military and secret-service training of West Germans. The network of bases in the Federal Republic with its 86 unofficial collaborators stretched from List on the North Sea island of Sylt all the way down to the Black Forest. Its depots contained 220,000 deutsche marks in cash and objects valued at 52,000 deutsche marks; its weapons stockpile 700 handguns and rifles, 67 submachine guns, 17 machine guns, and more than 1,600 hand grenades.

In 1964, Mielke once again expanded his plans for partisan warfare. A separate unit led by MfS training officer Heinz Stöcker and later referred to as the Minister's Working Group/S (Arbeitsgruppe des Ministers/S, or AGM/S—S for "Stöcker" or "Special Issues," i.e., *Sonderfragen*) was to systematically train officers in every unit as radio operators, explosives experts, combat divers, etc. for rapid deployment behind enemy lines in the event of an emergency. The MfS was simultaneously expanding its special IM network in the West to support single combatants or "task forces" (*Einsatzgruppen*[25]) to be smuggled in or dropped by parachute. They served as contact persons and liaisons, set up and maintained supply depots, and spied out potential targets. Some of them were even specially trained and held in reserve for combat missions in the case of attacks or invasions.

Between 1964 and 1984 about 3,500 employees were trained as solo combatants or specialists. This enabled the active reserves to be continually replenished with younger cadre. Apart from this there were permanent task-force units ("specific forces") comprising 623 full-time employees of the AGM/S in 1988. There is no precise information for the Western network of the 1970s and 1980s. The AGM/S defined 346 targets in the civil and military infrastructure for 1981. This, of course, required considerable logistical support.

A key West German support was the clandestine military organization of the DKP, the so-called Forster Group, named after its East German director Harry Schmitt, code name Ralf Forster. It was founded in 1968–69 and was said to have had about 200 members in 1989, likewise trained by the NVA and MfS—initially in Hungary and Poland, then, as of the mid-1970s, in camps on East German soil. As conceived by the AGM/S, this cadre formed part of the "patriotic forces" that were to collaborate with MfS fighters in crisis situations. Its headquarters were in Berlin-Grünau.

The role model for MfS troops in the 1960s was Directorate V of the KGB's First Main Directorate. Directorate V ("V" for Vympel) was present with its liaison officers and, in 1969, offered the head of the AGM and later deputy minister, Alfred Scholz, himself a former partisan, exclusive glimpses into their work by way of consultations. Unlike the partisans of World War II, their operations were no longer supposed to be aimed at large military targets (an incomparably stronger arsenal in the form of regular armed forces had meanwhile been created for this purpose); only critical points in the military infrastructure were targeted, ones which could be fought efficiently with special operations of this sort. Apart from this, they were to focus on targets important to "political morale," i.e., civilian targets: government institutions, political organizations, secret organizations, and "political-ideological centers." Underlying this concept was the assumption of a civil-war scenario. In the case of war or conflict, "resistance movements" were to be stirred up in the enemy's hinterland and used to their advantage. In times of peace, the troops were to be used for "physical operations." In this case, however, they were to act "under their respective national or third-country flags while consistently disguising their own involvement" using enemy weapons and equipment.[26] KGB plans encompassed the entire arsenal of undercover warfare, and the MfS was keen to follow suit. Scholz explained while inspecting the unit in 1972:

> The most important thing is to prepare operations for the early phase of a war. . . . There can be no formal resumption of partisan warfare; new targets of attack need to be chosen in the political and secret-service sphere. Appropriate cadre need to be trained for this purpose that are capable of acts of diversion, individual terror, the procurement of technical equipment, the capturing of individuals, the support of antiauthoritarian forces.[27]

This concept was elaborated with Prussian thoroughness in a 3,790-page AGM/S "handbook," which has only survived in fragments. The manual makes neat distinctions between damaging, destroying, and wrecking objects, but also between the disorganization, demoralization, elimination, and liquidation of individuals. On the latter it says: "Liquidation comprises the physical destruction of individuals and groups of persons. Attainable by shooting, stabbing, burning, blowing up, strangling, beating, poisoning, suffocating.[28]

These sabotage and murder commandos were never deployed under conditions of war. But in the "deployment principles" of 1981 they explicitly adopted the Soviet principles of peacetime operations. Under "relatively peaceful conditions" they were to be deployed for the "liquidation or capture of traitors, the liquidation or elimination of leading figures in terror organizations whose activities are directed against the state security of the GDR," as well as for "unsettling [*Verunsicherung*] leading figures in centers of political-ideological diversion by disrupting or obstructing their work routines and damaging or crippling facilities, equipment, and files." The assassinations and unresolved deaths depicted above give reason to assume that these were not mere theoretical considerations.

Though the AGM/S was not a service branch of the HVA, the two were linked in manifold ways. Like all other units, the espionage departments of the HVA sent employees to be specially trained as solo combatants, radio operations, divers, etc. Moreover, in 1981, HVA chief Markus Wolf requested the AGM/S to train three to four "young operational employees" as "permanent reserves for special duty" and deploy them in the "operation area" to, among other things, "fight enemy persons with the entire range of available measures for their punishment, neutralization [*Unschädlichmachung*], and transfer to safe custody." Deputy Minister Wolf apparently set great store in having a handful of agents vested with a "license to kill." In 1987, an HVA unit (Department XVIII) once again took on the task of scouting out targets for possible operations.[29]

None of the participants were ever actually put to the test—the task forces never had to engage in military operations in a war situation with the support of the Western stay-behind network. Although map exercises and preparatory training of this sort certainly existed on both sides of the Iron Curtain, the intensity and systematicness displayed by East German State Security in doing so is nonetheless quite striking. This was probably a throwback to the romantic notion of partisan warfare held by the older generation, as well as an expression of the violence-prone spiritual core of Chekism being given room to develop here—if only in the form of training exercises.

Chekist Development Aid and "Anti-imperialist Solidarity"

East German State Security distinguished itself as a junior partner of the KGB in the 1960s. With its stay-behind networks and undercover operations, it was nearly on par with the world's major international intelligence agencies (even though its operation area was basically restricted to the Federal Republic and West Berlin). It had already made quite a name for itself as a domestic secret-police force. It was thus that the MfS assumed an important role in the Eastern bloc's Third World policies: while the Soviet Union was providing massive military aid, the GDR became firmly established as a source of training and development assistance in the domain of internal security and guerilla warfare.

In terms of foreign policy, this new role was particularly attractive to the GDR in the 1960s, as contacts of this sort helped promote and consolidate its strategy of seeking recognition in the face of West Germany's Hallstein Doctrine. Its secret-police and secret-service expertise would later become a coveted "export commodity" to varied liberation movements, as well as to postcolonial and socialist states. Though rather heterogeneous in terms of ideology, these organizations and regimes actively sought the support of Soviet communism in their fight against domestic and foreign enemies that enjoyed the backing of the United States and other Western states. Apart from political advantages, international exchanges offered the chance to learn from others and study local conditions. In 1975, for instance, an AGM/S delegation went to Vietnam to evaluate the practical experiences of the Viet Cong in occupying the South Vietnamese capital, Saigon. The MfS delegates also took a wish list with them in the hope of enhancing their own capabilities for covert operations. Thus, for example, in Vietnam they requested 33 American uniforms, along with steel helmets and combat packs. Weapons of Western manufacture were also much in demand. The AGM/S was also more than willing to dispatch commandos for the protection of East German diplomatic missions in crisis and conflict regions—to Damascus, Islamabad, Baghdad, Cairo, Beirut, Mogadishu, and Teheran in the 1980s—and to gather valuable experience.

The first such cooperation began in 1964, with the African island state of Zanzibar, following a revolt against the ruling sultanate. The MfS dispatched a five- to six-man advisory group, including Markus Wolf and the regional boss of Dresden, Rolf Markert, which stayed there for several months. A liaison officer stayed behind once the advisory group departed. The security apparatus of Zanzibar remained strongly oriented towards the GDR, soon became "disproportionately large,"[30] and ultimately did the bidding of revolutionary leader Abeid Karume, who ruled despotically over the country. A similar commitment began the same year between the MfS and Ghana. It ended abruptly in 1966 with the overthrow of Kwame Nkrumah. The leader of the advisory group and subsequent HVA department head Jürgen Rogalla was arrested at the time and later released in a prisoner exchange. With that, the covert nature of the GDR's African policy had entered the public eye. Additional foreign deployments took place as of 1969, in Sudan and South Yemen, among other places, as of 1975 in Mozambique and Angola, and as of 1977 in Ethiopia, where the GDR spent around four million marks setting up a school for the local security apparatus and assisted in its training efforts.

The MfS also gave support to Communist parties and liberation movements. In southern Africa, the GDR promoted the underground and military organizations of the African National Congress (ANC), the ZAPU (Rhodesia/Zimbabwe), and the SWAPO (South-West Africa/Namibia) starting in the late 1960s. For the period from 1976 to 1979 alone, the aid provided to these three organizations amounted to more than 43 million marks. Cadre from all cooperating countries and organizations came to the GDR for training, most of them trainers themselves or commanders. The content of this training comprised a variety of aspects: personal and building security, classic secret-service methods, military combat training, radio operation, and explosives. The MfS also attached importance to conveying the basics of Marxism-Leninism and, especially, to indoctrinating its trainees in "counterintelligence thinking" (*Abwehrdenken*) in line with its own ideological concept of the enemy. A wide range of MfS units and training facilities were therefore involved here: apart from the AGM/S, the HVA, the MfS university with its own separate Institute for International Relations, the Main Department for Personal Security, the Guards Regiment, and the Main Department for Cadre and Training.

The ANC alone had several thousand fighters trained in a camp close to Teterow in Mecklenburg. The GDR became its second largest training destination after the Soviet Union, particularly in the wake of the Soweto Uprising of 1976, when hundreds of young people flocked to the ranks of the Umkhonto we Sizwe (MK), the ANC's military organization. ANC instructors came for political training, including the subsequent head of MK's military secret service and later South African minister of intelligence services, Ronnie Kasrils, who was impressed by the "creativity" and "practical relevance" of the training courses.[31] Other top cadre such as ZAPU security chief and later Zimbabwean minister of the interior, Dumiso Dabengwa, were likewise trained in the GDR.

Apart from the ANC, its largest cooperation partner, as well as other liberation organizations and Communist parties, there was a steady stream of sizable training groups from states that had just begun to build up their own security apparatuses, including a contingent of 110 Mozambicans in 1975, and several dozen state-security cadre from Nicaragua in the early 1980s. The MfS seemed to offer these apparatuses a kind of "developmental push," encouraging in them a tendency to ruthlessly "battle the enemy" with complete disregard for the underlying causes of local indigenous conflicts. Likewise part of these national liberation movements, at least in their self-perception, were the various Palestinian organizations, which in 1980–81 alone had 81 fighters against Israel trained by East Germans.

All in all, from 1970 to 1989 almost 1,900 resistance fighters and state-security cadre from 15 states received training from the AGM/S. The number of participants sank in the 1980s. In 1980 there were 230; by 1986, the last figure on record, there were only 92. The MfS might have been trying to cut costs, and anyway, with regard to the Third World, was more concerned about its own financial interests, e.g., increasing its arms trading. The protracted negotiations between Ethiopia and the MfS, begun in 1979 and concluded in 1987, over continued financial support are one indication of this.

Finally, the varied support offered to Arab terrorists, who had unobstructed access to the GDR as a safe haven and transit country, should be mentioned here as well. These forms of "anti-imperialist solidarity" also gave rise to cooperation with the notorious West German terrorist group the Red Army Faction (RAF). Both were the responsibility of MfS terror defense (Department XXII). The West German terrorist scene had been under close Stasi surveillance since the 1970s, and sporadic contacts were made through the associated PLO and the security apparatus of South Yemen. Known terrorists were able to travel unhampered to and from West Berlin through the East German airport of Berlin-Schönefeld. In 1979, State Security offered asylum to RAF members wanting to break away from the group, ten of whom took up the offer and settled in the GDR. Between 1980 and 1982 there were several meetings in the GDR with active RAF members, who were given the chance to practice firing a grenade launcher at an automobile. Whether this took place before or after the similar (failed) attack on U.S. General Frederik Kroesen has yet to be clarified. What is certain is that State Security made every effort to use these terrorists as sources of information about West German dragnet operations, assassination procedures, etc., offering knowledge of their own in return. At the same time, though, the Stasi endeavored to influence and control the RAF.

Intensive cooperation seems to have stopped by 1984, with the exception of the "asylum-seekers." Many of the latter, spotted by East German citizens or recognized during visits to the West, had to change addresses and identities on multiple occasions. For this the GDR took the risk of seriously harming its international image. There are some indications that West German security officials eventually knew the general whereabouts of some of these individuals. One of them, Silke Meier-Witt, even underwent facial surgery after being warned by the MfS. But the Federal Government eschewed requesting their extradition—perhaps to avoid diplomatic entanglements, perhaps for a lack of hard evidence.

Achievements and Limits of East German Espionage

The unofficial Western network was quite large, with 3,000 persons at last count. This reflected both the personnel-intensive, highly professional structure for handling and protecting the actual spies, as well as the great variety of targets. Added to this were the information channels via legally covered contacts and—not to be underestimated—the considerable amount of information procured through telephone and radio espionage. East German foreign espionage was particularly successful thanks to this network—especially in the areas of military and economic espionage, but also in spying out politics, state, and society in West Germany. By engaging in "active measures" and deploying agents of influence, State Security did its utmost to support the SED's propaganda line, sometimes using inner-party conflicts to sow the seeds of discord. In matters such as the failed vote of no confidence against Willy Brandt in 1972, the MfS indeed had a hand in turning the wheels of history.

What was the recipe for success of East German espionage against the West? As suggested by the verdict of Heribert Hellenbroich, a former official at the West German Federal Office for the Protection of the Constitution, these achievements were due to the peculiarities of inter-German relations, the high degree of professionalism, the patience and persistence of case officers, but not least of all the many advantages to be had from the differences between an open society and a dictatorial regime. Hunting for spies and other enemies was virtually elevated to a guiding principle of the SED's political system. The MfS could therefore conduct its counterintelligence with almost unlimited resources and without being hampered by the rule of law, while simultaneously taking advantage of the opportunities afforded by Western democracy and the legal protections of Western civil rights. By the 1960s at the latest, the scope of action of Western intelligence services in the GDR had almost entirely dried up for the opposite reason. To the best of our knowledge, the West German Federal Intelligence Service and Offices for the Protection of the Constitution had no genuine moles the likes of Gast, Spuhler, or Kuron, who would have enabled them to foil the strategies of their secret-service adversary (however much they tried to convey this impression after the defection of Werner Stiller).

A successful strategy in the 1950s, given the existence of two German states, was the resettlement of agents (or agent couples) in the West amidst the stream of refugees headed there. As shown by the case of Guillaume, the spy in the Federal Chancellery, persistence could pay off and lead to the highest echelons of power. This perspective-agent strategy was continued by the MfS even after the tide of refugees ebbed in 1961. For one thing, they could rely on the tips of existing agents, recruiting new agents from their circle of friends and relatives. For another, they often sent their recruiters to universities and technical colleges to approach young people (usually men) or approached them on their visits to the GDR. There were two advantages to this technique. First, the Moscow-oriented DKP was quite strongly represented there thanks to the "Spartakus" Marxist Students' League. Many a left-leaning young person could be "redirected" (*umgelenkt*) before he joined a Communist organization and "burned" (*verbrannt*) himself for a career in the secret service. Second, students were generally more amenable materially and ideologically to venture into the illegal world of espionage and had promising career perspectives. The likelihood that they would later end up in leadership positions in West German society was comparatively high. Once this step had been taken, moreover, the fear of exposure and punishment took effect and did its part to secure their loyalty. The Stasi clearly and unabashedly went for quantity over quality, well knowing that the vast majority of the students (and other West German citizens) it approached would reject its advances out of hand or after a little while.

Other penetration techniques were likewise facilitated by the situation of a divided Germany. Though cross-border secret-service connections were not discernible in the majority of inter-German contacts, the travels and personal contacts of West Germans to the GDR offered manifold points of contact for recruiting. East German agents (unlike, say, a Soviet agent in the United States) could easily assimilate language-wise and carry out undercover assignments while working as a journalist or businessman. Identity theft of unwitting West Germans was also an easy game.

Despite its impressive track record in the West, the MfS did have to deal with defeats and weaknesses. As long as the espionage and counterintelligence activities of the West remain under wraps, a final balance will be impossible. Our current level of knowledge allows us to make two observations, however—one about the balance of power between intelligence agencies in the narrow sense, another about the role of competing secret services in the framework of system conflict.

As shown above with respect to the West's cognizance of the military potential of the Warsaw Pact, the West evidently found other ways to offset the inherent advantages of the GDR, i.e., the placement of human sources and the sheer size of its apparatus due to the perceived exigencies of counterintelligence in all areas of society (in the narrow sense of combating real enemy agents, and the broad, Stalinist sense with its paranoid fantasies of ubiquitous infiltration). The use of state-of-the-art spying technology in the age of the microelectronic revolution, in particular, gave the West a clear advantage. Furthermore, the GDR's intertwining with the Federal Republic, deemed highly problematic by the MfS from a counterintelligence perspective, offered new opportunities as well.

The second aspect was the most deleterious to the GDR. The Eastern bloc, with its enormous investment in military power, vigilance, and armed security, and thus in espionage, had simply backed the wrong horse. This was not without reason, and had to do with the conflict-oriented worldview of Communist leaders. In principle one can assume that the services rendered by espionage and counterespionage can have a decisive influence on victory or defeat in the case of war and military confrontation. With the perspective of "mutually assured destruction," it was only logical that great importance was attached to secret services. The more civilian the system conflict became, however, the less influence secret services had. In the end it was not military prowess that determined the outcome of the Cold War but the ability of competing systems to modernize in the economic, technological, and social domains.

A militarized worldview and social thinking turned out to be quite a hindrance from the 1960s on. In the context of the Cold War and the efforts at détente, it was not the arduous arms-control negotiations of the 1970s but, rather, the concessions made by the East in the CSCE process and the attendant demands for humanitarian and civil rights that exacerbated the inner erosion of the Communist systems.[32] Classic espionage was powerless against this—and the internal secret-police forces would later founder because of it too.[33]

Against this backdrop, the frequently invoked advantages of the closed societies of the Eastern bloc, as opposed to the more liberal model of society practiced in the West, turned out to not be very compelling. It was precisely the pluralistic and complex decision-making processes of democratic civil societies that were not susceptible in the long run to covert action by fifth columns. To stick to the German case: the greatest weakness of East German espionage presumably had to do with the fact that the SED state was utterly devoid of charm for the majority of West German citizens. Even in the political left of the 1970s or the peace movement, it never had a pivotal influence on the many (sometimes fiercely warring) organizations—not least of all because the predominantly drab and dreary images of daily life in the GDR that trickled over to the West had little in common with the "wild and dangerous" lifestyles imagined by Western revolutionaries. The view expressed in 1984 by SED Politbüro member Hermann Axen in Moscow, "that we have a stronger influence [*stärker einwirken*] on the FRG [Federal Republic of Germany] nowadays than they do on us"[34] therefore seems like a combination of wishful thinking and blindness to reality. The practical experiences of the HVA looked quite a bit different in the 1980s. Recruiting new agents became more and more difficult, while the pressure mounted to prove that the GDR's internal opposition was being steered from outside and to neutralize these supposed external influences. By the same token, any sober assessment can scarcely maintain—as argued by some West German authors[35]—that the Federal Republic or, at the very least, considerable parts of the political mainstream or the (in the broadest sense) leftist social movements of the 1970s and 1980s were secretly being controlled by East Berlin, that the open society of the Federal Republic had been too lax in the face of its "enemies."

Second, the hope of using economic and technological espionage to compensate for innovative weakness and poor economic performance turned out to be an illusion. The Stasi's surreptitious feeding of East Germany's microelectronics program in the 1980s smacked of the desperate search for a *Wunderwaffe,* a "wonder weapon," to save the GDR from ruin.

Finally there was a third functional weakness with regard to decision-making processes, which American historian John Lewis Gaddis pointed out as early as 1989: "Intelligence coups are one thing; the uses of this intelligence are something else again."[36] There is not even the slightest indication of the Stasi functioning as a foreign- and military-policy think tank, coming to its own conclusions or at least taking part in the decision-making process. Compared to the National Intelligence Estimates of the CIA,[37] for example, MfS reports were much more limited to a sober regurgitation of the "hard" facts. Even the most realistic assessments of the enemy had little noticeable impact on the military doctrine of the Warsaw Pact, nourished as it was by unshakable ideological maxims about "aggressive imperialism" and by the bitter experiences of the German invasion of 1941. Networking with other government authorities, academic think tanks, and political organizations, as in the case of the intelligence services of the United States, are barely discernible here.

Chapter 7

FINAL CRISIS AND COLLAPSE, 1989–90

The Debilitated Dictatorship

On 7 October 1989, the fortieth anniversary of the GDR's founding, the state and Party leadership once again had their "armed organs" parade down Karl-Marx-Allee in East Berlin. Unit by unit, the soldiers, tanks, and missile carriers filed past the packed reviewing stand: the National People's Army and the "combat groups of the working class" (factory militias), border troops and the guard units of State Security. For months SED leaders did all they could to make sure the birthday of the republic was dignified and ceremonious. They wanted to present themselves to their own people and to the world as a stable state, confident of the future.

Six months later it was hard to even remember this anachronistic spectacle. The last MfS employees were getting their pink slips while the People's Police was struggling with its loss of authority, just trying to get a handle on traffic. The National People's Army clung to the hope of a second, bloc-free army in a reunified Germany as propagated by the new minister for disarmament and defense, Rainer Eppelmann. Frontier troops regulated the smooth passage of streams of travelers at the numerous border crossings to the Federal Republic. The "combat groups" were preparing their final report before disbanding.

A revolution had taken place. In the preceding six months, mass demonstrations had formed against Party rule, state and Party leaders were toppled, and the Wall was opened. The Volkskammer laughed at the minister for state security and expunged the leading role of the SED from the East German constitution. Opposition groups assumed responsibility at Round Table talks and in cabinet positions. The first free elections in the history of the GDR ultimately led to the overwhelming victory of a man who was not even on the ballot: West German Chancellor Helmut Kohl with his concept for the immediate accession of the GDR to the Federal Republic of Germany.

How could it have come to this? There was certainly no lack of manpower and equipment for East German rulers to strike back. In 1989, the GDR had over half a million people under arms for its internal and external defense, besides which there was the West Group of the Soviet armed forces with about 400,000 soldiers stationed in the country. But State Security and all of the other armed forces did not bring their strength to bear.

This curious turn of events gave rise to much speculation. Had State Security been so farsighted as to make provisions for the moment of collapse, fading into the woodwork, and girding themselves for inevitable reunification? It knew better than anyone, after all, how things stood in the country, with all the information at its disposal. Or had the Stasi itself put out its feelers to the West, on the lookout for possible partners?

The scope of maneuver of State Security had continually narrowed since the early 1980s. Considerable pressure had been building up in the population for years. Supply shortages caused by the lack of investment and worsening export conditions wore down the people's patience. Added to the discontent over material scarcities was a growing resentment among the younger and middle generation against the "tutelary state," which severely restricted any attempt to live a self-determined life. Many of these individuals turned to youth subcultures and the peace groups in numerous church communities, which, among other things, advocated the option of a civilian alternative service instead of compulsory military service in the NVA. The younger generation was less afraid of sanctions than were their older counterparts, who still remembered the bitter lessons of the June uprising and the building of the Berlin Wall.

The consequences of gradually opening the GDR to the West from the 1970s on were beginning to be felt by policy makers. Thanks to Intershops and black-market trade, the West German deutsche mark had become a veritable second currency. Consumer demands and the desired mode of living were measured against the standards of the Federal Republic. The tacitly tolerated evening visit to the class enemy through the medium of television no longer had a subduing effect, but was mobilizing instead. On top of this was the sudden jump in the number of permits issued for private visits to relatives in the West in 1986 and 1987, in the run-up to Honecker's visit to Bonn. The result would merely feed new desires—because of the possibility to travel but also because of the impressions gathered on the other side, which were passed on in the GDR. The ruled increasingly terminated the "toleration agreement" they had made with their rulers. The number of applications to emigrate is telling evidence of this discontent.

Rifts were also developing among the functional elites of the party-state. SED Party members, bound to their leaders "through a special relationship of discipline and loyalty" and part of an "omnipresent executive staff" (*allgegenwärtiger Herrschaftsstab*),[1] were supposedly free from these influences thanks to special provisions like the prohibition on Western contacts for bearers of state secrets, but in practice things were often different. What's more, Honecker's "really existing socialism" went hand in hand with a massive renunciation of utopian ideals, so that the promise of a better future as a source of legitimation and power necessarily faded away. What remained was antifascist rituals and the organizational pressure of the Unity Party.

The real qualitative leap came with the new reform policies of Soviet party chief Mikhail S. Gorbachev, who took office in 1985. For many East German citizens, glasnost and perestroika were projection screens for their own desires. The socialist Party intelligentsia and many a frustrated idealist saw Gorbachev as the long-awaited programmatic leader, propagating greater intellectual freedom as a lever for overcoming the "period of stagnation." Other functionaries and Party members who endeavored to toe the current Party line had a hard time finding their bearings between Moscow and East Berlin.

The transformation in the Soviet Union put the Chekists in the Ministry for State Security under enormous pressure. Their tasks had multiplied over the years, including security checks for bearers of secrets and travel cadre, as well as stemming the flow of applications to emigrate. At the same time, their margin of maneuver for repression was dwindling, since the Party refused to take a hard line. The contradiction between continued militancy in the Stasi's self-image and the restrictions placed on their actions on account of "orders from headquarters" (*zentrale Weisungen*)—or so the set phrase for the mutual decisions of Honecker and Mielke—resulted in "operational frustration." This could take any number of forms, from aggressive *Zersetzung* measures to an increased retreat into the private sphere or alcohol abuse.

As disciplinary crackdowns in the "total institution" (Erving Goffman) of State Security were once again heightened in the 1980s, there was virtually no space to articulate or reflect upon doubts or problems of orientation. If mounting "enemy activity" and the problems arising from it were long made out as the result of the West's "imperialist global strategy," the tables turned here as well with Gorbachev, especially in the wake of the Twenty-Seventh Party Congress of the CPSU in 1986. The initiative for open public debate and a critical assessment of communism's own system deficits challenged the worldview of State Security. Furthermore, voices in the Soviet Union increasingly began to use arguments once attributed to the propaganda arsenal of imperialism. Soviet "New Thinking" left its mark in international relations as well as in a statement adopted by the SED and West German SPD in August 1987 on the "Battle of Ideologies and Joint Security," in which both sides pledged not to stereotype the enemy. Many Chekists already thought Gorbachev a traitor back then, and some younger Stasi men, confused by the fading image of the enemy, asked: "Is it possible to hate a foe you cooperate with? . . . Does imperialism, which has already brought so much misery to humanity, have values that are worth preserving?"[2]

Just as variable as its ideological orientation was Chekism in actual practice. After loosening up the reins before and during Honecker's visit to Bonn in September 1987, even tolerating the participation of independent peace groups in the "Olof Palme Peace March," the SED then tightened the screws. The "Battle of Zion" began. On the night of 24 November 1987, state prosecutors and MfS agents forced their way into the premises of the Zion Church (Zionskirche) in the Berlin district of Prenzlauer Berg. Going on information from IM reports, they wanted to apprehend activists of the "environmental library" housed there and hoped to catch them red-handed, printing the underground magazine *Grenzfall* (an evocative and suggestive title meaning "borderline case," but also "border incident" or conceivably even "fall of the border") illegally published by the Initiative for Peace and Human Rights. They arrested seven people, but their house search was fruitless. Instead of a samizdat periodical, all they found in the printing press were the church-internal and therefore legal *Umweltblätter* ("Environmental Pages"). The days that followed saw a huge wave of solidarity. Several hundred demonstrators protested in front of the Zion Church, and a candlelight vigil was started. Of the seven people arrested, five were released by State Security on 25 November. The two "main culprits," Wolfgang Rüddenklau and Bert Schlegel, were set free three days later, after further protests in the GDR and numerous displays of solidarity in the Federal Republic and abroad. Though SED and State Security had bared their teeth, they hardly scored a victory:

> The security organs had failed to achieve their operational goal of criminalizing the UB [environmental library] or smashing the clandestine editorial office of *Grenzfall*, nor could they continue their measures under the pressure of candlelight vigils, the opposition movement throughout the country, and especially international public opinion. Though it is true that they did not keep all the promises they made to prevent the protests from escalating even further, they nevertheless made complete fools of themselves.[3]

There was renewed confrontation on the occasion of the official "Combat Demonstration in Honor of Karl Liebknecht and Rosa Luxemburg" on 17 January 1988. Leading opposition members and would-be emigrants wanted to take part with homemade banners. State Security detained about 160 potential "disturbers" (*Störer*) prior to the event, including dissidents Stephan Krawczyk, Bert Schlegel, and Vera Wollenberger. While the arrested would-be emigrants were deported to the West the very next day, the members of the internal opposition remained in custody. On 27 and 28 January, State Security had four of the opposition members sentenced to six months in prison each for attempted "riotous assembly" (*Zusammenrottung*). Again, a wave of solidarity ensued, which State Security reacted to with a second blow. On 25 January they arrested Krawczyk's wife, the theater director Freya Klier, along with leading members of the Initiative for Peace and Human Rights: Bärbel Bohley, Werner Fischer, Ralf Hirsch, as well as Lotte and Wolfgang Templin. The MfS initiated proceedings against them for "treasonous relations," which potentially carried long prison terms.

The Party and secret-service apparatus made full use of their powers in this situation. The detainees, in their isolation, knew nothing of the broad wave of support for them in the GDR and abroad. Their only outside contacts, and the only avenue to reaching a mutual agreement, were controlled and manipulated by State Security, as in the case of attorney Schnur's clients. And yet State Security could no longer do as it pleased, either. Behind the veil of intimidation, it was seeking negotiations with lawyers and church representatives in light of the protests going on around them.

For days both sides strove to reach a solution to the conflict, and here too State Security had unofficial collaborators active on all sides. Instead of long prison terms, the negotiations finally ended with the "permanent disposal of hazardous people abroad."[4] In some cases, such as those of Bärbel Bohley and Vera Wollenberger, it turned out to be merely "temporary storage," as they were able return after a period of six months to two years.

The SED had attained one of it goals: important representatives of the opposition had left the country against their initial will, and some of the dissidents left behind were disappointed by these "feeble revolutionaries." Furthermore, the dreaded joining of forces of opposition members and would-be emigrants had been thwarted. But the price for this counterstroke was high: the wave of solidarity mobilized thousands of people, who gathered together in churches and other places despite the fact that well-placed agents of influence such as Schnur and Wollenberger's husband, Knud, were doing their best to sow frustration and dampen the spirit of protest. What's more, though banishment may have been a cause of disappointment for many people in the GDR, it hardly acted as a deterrent. A two-year study trip to Cambridge, England, which Vera Wollenberger managed to organize with the help of the church, obviously seemed less threatening than the prison term she'd been sentenced to in a summary trial beforehand. Mielke again sketched out the line of approach for the MfS in the fall of 1988: "We mustn't give the enemy any ammunition that would allow him to call our organs troublemakers [Störenfriede] in the process of peace and détente."[5]

The tensions between the sometimes finely dosed, sometimes demonstrably harsh instruments of State Security and politically motivated concessions in the struggle to keep down unrest in the country were quite palpable in the Stasi's final years of operation. The MfS officers who repeatedly devised effusive measures, which Party leaders then proceeded to write off as politically inopportune, had to exhibit great Party discipline in order to deal with this tension. They could have consulted Lenin and recognized their situation: "[F]or a revolution to take place it is not enough for the exploited and oppressed masses to realize the impossibility of living in the old way, and demand changes; for a revolution to take place it is essential that the exploiters should not be able to live and rule in the old way."[6]

Though the circumstances surrounding subsequent events are understandable in hindsight, the peaceful route to system breakdown was by no means a foregone conclusion. It almost seems a mystery that the GDR's internal armed forces gave in to defeat without a fight, a reaction that fundamentally contradicted their interests in the narrow sense.

In the spring of 1989, the situation spun out of control for the SED. It started with Soviet foreign-policy makers abandoning the Brezhnev Doctrine, i.e., the claim to hegemony over the Eastern bloc. The individual countries in the East were henceforth allowed to go their own ways—a position that a speaker of the Soviet Foreign Ministry jokingly referred to as the "Sinatra Doctrine," alluding to the "My Way" song. Thus the Warsaw Pact organization disbanded in its function as a "frontier-securing community"[7] for the GDR. A hole in the Iron Curtain had effectively opened up on the Hungarian-Austrian border.

The GDR, too, had silently made its own contribution to this process, the use of firearms at the border being prohibited by personal order of Honecker, first to the frontier troops, on 4 April, then to the MfS passport-control units, on 28 April. The SED was reacting to the death of twenty-year-old Chris Gueffroy, who was gunned down at the Wall in Berlin-Treptow on 5 February 1989. The incident had sparked a furor in the West. Representatives of the Federal Government cancelled their planned visit to the Leipzig Spring Fair. The interplay of flight/emigration and internal opposition thereby gained a new dynamic. The number of East German citizens who did not return from vacation in Hungary multiplied throughout the course of the summer. Added to this were the growing number of people who occupied the embassies of the Federal Republic in Budapest, Warsaw, and Prague.

Domestic disturbances were growing as well. Opposition groups had sent observers to many polling stations during local elections and denounced the nearly unanimous results (98.85 percent in favor of the Party) as verifiably rigged, the 5 to 10 percent of negative votes they recorded having simply been swept under the table. On 13 August 1989, physicist Hans-Jürgen Fischbeck called for the formation of a coalition movement to try to contain the exodus movement. The "We want out!" (*Wir wollen raus*) of the emigration movement was countered by the "We're staying here!" (*Wir bleiben hier*) of the internal opposition, which called for the formation of a New Forum (Neues Forum) whose manifesto stated:

> Refugee movements on this scale are elsewhere caused by poverty, hunger, and violence. . . . The dysfunctional relationship [*gestörte Beziehung*] between state and society paralyzes the creative potential of our society and hinders the solution of local and global tasks. . . . This is why we are building a common political platform for the whole of the GDR, enabling people of all professions, walks of life, parties, and groups to participate in discussions and work on vital social problems in this country.[8]

This appeal served as a catalyst for mass demonstrations. It was distributed and discussed everywhere. From week to week, more and more dissatisfied citizens assembled at the "Monday demonstrations" in Leipzig.

The initiators of New Forum had deliberately left the SED unmentioned, probably for tactical reasons. But this silence about the "leading role of the Party" was quite in line with the real situation, for the Party led no more. Throughout the summer it tried out a variety of threatening postures but only revealed itself to be hamstrung. When a few weeks later the Chinese army brutally suppressed a democratic protest by students at Tiananmen Square in Beijing, the East German Volkskammer pointedly expressed its approval. Politbüro member Egon Krenz later headed to China for an extensive goodwill visit.

Despite the many inherent obstacles faced by the opposition and the seeming unlikelihood of success, not to mention the large number of agents such as Schnur and Böhme planted in the opposition movement, the SED and State Security did not manage to prevent the founding of New Forum, the Social Democratic Party of the GDR (SDP), and other civil-rights groups (Democratic Awakening, Democracy Now, United Left, etc.). Party leaders and their organs of repression were just as helpless in the face of mass exodus via West German embassies and the Hungarian border. After weeks of trying to fight the situation, attempting, in particular, to persuade the Hungarian government to reverse its stance, the GDR eventually gave up on 30 September and permitted the emigration of embassy refugees. The GDR's insistence that the trains conveying these refugees pass through East German territory on their way to the Federal Republic as a symbol, as it were, of the GDR's sovereignty, turned out to be disastrous, however. There were violent disturbances along the way, especially at Dresden Main Station, when other East German citizens tried to board the trains.

A lesson learned in the daily business of persecution—that *Zersetzung* measures "usually have a limited" effect and cannot prevent "enemies from banding together with other enemies", in the long run—was borne out here.[9] With the new situation since the summer of 1989, such instruments were no longer effective. Instead of weakening those who stayed behind, the refugee and emigration movement encouraged them to put up a fight—against further outmigration and the intransigence of the country's leaders. The small group of dissidents became the mouthpiece of a mass movement. Thus, before and during the fortieth anniversary of the GDR on 7 October 1989, the SED resorted to the use of direct police-state repression. It dispersed the protesters in East Berlin and many other cities with truncheons and water cannons, and arrested thousands. Especially in Dresden, in the first weeks of October, and on the night of 7 October in East Berlin, it tried its best to make a show of humiliating its arrestees. Even this was a limited use of violence, however. The opposition was to be "forced out" of the public sphere and "beaten" (*gedrängt und geprügelt*), but not decapitated.[10] State Security collected what information it could about the activists of New Forum and other groups, and kept its arrest lists updated daily in the event of Armageddon. But when the decisive moment came, it failed to intervene.

Turning Point, 9 October

On October 9, 1989, 70,000 people gathered in Leipzig for the (by this point almost traditional) Monday demonstration and began a protest march on the ring road around the center of town. While Party leaders in East Berlin were in a state of confusion, the Leipzig SED regional administration decided against the use of force to break up the demonstration. On the following Monday, Honecker toyed with the idea of having a tank regiment roll through the streets of the trade-fair city to set a warning example, but other Politbüro members dissuaded him from doing so. Many former NVA soldiers with training in fighting tanks at close range were among the crowd of protesters, they argued, and, besides, the tank tracks would destroy the cobblestone streets, and that would only incense the people more. There is no doubt that the National People's Army, the People's Police, and State Security could have managed to disperse the protesters. But this would have involved two risks: an internal civil war, and external isolation and confrontation with unforeseeable consequences.

A power struggle meanwhile ensued in the Party leadership, ending on 18 October with the fall of Honecker and the rise of Egon Krenz as general secretary. Krenz proclaimed a "turn" (*Wende*) to "dialogue" between party-state and population. True to its self-understanding as "shield and sword" of the Party, the MfS yielded, restricting itself to defensive measures, observing the demonstrations, and infiltrating opposition groups.

From the perspective of the MfS there were several good reasons to react this way. For one thing, the course set out by Krenz after Honecker's fall promised a way out of the lethargy of the preceding months and seemed the only feasible way to regain the political initiative. For another, the declared intent to henceforth solve conflicts politically instead of administratively meant an easing of the burden of responsibility for State Security.

On the other hand, the Party no longer tried to justify its use of force against protesters before 9 October but tried to play it down as isolated attacks by certain individuals; the will to severity it had always preached was now no longer being rewarded. What's more, solidarity in the ranks of the SED was visibly eroding, and this increasingly at the expense of the Stasi, e.g., in the form of articles criticizing the MfS written by hitherto loyal journalists and published in Party newspapers. State Security would have had to organize its own counterstrike. This would have run counter to the role of the Party in the Marxist-Leninist view, however, and the chances of finding other allies for such a move were slim. Thus the Stasi kept its clenched fist in its pocket. Its last hope was that the Soviet Army would intervene like it did on 17 June 1953.

In November 1989, the SED lost its leadership role. The old guard of the Politbüro, Erich Mielke included, stepped down, and the center of power was shifted from the Party to the state apparatus under its new state premier, Hans Modrow. Then, with the opening of the Wall on the night of 9 November 1989, the old order was upended for good. Here, too, the MfS was at the front lines with its passport-control units but was powerless to stop the tide of events; the hope of reestablishing a dictatorship through Soviet military intervention had been rendered obsolete. A devastating blow within the ranks of the MfS was Erich Mielke's Volkskammer speech on 13 November. His stammering about "close contacts" to the working people and his admission "I really do love everyone, all people" was, in the words of the regional head of the MfS in Karl-Marx-Stadt, Siegfried Gehlert, the "coup de grâce for the Chekists."[11]

State Security in the Limelight

Confronted with the massive pressure of demonstrations, State Security was unable to get back on the offensive. The protesters' demands increasingly and directly targeted the Stasi as an institution. Its employees had to put up with being called "lazy bums" and "rubber ears." As of late October, the protest marches began heading straight for Stasi offices in regional and district towns, if they were not already on the traditional march route, as in the case of the so-called "Round Corner" (Runde Ecke) on Dittrichring in Leipzig. One of the protesters' main demands was the disbanding of the Stasi, for well into January

1990 the secret apparatus was thought to have the greatest potential for a counterstrike. Moreover, they wanted to bring to justice those who had trampled on human and civil rights for so many years.

From the perspective of Stasi employees, catastrophe was now playing out. Mielke ordered files revealing the extent of surveillance to be taken out of storage or destroyed. Meanwhile, the Modrow government tried to stay on its feet by making concessions, while developing new concepts together with the leaders of State Security. On 17 November the new premier announced in a government statement that the Ministry for State Security would be transformed into the Office for National Security (Amt für Nationale Sicherheit—AfNS) and placed directly under his command. The previous deputy minister, Wolfgang Schwanitz, was to be its director. Schwanitz planned to make the office outwardly conform to Western models based on the rule of law—by disentangling state and Party, by anchoring AfNS work in a statutory regulation, and by focusing on "enemies of the constitution." At the same time, though, he endeavored to keep the network of unofficial collaborators intact as far as possible, preserving the staff and core structures of the ministry. Only tasks that were relatively far removed from normal secret-service activities, such as personal security or passport controls, were to be eliminated. The new leaders were not willing to give up their ingrained habits of thought and clichés of the enemy, and did not dare to significantly downsize the apparatus, effectively restricting its margin of maneuver.

The revolutionary transformation reached a new highpoint in early December. On 1 December, the SED forfeited its "leading role" as set out in the East German constitution. On 3 December, the SED Central Committee expelled Erich Honecker, Erich Mielke, and the former chairman of the Council of Ministers, Willi Stoph, from the Party. The very same day, the head of the Area of Commercial Coordination, Alexander Schalck-Golodkowski, fled the country, stoking rumors of stolen assets. Billows of smoke caused by the burning of files ultimately gave rise to renewed protests outside Stasi offices. On 4 December 1989, civil-rights activists occupied the regional office for national security in Erfurt to prevent the further destruction of files. In the course of this and on the following day, spontaneously formed citizens' committees commandeered numerous other district and regional offices, sealing off the files with the help of state prosecutors and the People's Police. The executive board of the AfNS unanimously resigned the very same day. Two days later Schwanitz discharged eighteen top cadre from their positions. The disbanding of the AfNS demanded by the Central Round Table on 7 December 1989 was put off for a number of days, but the Council of Ministers eventually complied on 14 December.

Once the first line of defense was broken, the government and the remaining leading figures in the former ministry made plans to set up two considerably smaller successors, outwardly confirming to the West German organization model. The HVA was to continue as the Intelligence Service of the GDR (Nachrichtendienst der DDR) under HVA chief Colonel-General Werner Grossmann, with 4,000 employees. An Office for the Protection of the Constitution of the GDR (Verfassungsschutz der DDR), with a staff of 10,000, was to be created for internal security under the direction of Major-General Heinz Engelhardt, the former chief of the regional administration for state security in Frankfurt an der Oder. Engelhardt was promptly given the task of disbanding the AfNS. But on 12 January Minister-President Modrow was forced to abandon these plans as well. The public pressure of citizens' committees and the opposition groups at the Central Round Table was simply too strong.

Finally, on 15 January 1990, a citizens' committee working in collaboration with the state prosecutor's office and the People's Police (a so-called "security partnership") took custody of State Security headquarters, in the Lichtenberg district of Berlin. That same evening, an enraged crowd stormed the premises under as yet unexplained circumstances, laying waste to some of the rooms. Its employees were given notice by 31 March 1990 or, in a minority of cases, transferred to other state authorities. The passport-control units were among the latter, being reassigned to the border troops of the GDR. The permanent dissolution of the Office for National Security was declared by the East German government with accession to the Federal Republic on 3 October 1990.

It all happened so fast that none of those involved really fathomed what was happening. The full-time employees were distraught by the sudden collapse of the party-state and the vanishing of their ostensibly predetermined paths in life. They desperately tried to blot out their past and find new ways of making a living. The civil-rights activists were wary of their own success and feared a potential backlash, secret weapons caches, and plans for a coup d'état. Aside from these concerns, the citizens' committees and dissident representatives at the Round Table were particularly worried about two possible dangers: first, the cover-up of MfS intrigues through the destruction of material, and, second, the manipulative attempts of MfS employees to feather their nests while simultaneously creating structures to cushion their fall. There were enough reasons to fear this, as the remaining

MfS employees did everything they could to outfox those watching over them. It was indeed quite a chore to get an overview of the many-tentacled apparatus with its secondary facilities and emergency headquarters. The rumors and conspiracy theories that cropped up at the time, insisting that there were "survival instructions" (*Überlebensordnungen*), secret chains of command and the like, have survived down to the present.

Chapter 8

Legacy—*Aufarbeitung*— Culture of Memory

The Second Life of the Stasi

Fundamental Decisions in Reappraising the History of the Stasi, 1990–91—The Special Agency Model

The dust slowly settled after the battle. Just a few weeks after the decision to disband it, the second life of the Stasi began with the case of Wolfgang Schnur—a burdensome legacy during the last, democratically ruled six months of the GDR and even in present-day reunified Germany. A sense of insecurity spread among the representatives of the opposition at the Round Table after the final decision was reached to dissolve State Security. There was no way of knowing what potentially explosive material the files contained and who would get their hands on it in the future. The rapid course of German reunification awakened fears that the West German intelligence services might wrest the files from civil-rights activists and use the illegally gathered, often sensitive information for their own purposes. The various civil-rights activists also found themselves in conflict with the representatives of the old SED ministerial bureaucracy, who called the shots in the State Liquidation Committee appointed by the Modrow government and who, together with the former MfS employees working in it, were suspected (not without reason) of wanting to give the Stasi issue as quiet a "burial" as possible. Added to this were the insecurities caused by the first IM exposures in the opposition's own ranks.

In February and March 1990 a number of citizens' committees were inclined to follow the arguments of the state liquidators and pleaded for the immediate destruction of all databases:

> Who, after all, is entitled to store and pass on to state archives information gathered unconstitutionally? Who dares to take personal responsibility for the safe storage of material compiled throughout forty years of Stasi spying?[1]

Other citizens' committees advocated the systematic safeguarding of Stasi materials. In Leipzig they even refused to turn over the foreign-espionage files slated to be sent to Berlin for their subsequent destruction by the HVA committee responsible for dissolving this branch. The Central Round Table offered two contradictory answers to the questions raised. First it voted to physically destroy the MfS central files stored on magnetic tape, in the (partly erroneous) belief that all of the information on them was also available on paper. This resolution was immediately adopted by the Council of Ministers. Hence the first television images of shredded reels of magnetic tape went around the world in early March. Further moves to destroy MfS files met with resistance, however. As Werner Schulz of New Forum concluded, it was not up to the citizens' committees to make irrevocable decisions regarding the destruction of files; despite its revolutionary legitimation as a transitional institution, it had no democratic mandate, which was true of the Round Table as well.

A step-by-step plan, drawn up by the Round Table's Working Group for Security and approved by Minister-President Modrow, proposed as a second step the removal of cross-references to and secondary files on personal data. The third step, the "destruction of all records and files containing personal data," was prepared in draft form, but the final ruling was to be left to the not-yet-elected parliament. The Round Table agreed on this in its final session, on 12 March 1990.

But even at this meeting, the voices against destroying the files were getting stronger. East Germans might be interested, they said, in taking a look at their own files. The distinction, posited until then, between files of general historical interest and historically "irrelevant" personal files was beginning to look questionable once the files had been partially opened. What's more, the dimensions of the IM network suggested by the Schnur affair were raising entirely new issues. The Round Table thus recommended to the future parliamentarians that they have themselves vetted for collaboration with the former Stasi.

Two conflicting camps rapidly formed after the Volkskammer elections and were present in subsequent discussions about the legacy of the MfS, surviving in a way even down to the present day. On the one side were the new minister of the interior, Peter-Michael Diestel (DSU/CDU); the Liquidation Committee appointed by him, with its numerous Council of Ministers cadre; the officers taken over from the MfS and its leading lobbyists; and finally the experts for "internal security" from the Federal Ministry of the Interior in Bonn assigned to Diestel as consultants. All of them advocated the immediate closing and destruction of Stasi records. They drafted a bill to centralize and largely seal off the files. There was no provision allowing access to the files, neither for private nor professional reasons. Inquiries would be answered for a period of one year, and this only in the case of individuals who suffered severe disadvantages because of Stasi persecution. Eckhart Werthebach (CDU), an advisor from the Ministry of the Interior in Bonn, argued for the archive to be directed by the president of the Federal Archives and for a "nuanced regulation of destruction" (*differenzierte Vernichtungsregelung*).[2] These plans apparently reflected shared interests: on the one hand, the efforts of former East German functionaries from the state and security apparatus not to reveal their techniques of rule and their many ties to each other, as well as ensuring continuity in the transition to a unified German state; on the other, the attempts of the Federal Government to keep the risks of potential disclosures under control, for the sake of its own national interests or raison d'état and with a view to internal peace—in other words, with a view to the political class of the Federal Republic and in an effort to prevent uncontrolled access to the world of secret services.

In the course of discussions in the summer of 1990, these representatives of overarching state interests found themselves opposed by the advocates of a broad social *Aufarbeitung*, a reappraisal and reconciliation of the past. The latter included the citizens' committees (marginalized by the new government) and local initiatives, but above all the overwhelming majority of Volkskammer parliamentarians, especially in their Select Committee on Controlling the Dissolution of the MfS/AfNS (Sonderausschuss zur Kontrolle der Auflösung des MfS/AfNS). They found support from West Germany in the form of forces with a civil-society orientation that added a new dimension to the debate, in particular the federal constitutional ruling on the "right to informational self-determination," encouraging a greater protection of personal data. The Volkskammer had already voted on

5 April to have itself screened for MfS activities. Fierce resistance to the government's draft bill erupted across party lines. The Select Committee led by Rostock representative Joachim Gauck (Alliance 90) drafted its own bill, which cited as its main purpose the "political, historical and legal reckoning [*Aufarbeitung*] with the activities of the former Ministry for State Security." Officials and public figures were to be vetted, the perpetrators called to account for their misdeeds, those persecuted and spied on were to be informed about their files and—if possible—awarded compensation for the injustice they suffered, and, lastly, the public was to be given a qualified assessment of the past through a look at the now-defunct world of the East German secret police. The Volkskammer representatives were thus endorsing the argument of enabling access to one's own file as a step toward a self-determined life true to the principle of the sovereign citizen. The law was passed by the Volkskammer on 24 August 1990 with one dissenting vote.

But the resistance of the "statists" was not yet broken. A few days later, word spread that the negotiators of the GDR and the Federal Republic had decided at the last minute not to include the law in the Unification Treaty—in other words, that in a couple of weeks the law would no longer be in force. It took considerable protests, another Volkskammer resolution, and the occupation of buildings at the former MfS headquarters in Berlin-Lichtenberg by Stasi liquidators and civil-rights activists for the reluctant government officials to belatedly add the principles of the Volkskammer law to the Unification Treaty. These principles later formed the core of the Stasi Records Act (Stasi-Unterlagen-Gesetz—StUG) passed by the German Bundestag in 1991. Thus the path was finally clear for the opening of secret-service files, a process unique in kind and degree in the post-Communist countries and, indeed, around the world. In 1991 Joachim Gauck was elected by the Bundestag as the "federal commissioner for the Stasi archives" (*Bundesbeauftragter für die Stasi-Unterlagen*). He had already been administering the files as a "special commissioner of the Federal Government" (*Sonderbeauftragter der Bundesregierung*) since 3 October 1990.

More than twenty years have passed since then. As late as September 1990, Minister-President Lothar de Maizière had prophesied disaster to the disobedient parliamentarians and their desire to reckon with the past: "Then there will be no more neighbors, friends, and colleagues, then there'll be hell to pay."[3] History would prove him wrong. But of course the process of *Aufarbeitung* would not be without its consequences.

The Post-Chekist Milieu

One of the most astonishing things about the revolution was the way in which, within a few weeks, the approximately 91,000 MfS employees resigned themselves to their fate, accepting the new situation without complaint. This enigma fueled two kinds of rumors and speculations. Fears of an imminent putsch were widespread in December 1989 and January 1990, but were rendered obsolete with the occupation of MfS headquarters on 15 January. The second tendency was the theory—embellished with countless alleged discoveries in the files made by the citizens' committees—that the MfS was the actual initiator of the revolutionary events, that it had seen the downfall of the system coming, prepared itself with "survival instructions," and was still calling the shots from behind the scenes.[4] Behind this discrepancy between the population's fears about the security apparatus's willingness to fight and its operational capabilities on the one hand as opposed to the actual course of events on the other was a shift in the self-understanding of MfS employees, indiscernible to the casual observer and concealed by the rituals of Chekism.

The hard core of Chekism, the unconditionality of its "revolutionary" claim to power and will to action—as depicted in its founding myth about the early days of 1917–18, around its leader Dzerzhinsky, and continued in the "Antifa" (antifascist) tradition of the militant German Communists—was, in abstract terms, certainly an important reference point, but in practice it had all but faded and had little to do with the living reality of a Chekist in the latter days of the GDR. "Red fervor" could no longer eclipse the crises unfolding in the economy and society, and the loss of orientation concerning the right ideological line. Deep entanglement with the Western enemy was not only evident in the economy; the value system of this hostile world had also pervaded much of East German society. Beneath the veneer of revolutionary rituals, a form of power-conscious statism had become the core of the Stasi's identity. MfS employees reacted with a kind of sulkiness to the democratic movement and the GDR's subsequent loss of legitimation as a dictatorship of the proletariat supposedly executing the "will of the people." They retreated into their class-consciousness as state representatives and guarantors of order and security. At the same time, however, they suddenly perceived the (always existent) problem of Party rule and its lack of legitimation: "We have the power, but not the majority," as Neubrandenburg regional chief Peter Koch put it on 23 October 1989.

A look at the other secret-police forces of the Eastern bloc shows that there was a great willingness under these circumstances to consider shedding Communist ideology. This went hand in hand with the removal of old leaders and a considerable downsizing of these apparatuses. Nonetheless, the police forces and secret services of the post-Communist states of Eastern Europe reveal a high continuity of institutions and staff, more or less independent of the respective political system. The transition of secret-service employees to other sectors of the state and economy was often successful there as well.

As far as East German State Security is concerned, there are no indications of any kind of central steering or anticipatory behavior. The mass dismissals alone posed almost insurmountable logistical problems. True, there were some successful attempts to transfer larger or smaller units into other state structures. For the mass of employees, however, starting a new life after the MfS was an unpleasant task they had to face, either on their own or in small, improvised groups.

It took several weeks to recover from the shock of having their apparatus dissolved before the remnants of the MfS leadership tried, under wholly new circumstances, to seek an understanding with Minister-President Hans Modrow and, after the Volkskammer elections in March 1990, with the minister of the interior of the GDR, Peter-Michael Diestel, as well as with the West German Ministry of the Interior. A group of generals around former main department head Edgar Braun, following a concept paper by Major-General Gerhard Niebling, attempted to negotiate a deal with the two German governments: amnesty and a new basis for their future existence in exchange for keeping their inside knowledge secret and a limited willingness to cooperate with West German secret services.[6] Both governments had an interest in such a deal, wanting to neutralize the Stasi complex—a potential destabilizer. These negotiations failed, however, due to the fierce resistance of the citizens' committees and the general mood of the populace, which, frankly, had no understanding for such arrangements.

Of the 91,000 employees in October 1989 who were suddenly seeking a new professional and social existence, more than 90 percent were under the age of fifty, which is to say far from retirement age. Almost half of them (about 46 percent) had not even reached the age of thirty.[7] Well more than two-thirds of former MfS employees are still of working age today. There are no sociological studies about their whereabouts. Press reports and occasional analyses by truth and reconciliation commissions (*Aufarbeitungskommissionen*) offer an incomplete picture.

The perspective of leaving behind their Chekist past and continuing their work in a related field in the service of the state, though by no means merely an illusion, only came true for a minority of MfS employees. The Federal Intelligence Service—by its own account—did not take on any former MfS members as full-time employees, but did reward several hundred defectors with honoraria and, in cases of mutual interest, continued their cooperation in an unofficial capacity. The willingness to take on MfS employees was greater in the federal and regional ministries of the interior. At least 1,500 Stasi employees were absorbed more or less directly by the police—about 1,000 of them in the Federal Border Guard, and about 150 to 200 in each new federal state (*Bundesland*) of eastern Germany.[8] There is no reliable data for other areas of the public-service sector, only the occasional news report indicating, for example, that many of them found mid-level positions at East German unemployment offices. Even the Presidium of the German Bundestag found it unproblematic to employ a former MfS office secretary. This notwithstanding, the metamorphosis from Chekist to post-Communist civil servant of the Federal Republic was far less common in Germany than in the rest of Eastern Europe.

In terms of occupational identity, it is apparent, first of all, that these individuals evidently did not have a problem serving the "imperialist" states they once decried as the enemy—whether as a police station chief in Cottbus, the bodyguard of an East German minister-president, a passport inspector at the German-Polish border, or a receptionist at the Stasi Records Office. Behind this seemingly opportunistic attitude was not only a willingness to conform in the struggle to make a living, but also a self-understanding that upheld the values of disciplined professionalism and a close identification with the state (*Staatsbewusstsein*). Many of them found a new collective home in professional organizations such as police unions. Part of reinventing their own social identity, however, was repressing all memory of their pre-1989 professional past and the responsibility stemming from this, which both new employers and employees succeeded in doing, as long as it remained out of the public eye.

Clusters in typical occupational fields can be made out in the private and semi-public employment sectors: private security companies, independent professions in the broker business (insurance, financial services, real estate, etc.), as well as job-placement agencies and other service providers associated with the public sector (hospital associations, nursing services, housing associations, etc.). Employees from special divisions like the Schalck complex of KoKo and the HVA would later go on to fill managerial positions at international trading companies or in German-Russian enterprises.

In terms of social status and self-image, an ambivalent profile emerges. Compared to the elitist sense of power and status they enjoyed in their former positions, these new careers have for the most part been accompanied by a sense of personal humiliation. On the other hand, former officers could sometimes use their professional skills—those acquired in handling IMs, the assertiveness and agility required of a secret policeman—in selling insurance or as the head of security at a factory site. Moreover, these former officers benefited from their good connections in the East German administrative structures that persisted after reunification.

The lack of a sociological topology also means that there is no data on unemployment and precarious employment circumstances—predominant features of crisis-ridden postunification East Germany. Older MfS officers, in particular, cite their work as parking attendants and night watchmen, promotional leaflet distributors, etc. as proof of their social marginalization. But the most profound act of social exclusion, materially and symbolically, was the cut in pension benefits for MfS employees—to 990 marks—that was passed by the Volkskammer in June 1990, later adopted by federal German lawmakers, and upheld as constitutional by the Federal Constitutional Court of Germany in 1999. Though the court did combine this with a slight increase in pension values to match the East German average, it still amounted to a considerable net loss, given the well-above-average salaries and pensions paid to them during the GDR.

If all these factors are balanced out, the professional and material situation of former MfS employees is probably much better than their symbolic social exclusion in the public sphere and the media would suggest. They tended to still be well networked, which now found expression in their own companies, etc. Thus, for example, in the Lichtenberg and Hohenschönhausen districts of Berlin, one can be cared for by the "in-house" nursing services of the last main department head for economic surveillance, and have one's deceased comrades put to rest by a spin-off of the "Firm's" funeral home. The "company outing" of a more than 90-person delegation of former MfS agents to a conference in the Danish city of Odense in 2007 was undertaken in buses from the tour operator of a former NVA officer with unofficial ties to the Stasi. Despite these opportunities, however, they never attained a central position of power like former security agents in Russia, and never experienced the "wintering" of a core group in the new security apparatuses, as was the case in East-Central Europe.

Little can be said about today's political role of the mass of former Stasi employees. Most of them shun public appearances on account of their "contaminated" lives. If they do embark on a political career, as in the case of PDS Bundestag member Lutz Heilmann, they do everything in their power to conceal their MfS involvement.

Their strongest lobby group is the "Joint Initiative for the Protection of the Social Rights of Former Members of the Armed Organs and the Customs Administration of the GDR" (ISOR) whose main purpose is fighting what they call the "punitive pension" plan. ISOR at one time had around 26,000 members, but in 2010 its membership ranks fell to about 22,000. That the group is primarily a pensioners' association is evidenced by the fact that since its founding in 1991 about 10,000 of its members have passed away. In 2010 the average age of its members was just under 73. ISOR has a remarkable reach. It has 187 local chapters and is in most cases exceptionally well represented in local senior citizen advocacy groups.[9] It has good contacts to other historical revisionist groups in East Germany, but also to the all-German professional associations for security forces, such as the "German Bundeswehr Association/East," which basically serves as a veterans' organization for the NVA.

A few of these associations are politically active beyond the pension issue. The largest of these is the "Society for Legal and Humanitarian Support" (GRH), which, apart from MfS employees, mainly unites former state prosecutors, judges, and border-troop officers who deny or try to justify the state crimes of the GDR. Also noteworthy in this context is the so-called MfS "Insider Committee" (Insiderkomitee), which maintains its own grotesquely aggressive website and regularly agitates against the critical reappraisal (*Aufarbeitung*) of MfS history at discussion events in Berlin. These associations are extremely active in the media. They publish memoirs and apologia with dubious publishing houses such as "Edition Ost," as well as frequent articles in the radical left-wing press—*Junge Welt* and the online periodical *Rotfuchs*, for example. These organizations are logistically headquartered in the editorial offices of *Neues Deutschland,* on Franz-Mehring-Platz in Berlin.

Journalists will occasionally claim that this scene has grown stronger in recent years. This is not the case. The circle of activists is stagnating, and many of its main protagonists, such as former professor at the MfS university Wolfgang Edelmann or longtime speaker of the Insider Committee and former HVA resident Wolfgang Hartmann, have died in recent years. The number of active personnel has successively shrunk since 1990, and the present leaders of this informally enduring hierarchy—deputy ministers Schwanitz and Grossmann—are now octogenarians.

One of the paradoxical things about this revisionist scene is its progressive isolation since the early 1990s. The Insider Committee, originally founded with the purpose of "critically reappraising" the history of the MfS and showing a certain willingness to engage in self-criticism, quickly corrected its course when it became clear that no arrangement with the West German establishment was forthcoming. The perhaps hundred-man-strong core of this scene is meanwhile firmly established in the antidemocratic radical left-wing spectrum, and has since begun to reminisce about the "good old-fashioned" values of Chekism.

Its cross-connections to the democratic spectrum of the political landscape are almost solely based on its cooperation with the "Left Party.PDS" (Linkspartei.PDS), which supports its demands to rescind the pension cuts and is networked with former Stasi officers through East German functionaries and former unofficial collaborators. The hard core of this scene is generally critical of the Left Party, the latter having increasingly distanced itself since its founding from the activities of the MfS and thus, in their view, being guilty of espousing "reformist" positions. Most of them are active in the KPD or the DKP. How important this clientele of former MfS employees is for the Left Party as a bridge organization can be seen in its voting behavior. In the main residential area of former MfS employees, Lichtenberg/Hohenschönhausen, Gesine Lötzsch, the future chairman of the Left Party, received 47.5 percent of the vote as direct candidate for the Bundestag in 2009.

The Overall Balance of *Aufarbeitung*— The Special Agency Model

The second life of State Security is inextricably linked to the establishment and continued existence of the special agency that was soon referred to colloquially by the names of its respective directors: the "Gauck," "Birthler" and, most recently, the "Jahn Authority." The eponymous nickname of the Stasi Records Office is not only a result of the agency's complicated official title, but also an indirect expression of the fact that a slew of functions are bundled together here under one roof, thus defying a common denominator: archive, vetting agency, political-educational institution, and academic research institute. This fusion is the trademark, as it were, of the Stasi Records Office, and has been adopted in other post-Communist countries as well.

The model has strengths and weaknesses. It was the guarantee for averting strategies of "quiet disposal" and "creeping liquidation." The talk of a "nuanced regulation of destruction" under the aegis of the Federal Archives, which the Federal Ministry of the Interior was considering in 1990, is an indication of the kind of alternatives that were up for discussion back then. Despite manifold data-protection regulations, the idea of *opening* the files was much more of an option to a special authority than it would have been were it subject to general archive laws, especially in a domain so controversial with regard to the protection of personal privacy and confidentiality. The model of a special agency likewise meant that the exposure of MfS employees was at the forefront of its work—a mission that went well beyond the general administration of files. It was no coincidence that a hot potato of this sort made the first federal commissioner, Gauck, a political figure of the first order.

One of the essential conditions for the success of the Stasi Records Office was the relative autonomy of the agency from day-to-day party politics. Plans for binding the agency more closely to the respective government policy and winding it up, as attempted in 2004 with the shift of portfolio from the Ministry of the Interior to the Federal Chancellery and its state minister for culture and media, proved to be unfeasible. Such initiatives have always ended with the realization that winding up this agency would be detrimental to the aims of *Aufarbeitung*. The Federal Commissioner also clearly distanced itself from the proportional representation of political parties seen in other institutions of *Aufarbeitung*, such as the Commissions of Inquiry (Enquetekommissionen) of the Bundestag, the Federal Foundation for the Reappraisal of the SED Dictatorship (Bundesstiftung zur Aufarbeitung der SED-Diktatur), or the Federal Agency for Civic Education (Bundeszentrale für politische Bildung). As shown by the discussions around the candidacy of Joachim Gauck for the office of federal president in 2010 and 2012, his republican credo of civil society has meanwhile come to represent a broad consensus on democratic values.

On the other side of the equation are the frictional losses and the lack of professionalism caused by the combination of various functions. These include the archive's deplorable organization and the difficulty in accessing files, the mixing of scholarly and political positions, and the lack of efficiency of a large-scale bureaucracy. Last but not least, the hybrid nature of the authority has given some of its employees access to inside information (*Herrschaftswissen*) that they freely inject into public debate, as some observers have noted with consternation.[10]

The most fundamental political aim of the Stasi Records Office was to openly talk about secret work for the Stasi and keep incriminated persons out of the civil service and political offices. More than 1.7 million inquiries about employees in the public sector have been made to date, primarily in eastern Germany. The screenings of elected political officials in the Bundestag as well as in state and communal parliaments number into the hundreds of thousands. The results have been varied. Individual cases require careful judgment, but sometimes the files are only fragments. Moreover, some public employers have decided only to screen high-ranking employees or to turn a blind eye to full-time or unofficial MfS work, even in clearly documented cases. It is ultimately not the Stasi authority that decides on the consequences, but the respective employer, representative assembly, etc. The results of vetting are therefore extremely heterogeneous. By no means has the discovery of an IM file automatically led to dismissal. The circumstances surrounding each case, but also the standards applied, have been too varied. But in the heat of debate about this or that individual case, we should not overlook the fact that a range of new and aspiring politicians have fallen into oblivion after their unmasking as IMs, individuals who would otherwise surely be holding important offices today. And when candidates for a public office proudly defend their IM biographies or flat out deny their complicity, people can decide for themselves before voting this or that person into office as a representative.

The statute of limitations on screening individuals for public service has applied in most cases since 2006. Only executive personnel, political-office holders, and employees at *Aufarbeitung* institutions can be formally "Gaucked," as the procedure is now called in common parlance. The statute of limitations has not been unproblematic, however, because, unlike employers, journalists and researchers can still investigate any person for former Stasi connections and subsequently report on their findings. In this context a separate subdiscipline of contemporary history has developed, which we might refer to as "lustration."[11] Historians and political scientists will arrogate to themselves the role of prosecutor, while at the same time attesting to the authenticity and credibility of the files. They advise political bodies, state administrations, the courts, and secret services, or comb through various walks of society looking for unofficial collaborators on behalf of radio and television broadcasters or professional organizations. This kind of "public history" can be taken for a windfall of historical scholarship—because, after all, how often does a historian have access to secret sources like this? But the blessing can also be a curse. In general, the categories of analysis and perception closely follow secret-police terminology. Attention is almost solely focused on formally recruited informers, whereas all other forms of cooperation with the apparatus of repression (official contacts, spontaneous denunciations, etc.) are virtually ignored. Moreover, the naïve principle often holds that the sources are a veritable fountain of truth. These effects have led historians to blindly adopt the vocabulary, thought patterns, and logic of case histories as recorded by police bureaucrats.[12]

Consulting one's own file is the most common form of Stasi *Aufarbeitung*. Since 1992 more than 1.5 million people have requested to see their files. Far removed from the big headlines, personal consultation of the files is the silent mass basis of *Aufarbeitung*. It involves the former inhabitants of the GDR in their erstwhile and sometimes present-day settings, which is probably the reason why many of them have only made inquiries fifteen or twenty years later. Contrary to all expectations during the founding period of the authority, when it was thought that interest in the files would quickly subside, the number of applications has been relatively stable—and quite high—for some years now. Since 2005 the figures have hovered between about 85,000 and 100,000 applications per year, with big public events such as the twentieth anniversary of the fall of the Wall in 2009 raising awareness even more. Of these requests a consistent 75 percent are first-time applications.

Behind these impressive numbers lie some highly complex psychological mechanisms. Employees at the authority have noted that many people only find the time and energy to take this step once they have gone into retirement. Family dialogue can be a motivator as well—when pupils go on a guided tour and bring back applications for their parents, for instance. But the inhibition threshold is still very high. This is especially true for those whose lives were derailed by imprisonment, direct interference, and other humiliations at the hands of the Stasi and who have yet to overcome this trauma. But even less afflicted East Germans are reluctant.[13] Historian Jan Palmowski, in his microhistorical study on the villages of Dabel, in Mecklenburg, and Holungen, in the Eichsfeld region of Thuringia, was surprised to discover that hardly any of the inhabitants there had applied to see their files. Only in the course of his research did he begin to unearth this hidden dimension of village life, which caused many of his interview partners to considerably change their perspective on the past.[14] If the number of applications (which includes West German and foreign applicants) is measured against the approximately twelve million adult inhabitants of the GDR in 1989 or the approximately six million individuals listed in the central files of the MfS (about one-third of whom were not residents of the GDR), it is clear that the tide of applications will not be ebbing anytime soon. Whether or not this kind of remembrance can really lead to reconciliation seems very much to depend on the concrete circumstances. But the mere possibility of viewing the files has created a more truthful basis for continued coexistence through countless private confessions and conversations, well beyond the sphere of public debate.

Far less successful on the other hand, at least in quantitative terms, has been the criminal prosecution of Stasi injustices. Unlike the Wall-shooting trials against frontier soldiers and their commanders who carried out "shoot to kill" orders, most of the several thousand investigative proceedings against Stasi officers have failed because of lack of evidence, the often aged defendants' incapacity to be sued, or loopholes in the laws. Even Erich Mielke was not held accountable for the orders he gave as minister of State Security but for the murder of two policemen in 1931. He was sentenced to six years in prison. The West German agents working for State Security were punished more severely—for example, NATO spy Rainer Rupp, who received a sentence of twelve years. (He was released on probation after serving eight years.) His higher-ups in East Berlin, such as intelligence chief Markus Wolf, were given a clean bill of conduct. Exonerated in 1995 by the Federal Constitutional Court of Germany, they were not held accountable for their espionage work. To be sure, Wolf was convicted of coercion and deprivation of liberty in a kidnapping case, but the torture of the 1950s and the assassination of escape agents has remained unpunished in the majority of cases. All the same, criminal prosecution has not been insignificant from a qualitative perspective, yielding as it has a wealth of descriptions and insights into personal motives and other factors, an important fund of information beyond the wide stream of files.

Another unsolved, perhaps unsolvable task in retrospect is providing support to the persecutees. No law can give back lost opportunities in life. All that remains is rehabilitation, compensation for wrongful imprisonment, and a victim's pension for "needy" former political prisoners of up to 250 euros, which was only approved in 2007 after protracted resistance by several federal governments. The public focus on IMs and mass surveillance of the population at large has meant that these latter victims with their tragic fates have tended to recede into the background, not least of all because many former prisoners still have a hard time coping with the challenges of work and daily life.

The special agency for the Stasi records has become a symbol of the peaceful revolution and has had a massive effect—intentional or unintentional—on the way we see the Ministry for State Security today, its work and its role in East German society. The sheer mass of files has generated a force and dynamic of its own. The fact that about 60 percent of the files date from the 1980s and another 30 percent from the 1970s has had a formative influence on our image of State Security, even though the worst crimes of this secret apparatus were committed in the 1950s. The files have also shaped our perception of the protagonists of the SED dictatorship. State Security is always foremost in our minds, more present than the SED or the judges and state prosecutors of the political justice system. The widespread use of MfS jargon, which prior to 1989 no one outside the apparatus was familiar with, speaks volumes here.

The Stasi Debate in the Politics of History and the Culture of Memory

The historical reappraisal of the Stasi has become a distinct hegemonic force in the political public sphere. It is considered a role model for dealing with a dictatorial past. But this hegemony has its drawbacks. The ceremonial addresses, exhibitions, panel discussions, and many other forms of canonized narratives about perpetrators and victims in the GDR can also be interpreted as the product of an opinion-forming coalition of former East German civil-rights activists and the West German establishment of journalists and politicians, in which the latter endeavor to identify retrospectively with all those who refused to cooperate with the SED regime. The process behind this is not unlike the West German "rediscovery" of the conspirators of 20 July 1944, which journalist Johannes Gross once mocked with his remark that the "anti-Hitler resistance is growing every day."[15]

The Stasi debate is unique in that it offers a clear-cut and handy normative model for assessing the parts people play in a dictatorship. The files present their readers with a variety of roles, as it were, that allow participants to perceive themselves as the victims of persecution or surveillance beyond the real ambiguities involved. This perspective is plausibly rooted in the autumn revolution of 1989. The Stasi did not become the focus of protests in the fall of 1989 by chance, and not (contrary to a number of conspiracy theories) as a sinister diversionary tactic of the SED, but because large segments of the population viewed it as the very real embodiment of ideologically hidebound human abuse. The emphasis on MfS informers was also not without reason: they stood for the baseness of human betrayal. Anybody could size up the Party secretary at a factory, the kind of person he was and what you could expect from him; but the files revealed a more hidden and personal dimension of dictatorship: the many private individuals who secretly reported to the Stasi.

This hegemonic model has nonetheless produced some dissonance. Those who bothered to take a closer look recognized the complexity of individual cases and knew that it had long been just a miniscule minority who actually put up any resistance. They recalled the compromises and conformity, and the fact that SED rule, though perhaps not having a majority behind it, did, for whatever individual reasons, have a broad base of active supporters and an even broader level of acceptance in the population, who for the most part acquiesced to its rule. This experience of dissonance not only gave rise to the historical amnesia of *Ostalgie* ("nostalgia for the East"), but also a certain uneasiness, a sense of discontent or irritation over all those who judge the GDR and its people without having "lived it" themselves.

This conflict came to a head in the so-called *Literaturstreit* ("literature debate") centered on Christa Wolf. In 1993, the writer—who was under MfS surveillance for many years, had attempted a difficult balancing act as a critical member of the SED, locked horns with the Party leadership in several instances, and for many readers in the GDR was tantamount to a moral authority—was suddenly and viciously attacked by two major West German media outlets for her role in the GDR and her self-portrayal after 1989, when it was discovered that she had briefly pledged to work as an IM early in her career. She herself later concluded:

> You can destroy people this way. And I know what I'm saying. If everywhere I'm considered a "Stasi collaborator" now, reduced to the two letters "IM," as far as *Die Zeit* and *Der Spiegel* reach—which I saw coming, actually—I can only repeat: you can destroy people this way.[16]

The distortions and instrumentalization created a backlash of indignation, however. The attacks on Christa Wolf, in particular, triggered a broad wave of solidarity and pleas for more fairness in East and West.[17]

This sense of discontent has not diminished over the years. And so the consistent demand of people to see their files at the Stasi Records Office has been accompanied by sinking approval rates for the way this negative heritage of the MfS is being dealt with in the public sphere. Long-term surveys show that in 1991 a majority of East Germans were in favor of "inquiring into whether someone had worked for the Stasi or not during the old regime of the GDR." Only 36.3 percent were opposed to it back then. Just one year later, the voices against it had risen to 54.1 percent. This figure continued to rise to 70.6 percent in 1998 and (after falling to 64.7 percent in the year 2000) had reached 78.1 percent by 2006. The corresponding figures in West Germany were always at least 6 percent lower. In 1998, the highpoint of the heated conflict around Bundestag member Gregor Gysi,[18] the discrepancy between East and West shot up to 21.2 percent.[19] A temporary reversal of this trend after the turn of the century was evidently linked to speculations about Stasi agents in the West, as well as the dispute over the publication of Stasi files about the former chancellor, Helmut Kohl (which incidentally had nothing to do with the IM debate).[20]

A culmination of this hegemonic view of the Stasi was the movie *The Lives of Others* by West German filmmaker Florian Henckel von Donnersmarck. The movie perfectly captures this iconization of the *Erinnerungswelt*, the "world of memory," surrounding the Stasi today: the gray, cold security bureaucracy, the total surveillance and psychological perfidiousness, the juxtaposition of cynics and ideologues on the one hand and critical artists on the other, even the requisite smell samples (a staple of any artistic treatment of the topic nowadays) as a symbol for the pedantic invasiveness of personal intimacy. Even its dramaturgical irrealities and blank spots make the film an accurate reflection of the Stasi as an *Erinnerungsort*, a "place of memory." This goes for the main protagonist, the brooding and highly reflective Stasi officer, but even more so for the almost total absence of ordinary people in the movie's plot. Just as the American television miniseries *Holocaust* had a formative influence on the images of death in Auschwitz, this melodrama has shaped the image of the Stasi—and this worldwide, as British historian Timothy Garton Ash noted on the occasion of its winning an Oscar for Best Foreign Language Film:

> One of Germany's most singular achievements is to have associated itself so intimately in the world's imagination with the darkest evils of the two worst political systems of the most murderous century in human history. The words "Nazi," "SS," and "Auschwitz" are already global synonyms for the deepest inhumanity of fascism. Now the word "Stasi" is becoming a default global synonym for the secret-police terrors of communism.[21]

In the debate over von Donnersmarck's film, Henry Hübchen, a well-known East German actor, summed up his discontent as follows:

"I would prefer not to have more recent German history being dealt with like a fairy tale, American style." Apart from its black-and-white morals, he was disturbed by the one-sided picture it presents of the late GDR:

> See, that's just the problem: the constant generalizing, reduction, simplification. In the 1980s, popular artists were also extorting power, not just the other way around. The Stasi was not just an organ of intimidation; it was despised, mocked, and ridiculed more than anything.[22]

It is easy to judge such critiques as being one-sided too, but it does remind us that MfS *Aufarbeitung* is only truly successful when it faces the full complexity of historical reality.

A European Memory?

Germany's process of dealing with its Communist past had an international impact even before *The Lives of Others*. This goes above all for the institutional example set by the Stasi Records Office, which served as a model, among others, for the Institute of National Remembrance (IPN), founded in Poland in 1999. To be sure, the debate in Eastern Europe took an entirely different tack. Thus, for instance, from the very beginning the IPN was equipped with powers of prosecution, was much more of a plaything of day-to-day politics, and figured much more strongly in the politics of history. For one thing, being responsible for both the period of Nazi occupation and Communist "People's Poland" has meant that it is inevitably informed by the predominant mode of national self-perception in Poland, which sees the Poles as a fighting people under *double* foreign rule. For another, the sheer amount of staff resources at its disposal has lent it a determining influence on historical scholarship in a way much different than in a country like Germany, with its rather diverse academic landscape. With well over one hundred researchers, the IPN has more capacities than all university and nonuniversity-based research institutes for contemporary history in Poland combined.

The historical-political concept advocated by the IPN has become quite an influential one, spreading to the Baltic states and the Czech Republic, for example. At the European level this has led to a new debate that ultimately questions "1945," and with it the supreme significance of the Holocaust, as the "negative founding myth" of a unified Europe.[23] From this perspective, the end of the war was merely marked by the substitution of one occupying regime for another, and not by a moment of liberation. The crimes of communism are comparable to those of Nazism in the European culture of memory, argued Latvian politician and occasional EU commissioner Sandra Kalniete. At the 2004 Leipzig Book Fair she called for treating both big ideologies not only as criminal but as "equally criminal."

> For more than fifty years, the history of Europe was written without us, and the history written by the victors of World War II—how predictable—neatly divided everyone up into good and bad, correct and incorrect. It was only after the fall of the Iron Curtain that researchers gained access to the archived documents and life stories of the victims. The latter confirm that the two totalitarian systems—Nazism and Communism—were equally criminal. We must never let one of these two philosophies be considered less harmful than the other just because one of them was on the side of the victors.[24]

The debate has since gone back and forth, particularly at the level of EU resolutions on historical policy.

The perspective of a "Red Holocaust"[25] had its precursor in the *Black Book of Communism*. Joachim Gauck penned a rather reserved contribution, really more of a commentary, for the expanded German edition. Ehrhart Neubert, one of his employees, also represented in the German edition, went one step further than Gauck by extending the argument of Soviet mass murder to the post-Stalinist State Security apparatus of the GDR:

> The communist idea was and is lethal, it was a program of liquidation from the very start. . . . That is why there was no humanization or liberalization of Stalinism, of communism, of socialism. By the 1980s the death toll had diminished, but there was more control [*Herrschaft*] in its place. . . . This is why it was no longer necessary to chop off lots of heads. It was enough to get people to stop using essential functions of their heads and hearts.[26]

A similar triad of Holocaust, Gulag, and Stasi was established in 1991 by civil-rights activist Jürgen Fuchs, who raised the terminology of mass murder to a metaphorical plane with his notion of an "Auschwitz of the soul."[27] Memorial-site director Hubertus Knabe has followed this line as well, referring to the MfS prison in Berlin-Hohenschönhausen as the "Dachau of communism" and the "German Lubyanka."[28]

The Stasi Records Office has been moderate by comparison, emphasizing other aspects in its historical-political narrative. In the anniversary years of 2003 (the June uprising) and 2009 (the fall of the Wall), it aimed not to place a second history of suffering alongside the Holocaust as a negative starting point of German and European postwar history, but to assert a positive founding myth instead: the tradition of freedom in the East German struggle against communism, which, failing in the revolution of 1953, ultimately won out in 1989.[29] This was a double jab at the West, which was not only guilty of the "betrayal at Yalta"[30] and the subsequent division of Europe into spheres of interest, but failed, in addition, to achieve democracy in the East through any efforts of its own. In other words, so the argument goes, it is in a state of "revolution envy."

The "equally criminal" theory of Kalniete has not gained a foothold in the political landscape of the Federal Republic. What State Security was doing in the GDR, so the dominant position goes, was not the same as what the SS or the NKVD did. In the historical approach of the Federal Republic, this conviction has meanwhile been recast in the so-called "Faulenbach formula," under the influence of historian, SPD politician, and deputy chairman of the Federal Foundation for the Reappraisal of the SED Dictatorship Bernd Faulenbach: "Every act of remembering Germany's dictatorial past should start from the principle that Nazi crimes must not be relativized nor the injustices committed by the SED dictatorship trivialized." This formula of acknowledging both sides but of an ultimately asymmetrical memory of dictatorship was articulated in the final report of the Bundestag's second Commission of Inquiry, and has been set down in the currently valid memorial-site concept of the Federal Government outlined in 2008.[31]

There is no consensus in sight at the level of multinational historical debate in Europe, but no hegemony of particular concepts either. Joachim Gauck's reference to the von Weizsäcker speech of 1985 serves as the baseline for the Germans:

> The West Germans are one step ahead of the East Germans, having experienced how bitter it can be to leave it up to the next generation to work through a horrific past. They are once bitten, twice shy, so to say, and are not prepared to let this neglect become a negative tradition of the Germans. In his famous speech on May 8, 1985, the fortieth anniversary of the end of the war, Richard von Weizsäcker talked about the importance of remembering in shaping the present and the future. The task before us of working through our past [*Aufarbeitung unserer Vergangenheit*] is a good opportunity to refute the preconceived notion that the Germans, in general, deny their history and are "incapable of mourning."[32]

Defining oneself in this way, from a position of self-critical responsibility as a "nation of perpetrators" (*Tätervolk*), is, by nature, something foreign to most other societies. Thus, for example, the disclosures of U.S.-based Polish historian Jan T. Gross about the massacre of Jews in Jedwabne had a deeply disturbing effect in Poland, as they threatened to undermine the Poles' self-image as a nation doubly victimized.[33] An IPN documentation confirming his findings only added fuel to the fire. Behind all of this lies the question of one's own complicity in dictatorship and persecution—a question that cannot be answered by externalizing these horrible events.

A European culture of memory, if we take the idea seriously, is likely to remain pluralistic, heterogeneous, and changeable, and this not only because it is the product of highly diverse national experiences. Heterogeneity, and the ability to engage in debate within it, can be seen as a value in itself, one that enables us to overcome the dangers of a monochromatic view of history. It was Jürgen Habermas who noted—at the Bundestag's Commission of Inquiry in 1994—that now, after the end of system conflict, it might finally be possible to achieve an "antitotalitarian consensus" based on a "liberal outlook and democratic mindset."[34] In this respect, even in Europe, being antitotalitarian would then be the way and the goal.

APPENDICES

Budget of the Ministry for State Security, 1957–89 (in millions of GDR marks)

Legend:
- Revenues (incl. sales and visa fees)
- Appropriations from state budget

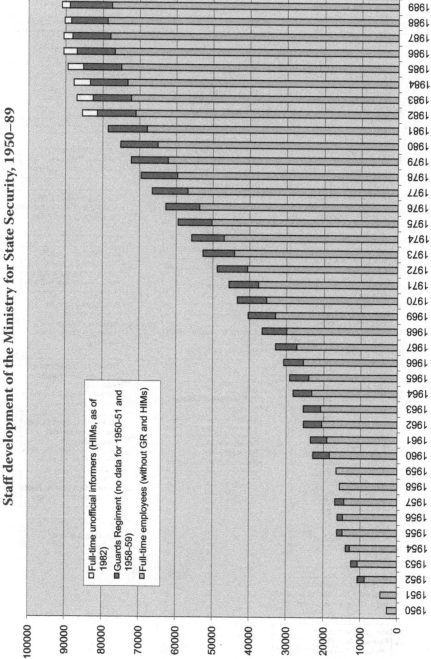

Staff development of the Ministry for State Security, 1950–89

Organizational Structure of the Ministry for State Security, 1989

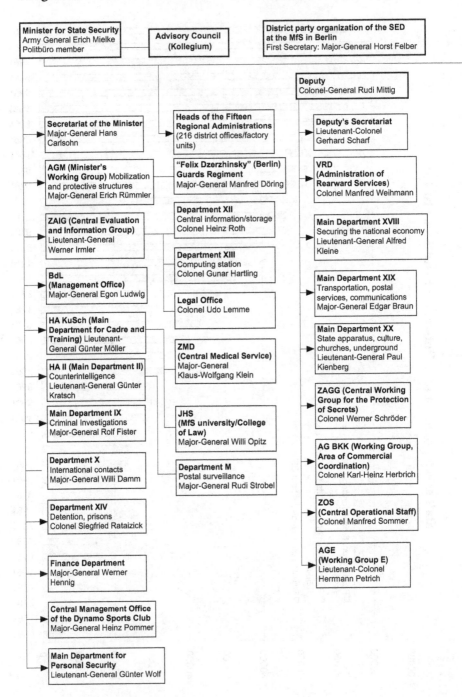

Minister for State Security
Army General Erich Mielke
Politbüro member

**Advisory Council
(Kollegium)**

**District party organization of the SED
at the MfS in Berlin**
First Secretary: Major-General Horst Felber

Deputy
Colonel-General Rudi Mittig

Secretariat of the Minister
Major-General Hans
Carlsohn

**AGM (Minister's
Working Group)** Mobilization
and protective structures
Major-General Erich Rümmler

**ZAIG (Central Evaluation
and Information Group)**
Lieutenant-General
Werner Irmler

**BdL
(Management Office)**
Major-General Egon Ludwig

**HA KuSch (Main
Department for Cadre and
Training)** Lieutenant-
General Günter Möller

HA II (Main Department II)
Counterintelligence
Lieutenant-General Günter
Kratsch

Main Department IX
Criminal Investigations
Major-General Rolf Fister

Department X
International contacts
Major-General Willi Damm

Department XIV
Detention, prisons
Colonel Siegfried Rataizick

Finance Department
Major-General Werner
Hennig

**Central Management Office
of the Dynamo Sports Club**
Major-General Heinz Pommer

**Main Department for
Personal Security**
Lieutenant-General Günter Wolf

**Heads of the Fifteen
Regional Administrations**
(216 district offices/factory
units)

**"Felix Dzerzhinsky" (Berlin)
Guards Regiment**
Major-General Manfred Döring

Department XII
Central information/storage
Colonel Heinz Roth

Department XIII
Computing station
Colonel Gunar Hartling

Legal Office
Colonel Udo Lemme

**ZMD
(Central Medical Service)**
Major-General
Klaus-Wolfgang Klein

**JHS
(MfS university/College
of Law)**
Major-General Willi Opitz

Department M
Postal surveillance
Major-General Rudi Strobel

Deputy's Secretariat
Lieutenant-Colonel
Gerhard Scharf

**VRD
(Administration of
Rearward Services)**
Colonel Manfred Weihmann

Main Department XVIII
Securing the national economy
Lieutenant-General Alfred
Kleine

Main Department XIX
Transportation, postal
services, communications
Major-General Edgar Braun

Main Department XX
State apparatus, culture,
churches, underground
Lieutenant-General Paul
Kienberg

**ZAGG (Central Working
Group for the Protection
of Secrets)**
Colonel Werner Schröder

**AG BKK (Working Group,
Area of Commercial
Coordination)**
Colonel Karl-Heinz Herbrich

**ZOS
(Central Operational Staff)**
Colonel Manfred Sommer

**AGE
(Working Group E)**
Lieutenant-Colonel
Herrmann Petrich

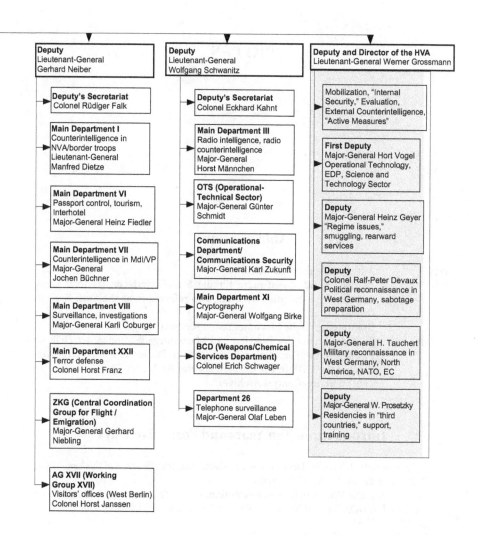

Deputy
Lieutenant-General
Gerhard Neiber

Deputy's Secretariat
Colonel Rüdiger Falk

Main Department I
Counterintelligence in
NVA/border troops
Lieutenant-General
Manfred Dietze

Main Department VI
Passport control, tourism,
Interhotel
Major-General Heinz Fiedler

Main Department VII
Counterintelligence in MdI/VP
Major-General
Jochen Büchner

Main Department VIII
Surveillance, investigations
Major-General Karli Coburger

Main Department XXII
Terror defense
Colonel Horst Franz

ZKG (Central Coordination
Group for Flight /
Emigration)
Major-General Gerhard
Niebling

AG XVII (Working
Group XVII)
Visitors' offices (West Berlin)
Colonel Horst Janssen

Deputy
Lieutenant-General
Wolfgang Schwanitz

Deputy's Secretariat
Colonel Eckhard Kahnt

Main Department III
Radio intelligence, radio
counterintelligence
Major-General
Horst Männchen

OTS (Operational-
Technical Sector)
Major-General Günter
Schmidt

Communications
Department/
Communications Security
Major-General Karl Zukunft

Main Department XI
Cryptography
Major-General Wolfgang Birke

BCD (Weapons/Chemical
Services Department)
Colonel Erich Schwager

Department 26
Telephone surveillance
Major-General Olaf Leben

Deputy and Director of the HVA
Lieutenant-General Werner Grossmann

Mobilization, "Internal
Security," Evaluation,
External Counterintelligence,
"Active Measures"

First Deputy
Major-General Hort Vogel
Operational Technology,
EDP, Science and
Technology Sector

Deputy
Major-General Heinz Geyer
"Regime issues,"
smuggling, rearward
services

Deputy
Colonel Ralf-Peter Devaux
Political reconnaissance in
West Germany, sabotage
preparation

Deputy
Major-General H. Tauchert
Military reconnaissance in
West Germany, North
America, NATO, EC

Deputy
Major-General W. Prosetzky
Residencies in "third
countries," support,
training

Adapted from Roland Wiedmann, ed.: *Die Organisationsstruktur des Ministeriums für Staatssicherheit 1989* (MfS-Handbuch, Teil V/1), Berlin 1995, 404f.

NOTES

Abbreviations

Introduction: Ten Years and Forty-five Days

1. Helmut Kohl: *"Ich wollte Deutschlands Einheit." Dargestellt von Kai Diekmann und Ralf Georg Reuth*, Berlin 1996, 520.
2. Walter Süß: Die Wendehälse der Revolution, in *Die Tageszeitung*, 8 March 1990, reprinted in *DDR Journal Nr. 2. Die Wende der Wende*, ed. Die Tageszeitung, Berlin 1990, 142–44.
3. Kohl, "Ich wollte Deutschlands Einheit," 521.
4. Petra Bornhöft: "Schnurstracks verliert Kohl seinen Stasi-Mann," in *Die Tageszeitung*, 15 March 1990, reprinted in *DDR Journal Nr. 2*, 148.
5. Kohl's assumption that Schnur reported to "the respective Stasi general" on the founding meeting of Alliance for Germany in early February 1990 is misguided given the available evidence; Kohl: "Ich wollte Deutschlands Einheit," 288.
6. See the detailed discussion of the Schnur affair in Walter Süß: *Staatssicherheit am Ende. Warum es den Mächtigen 1989 nicht gelang, eine Revolution zu verhindern*, Berlin 1999, 703.

7. Rainer Eppelmann: *Fremd im eigenen Haus. Mein Leben im anderen Deutschland,* Cologne 1993, 295. Wolfgang Schnur lost his license to practice law in 1993 for violating "basic principles of humanity and the rule of law." In 1996 the Berlin Regional Court (Landgericht Berlin) gave him a suspended sentence of one year for "casting political suspicion" (*politische Verdächtigung*) in connection with spying on his clients.

8. Klaus-Dietmar Henke: "Staatssicherheit," in Werner Weidenfeld, Karl-Rudolf Korte (eds.): *Handbuch zur deutschen Einheit,* new edition, Bonn 1996, 646–53, here 647.

9. Vladimir Il'ich Lenin: *Selected Works,* one-volume edition, New York 1968, 329.

Chapter 1. Antifascism—Stalinism—Cold Civil War: Origins and Influences, 1945 to 1956

1. Provisorische Volkskammer der Deutschen Demokratischen Republik, Protokoll der 10. Sitzung, 213.

2. "Ein großer Tag in der Volkskammer," in *Neues Deutschland,* 9 February 1950, 2.

3. "Die Hintermänner," in *Neues Deutschland,* 29 January 1950, 1 (lead article).

4. "Gangster und Mörder im Kampf gegen unsere Republik. Bericht des Generalinspekteurs der Hauptverwaltung zum Schutz der Volkswirtschaft, Erich Mielke", in *Neues Deutschland,* 28 January 1950, 4.

5. Ibid.

6. "Achtung, Agenten!" in *Neues Deutschland,* 29 January 1950, 4.

7. *Verfassung der Deutschen Demokratischen Republik* (7 October 1949), Berlin 1949.

8. "Ein großer Tag in der Volkskammer," in *Neues Deutschland,* 9 February 1950, 2.

9. "Die Volkskammer-Delegierten vor der Presse," in *SBZ-Archiv* 3, 18 (1952), 273–75, here 275.

10. Kurt Hager: "Die Aufgaben der Partei im Kampf um erhöhte Wachsamkeit (Zum politischen Bildungsabend)," in *Neues Deutschland,* 8 January 1950, 4.

11. Sigrid Meuschel: *Legitimation und Parteiherrschaft. Zum Paradox von Stabilität und Revolution in der DDR 1945–1989,* Frankfurt am Main 1992, 29.

12. Erich Kuby: *Die Russen in Berlin 1945,* Munich, Bern, Vienna 1965, 326.

13. Entry from 25 October 1948. Bertolt Brecht: *Arbeitsjournal, Band 2: 1942–1955,* ed. Werner Hecht, Frankfurt/Main 1973, 850.

14. "Memorandum des Chefs der SMA-Verwaltung des Landes Thüringen I. Kolesničenko für B. Ponomarev zu Fragen der politischen Praxis in Deutschland (Auszug)," in Bernd Bonwetsch, Gennadij Bordjugov, Norman M. Naimark, eds.: *Sowjetische Politik in der SBZ 1945–1949. Dokumente zur Tätigkeit der Propagandaverwaltung (Informationsverwaltung) der SMAD unter Sergej Tjulpanow (Archiv für Sozialgeschichte,* Beiheft 20), Bonn 1998, 183–98, here 193f.

15. "RIAS-Meldung vom 6. 8. 1949"; BStU, ZA, SdM 339, 2, cited in Monika Tantzscher: "'In der Ostzone wird ein neuer Apparat aufgebaut.' Die Gründung des DDR-Staatssicherheitsdienstes," in *Deutschland Archiv* 31, 1 (1998), 48–56, here 52.

16. Ann J. Merritt, Richard L. Merritt: *Public Opinion in Occupied Germany. The OMGUS-Surveys. 1945–1949,* Urbana, Chicago, London 1970, 32f. The survey methods used do not conform to modern-day sociological standards. The surveys were

not conducted in the Soviet Occupation Zone, but they do at least give an idea of the mood and atmosphere.

17. Cited in Damian van Melis: *Entnazifizierung in Mecklenburg-Vorpommern. Herrschaft und Verwaltung 1954–1948*, Munich 1999, 257.
18. Letter of 7 January 1950, cited in David E. Murphy, Sergei A. Kondrashev, George Bailey: *Battleground Berlin*, New Haven 1997, 130.
19. Gerald Hacke: *Zeugen Jehovas in der DDR. Verfolgung und Verhalten einer religiösen Minderheit*, Dresden 2000, 40–47.
20. "Beschluß der II. Parteikonferenz der Sozialistischen Einheitspartei Deutschlands zur gegenwärtigen Lage und zu den Aufgaben im Kampf für Frieden, Einheit, Demokratie und Sozialismus," in: *Protokoll der Verhandlungen der II. Parteikonferenz der Sozialistischen Einheitspartei Deutschlands, 9.–12. 7. 1952*, Berlin 1952, 489–97, here 492.
21. Letter from Kurt Müller to Minister-President Otto Grotewohl, 31 May 1956, documented in Wilfriede Otto: *Erich Mielke—Biographie. Aufstieg und Fall eines Tschekisten*, Berlin 2000, 557–59, here 559.
22. Werner Großmann: *Bonn im Blick. Die DDR-Aufklärung aus der Sicht ihres letzten Chefs*, Berlin 2001, 12.
23. "Richtlinie 21 vom 20. 11. 1952 über die Suche, Anwerbung und Arbeit mit Informatoren, geheimen Mitarbeitern und Personen, die konspirative Wohnungen unterhalten," in Helmut Müller-Enbergs, ed.: *Inoffizielle Mitarbeiter des Ministeriums für Staatssicherheit. Richtlinien und Durchführungsbestimmungen*, Berlin 1996, 165f.
24. These figures do not contain data on the regional administrations of Potsdam, Cottbus, and Schwerin, for which there are no records; see ibid., 35.
25. "Über die Maßnahmen zur Gesundung der politischen Lage in der Deutschen Demokratischen Republik. Dokumentiert bei Rolf Stöckigt: Ein Dokument von großer historischer Bedeutung vom Mai 1953," in: *Beiträge zur Geschichte der Arbeiterbewegung* 32, 5 (1990), 648–54, here 653.
26. Quote contained in "MfS, Wachregiment Berlin, PK-Abteilung, Referat Schulung vom 21. 6. 1953, 'Bericht über die Stimmung der Einheiten des Wachregiments beim Einsatz,'" BStU, ZA, SdM 249, 73–79. This and the following quotations from the archives of the Federal Commissioner for the Stasi Archives (BStU) are well documented and discussed. See Jens Gieseke: *Die hauptamtlichen Mitarbeiter der Staatssicherheit. Personalstruktur und Lebenswelt*, Berlin 2000.
27. Zentrale Kommission für staatliche Kontrolle: "Bericht über die Einrichtung und Verwaltung des Erholungsheimes Wolletz durch das ehemalige Ministerium für Staatssicherheit sowie weitere Feststellungen über den Verbrauch eines Teiles von Haushaltsmitteln durch dieses Ministerium," SAPMO-BA, DY 30 IV 2/4/391, 267.
28. "Anlage zum Bericht der Kontrollkommission. Schreiben von Willy Schläwicke an den Vorsitzenden der ZKK, Fritz Lange, vom 28. 10. 1953," SAPMO-BA; DY 30 2/4/391, 281–95, here 291.
29. "Referat des Genossen Hermann Matern auf der Dienstbesprechung am 11. 11. 1953," in Karl Wilhelm Fricke, Roger Engelmann: *"Konzentrierte Schläge." Staatssicherheitsaktionen und politische Prozesse in der DDR 1953–1956*, Berlin 1998, 260–71, here 266f.
30. Murphy, Kondrashev, Bailey: *Battleground Berlin*, 294.
31. "Referat von Ernst Wollweber auf der zentralen Dienstkonferenz im Staatssekretariat für Staatssicherheit, 11. und 12. 11. 1953," in Fricke/Engelmann ibid., 272–83, here 276.

32. G. G. Yagoda, N. I. Jezhov, L. P. Beria, V. N. Merkulov, V. S. Abakumov, and S. I. Ogoltsov were shot. Only S. D. Ignatiev (minister of state security from 1951 to 1953) survived the terror and died of natural causes in 1983.

33. "Brief des 1. Sekretärs des ZK an die Genossen und Mitarbeiter der Staatssicherheit, 5. 11. 1956," SAPMO-BA, DY 30 IV 2/12/102, 314–17, here 315f. Emphasis in the original.

34. "Handschriftliche Notizen Bruno Beaters über ein Gespräch Wollwebers mit seinen Stellvertretern Beater und Weikert, 10. 2. 1957," in Roger Engelmann, Silke Schumann: *Kurs auf die entwickelte Diktatur. Walter Ulbricht, die Entmachtung Ernst Wollwebers und die Neuausrichtung des Staatssicherheitsdienstes 1956/57,* BF informiert 1 (published by the BStU), Berlin 1995, 51–54.

Chapter 2. The Safest GDR in the World: The Driving Forces of Stasi Growth

1. For details cf. Jens Gieseke, Die hauptamtlichen Mitarbeiter der Staatssicherheit. Personalstruktur und Lebenswelt, Berlin 2000, p. 538.

2. Armin Mitter, "'. . . gegen das Volk regieren'—Der Ausbau des Disziplinierungsapparates nach dem 17. Juni 1953," in *Der 17. Juni 1953. Der Anfang vom Ende des sowjetischen Imperiums. 4. Bautzen-Forum der Friedrich-Ebert-Stiftung,* Leipzig 1993, 63–66, here 66.

3. Klaus-Dietmar Henke: "Zu Nutzung und Auswertung der Unterlagen des Staatssicherheitsdienstes der ehemaligen DDR," in *Vierteljahreshefte für Zeitgeschichte* 41, 4 (1993), 575–87, here 586.

4. "Diskussionsbeitrag" of Roger Engelmann, documented in Klaus-Dietmar Henke, Roger Engelmann: *Aktenlage. Die Bedeutung der Unterlagen des Staatssicherheitsdienstes für die Zeitgeschichtsforschung,* Berlin 1995, 191.

5. "Diskussionsbeitrag" of Lutz Niethammer, in Henke and Engelmann, *Aktenlage,* 190f.

6. "Befehl 385/61 des Ministers vom 7. 9. 1961," BStU, ZA, DSt 100323.

7. "Protokoll der Kollegiumssitzung am 15. 3. 1960," BStU, ZA, SdM 1556, 39–42, here 40.

8. "Schlußwort des Ministers, Protokoll der Kollegiumssitzung am 13. Und 20. 12. 1961," BStU, ZA, SdM 1558, 2–43, here 36.

9. Ibid., 37.

10. "Diskussionsbeitrag von Hermann Matern auf der 2. Kreisdelegiertenkonferenz des Ministeriums für Staatssicherheit," no date [December 1962], SAPMO-BA DY 30 A 2/12/128, 17f.

11. "Protokoll über die Dienstbesprechung am 12. 10. 1962," BStU, ZA, ZAIG 4907, 1–8, here 1f.

12. Paragraphs 1, 2, 4, and 5 of the Statute of the Ministry for State Security of 30 July 1969, in Karl Wilhelm Fricke: "Zur Geschichte der DDR-Staatssicherheit," in Bernd Florath, Armin Mitter, Stefan Wolle, ed.: *Die Ohnmacht der Allmächtigen. Geheimdienste und politische Polizei in der modernen Gesellschaft,* Berlin 1992, 139–45.

13. Klaus-Dietmar Henke: "Staatssicherheit," in Werner Weidenfeld, Karl-Rudolf Korte, ed.: *Handbuch zur deutschen Einheit,* new edition, Bonn 1996, 646–53, here 647.

14. "Unsere Kampfkraft stärken und vorwärtsschreiten zum Wohl des ganzen Volkes. Interview mit Erich Honecker, Erster Sekretär des ZK der SED, zum Beginn der Parteiwahlen 1973/74," in *Neues Deutschland*, 1November 1973, 3–5, here 4.

15. "Erich Mielke auf der Zentralen Dienstkonferenz am 16. 11. 1972," 37, BStU, ZA, Dst 102219, 82f.

16. *Studienmaterial zur Geschichte des Ministeriums für Staatssicherheit, Teil VII*, published by the Juristische Hochschule Potsdam-Eiche, Lehrstuhl Geschichte der deutschen Arbeiterbewegung und des MfS, Potsdam 1980, 67.

17. "Erich Mielke auf der Zentralen Dienstkonferenz am 16. 11. 1972," 37.

18. Ibid.

19. "Referat des Ministers auf der Dienstbesprechung in der HA Kader und Schulung zur Verabschiedung des Genossen Generalmajor Otto und zur Einführung des Genossen Oberst Möller als Leiter der HA Kader und Schulung, 31. 1. 1983," BStU, ZA, ZAIG 4815, 12f.

20. "Referat des Leiters der HA KuSch auf der Dienstbesprechung am 5. 4. 1983 zur Auswertung der erweiterten Kollegiumssitzung am 4. 3. 1983"; BStU, ZA, HA KuSch 219, 45.

21. "Erklärung von Egon Krenz zur Beziehung von SED und Sicherheitsapparat vor dem Zentralen Runden Tisch, 22. 1. 1990 in Berlin," in Uwe Thaysen, ed.: *Der Zentrale Runde Tisch. Wortprotokoll und Dokumente*, vol II, Wiesbaden 2000, 501–5, here 502f.

22. Reinhold Andert, Wolfgang Herzberg: *Der Sturz. Erich Honecker im Kreuzverhör*, Berlin/Weimar 1990, 366–68.

23. Erich Mielke: "Ich sterbe in diesem Kasten," (interview), in *Der Spiegel* 36/1992, 31 August 1992, 38–53, here 48.

24. H. Gordon Skilling: "Groups in Soviet Politics. Some Hypotheses," in H. Gordon Skilling, Franklyn Griffiths, eds.: *Interest Groups in Soviet Politics*, Princeton, N.J. 1971, 3–18, here 3.

25. Manfred Hildermeier: *Geschichte der Sowjetunion 1917–1991*, Munich 1998, 770 and 772f.

26. Ibid., 773.

27. Frederick C. Barghoorn: "The Security Police," in Skilling, Griffiths: *Interest Groups in Soviet Politics*, 93–129, here 99.

28. Markus Wolf: *In eigenem Auftrag. Bekenntnisse und Einsichten*, Munich 1991, 208.

29. Gerhard Schürer and Siegfried Wenzel: "Wir waren die Rechner, immer verpönt," in Theo Pirker et al.: *Der Plan als Befehl und Fiktion. Wirtschaftsführung in der DDR*, Opladen 1995, 67–120, here 107.

30. See the overview provided in the appendix, page [xxx].

31. Actual figures rounded, for 1989, Volkspolizei (People's Police) for 1987.

Chapter 3. The Unofficial Collaborator:
A New Type of Informer

1. The following looks at IMs in the GDR and not those working in the West. Special conditions undoubtedly applied to the latter, which will be dealt with in the section on MfS operations in the West.

2. "Richtlinie 1/79 für die Arbeit mit Inoffiziellen Mitarbeitern (IM) und Gesellschaftlichen Mitarbeitern für Sicherheit (GMS)," in Müller-Enbergs: *Inoffizielle Mitarbeiter*, 305.

3. Werner Korth, Ferdinand Jonak, Karl-Otto Scharbert: *Die Gewinnung Inoffizieller Mitarbeiter und ihre psychologischen Bedingungen*, dissertation, JHS Potsdam-Eiche 1973, BStU, ZA, JHS 21826, 68; cited in Müller-Enbergs: *Inoffizielle Mitarbeiter*, 15.

4. Korth, Jonak, Scharbert: Die Gewinnung Inoffizieller Mitarbeiter, 25; cited in: Helmut Müller-Enbergs: "Inoffizielle Mitarbeiter des Staatssicherheitsdienstes der DDR," in: *Jahrbuch Extremismus und Demokratie* 6 (1994), pp. 57–87, here p. 58.

5. "Richtlinie 1/68 für die Zusammenarbeit mit Gesellschaftlichen Mitarbeitern für Sicherheit und Inoffiziellen Mitarbeitern im Gesamtsystem der Sicherung der Deutschen Demokratischen Republik," in Müller-Enbergs: *Inoffizielle Mitarbeiter*, 242–82, here 266f.

6. "Statut des Ministeriums für Staatssicherheit vom 30. 7. 1969," in Fricke: *Zur Geschichte der DDR-Staatssicherheit*, 141. The foreign agents are likewise lauded here as "upstanding patriots."

7. "Rede des Abgeordneten Erich Mielke (SED) vor der Volkskammer, 13. 11. 1989," in *Deutschland Archiv* 23, 1 (1990), 121.

8. "Stichwort 'Vertrauensverhältnis,'" in Siegfried Suckut, ed.: *Das Wörterbuch der Staatssicherheit. Definitionen zur "politisch-operativen Arbeit,"* Berlin 1996, 405.

9. About 200 to 250 cell informers were recruited each year in the 1980s. Their "useful life" was usually about three months.

10. Not included in these figures are the IMs of Main Department I (military counterintelligence). The latter had an IM ratio similar to the district offices, being integrated down to the lowest levels of the military hierarchy in the NVA and not having corresponding departments and divisions in the regional administrations and district offices.

11. Gerhard Paul: *Staatlicher Terror und gesellschaftliche Verrohung. Die Gestapo in Schleswig-Holstein*, Hamburg 1996, 125.

12. Gisela Diewald-Kerkmann: *Politische Denunziation im NS-Regime. Oder Die kleine Macht der "Volksgenossen,"* Bonn 1995.

13. "In the Soviet case, manipulative denunciations should be considered part of a complex of informal mechanisms of citizen agency, including client-patron relations and 'pull' [blat], that were the sociocultural equivalent of the Stalinist 'second economy' or black market." Sheila Fitzpatrick: "Signals from Below: Soviet Letters of Denunciation of the 1930s," in Sheila Fitzpatrick, Robert Gellately, ed.: *Accusatory Practices: Denunciation in Modern European History, 1789–1989*, Chicago 1997, 85–120, here 117.

14. "Einführungsreferat auf dem zentralen Führungsseminar Dezember 1975," DSt 102261, 19; cited in Müller-Enbergs: *Inoffizielle Mitarbeiter*, 95.

15. "Die Bildung des MfS am 8. Februar 1950—eine historische Notwendigkeit beim Aufbau der DDR"; BStU, ASt Neubrandenburg, AKG 171, 8.

16. "Richtlinie 1/68," in Müller-Enbergs: *Inoffizielle Mitarbeiter*, 251.

17. "Richtlinie 1/79," in Müller-Enbergs: *Inoffizielle Mitarbeiter*, 368.

18. "Richtlinie 1/58," in Müller-Enbergs: *Inoffizielle Mitarbeiter*, 211f.

19. Cited in Helmut Müller-Enbergs: "Warum wird einer IM? Zur Motivation bei der inoffiziellen Zusammenarbeit mit dem Staatssicherheitsdienst," in Klaus Behnke,

Jürgen Fuchs, ed.: *Zersetzung der Seele. Psychologie und Psychiatrie im Dienste des MfS*, Hamburg 1995, 102–29, here 120f.

20. Cited in Müller-Enbergs: "Inoffizielle Mitarbeiter des Staatssicherheitsdienstes der DDR," 79.

21. "Richtlinie 1/79," in Müller-Enbergs: "Inoffizielle Mitarbeiter des Staatssicher-heitsdienstes der DDR," 325.

22. Cited in Müller-Enbergs: *Inoffizielle Mitarbeiter*, 120.

Chapter 4. Blanket Surveillance?
State Security in East German Society

1. Emphasis in the original; Henke: "Zu Nutzung und Auswertung der Unterlagen des Staatssicherheitsdienstes," 585f.

2. Thus, for example, the Office for the Protection of the Constitution of the state of North Rhine-Westphalia has covert branches but little staff and few responsibilities.

3. "Stichwort Territorialprinzip," in Suckut: *Wörterbuch der Staatssicherheit*, 364.

4. "Referat auf der zentralen Dienstkonferenz zu ausgewählten Fragen der politisch-operativen Arbeit der Kreisdienststellen und deren Führung und Leitung (Ma-nuskript), 26. 10. 1988," BStU, ZA, DSt 103527, 37; cited in Walter Süß: "Die Durchdringung der Gesellschaft mittels des MfS—Fallbeispiel: Jena im Jahre 1989," in Eberhard Kuhrt et al., ed.: *Die SED-Herrschaft und ihr Zusammenbruch*, Opladen 1996, 115–37, here 118.

5. Süß, Durchdringung, 118.

6. "Stichwort Schwerpunktprinzip," in Suckut: *Wörterbuch der Staatssicherheit*, 349.

7. "Stichwort Schwerpunktbereich," in Suckut: *Wörterbuch der Staatssicherheit*, 349.

8. See Bernd Eisenfeld: "Eine 'legale Konzentration feindlich-negativer Kräfte.' Zur politischen Wirkung der Bausoldaten in der DDR," in *Deutschland Archiv* 28 3(1995), 256–71.

9. We do not know what share of IMs in Main Department I did not belong to the armed forces. This also does not take into account the individuals who did not be-long to the NVA or border troops but formed part of the portfolio of the Defense Ministry and thus was in the area of responsibility of Main Department I. These figures also do not include the IMs and employees in regional administrations and district offices for the surveillance of territorial defense administration. The actual ratio of IMs might therefore be a little lower, without this appreciably af-fecting the overall magnitude.

10. "Erich Mielke auf einer Dienstbesprechung am 12. 10. 1962," BStU, ZA, ZAIG 4907, 1–8, here 5.

11. [Erich Honecker:] *Bericht des Zentralkomitees der SED an den XI. Parteitag; Pro-tokoll der Verhandlungen des XI. Parteitages der Sozialistischen Einheitspartei Deutschlands, 17. bis 21. April 1986*, Berlin 1986, 67.

12. "Zur Reaktion der Bevölkerung der DDR im Zusammenhang mit der Lage in der Volksrepublik Polen, Berichte der ZAIG vom 18., 21., 29. 8. Und 3. 9. 1981," BStU, ZA, ZAIG 4151, 152.

13. This and the following figures include GMSs but not IMKs.

14. Sonja Süß: *Politisch mißbraucht? Psychiatrie und Staatssicherheit in der DDR*, Berlin 1998, 192.

15. "Mielke auf der Dienstkonferenz zur zentralen Planvorgabe, 22. 1. 1975"; cited in Süß: *Politisch mißbraucht? Psychiatrie und Staatssicherheit in der DDR*, 167.

16. "Arbeitshinweise des Ministers für die politisch-operative Bekämpfung der politisch-ideologischen Diversion und Untergrundtätigkeit unter jugendlichen Personenkreisen in der DDR vom 4. 7. 1963," 26; BStU, ZA, DSt 100483; cited in Thomas Auerbach: "Desinteresse, Disziplinlosigkeit, Dekonspiration. Die Probleme des MfS mit jugendlichen IM," in Jörn Mothes et al., ed.: *Beschädigte Seelen. DDR-Jugend und Staatssicherheit*, Bremen 1996, 276–81, here 276.

17. "Redemanuskript des Leiters der HA XX/2 zu Problemen der Werbung und Erziehung von IM unter 25 Jahren [1989]"; cited in Mothes et al: *Beschädigte Seelen. DDR-Jugend und Staatssicherheit*, 280.

18. Ibid., 278.

19. Hans-Hermann Hertle, Franz-Otto Gilles: *Überwiegend negativ. Das Ministerium für Staatssicherheit in der Volkswirtschaft dargestellt am Beispiel der Struktur und Arbeitsweise der Objektdienststellen in den Chemiekominaten des Bezirks Halle*, Berlin 1994, 42.

20. Cited in Maria Haendcke-Hoppe-Arndt: "Wer wußte was? Der ökonomische Niedergang der DDR," in Gisela Helwig, ed.: *Rückblicke auf die DDR. Festschrift für Ilse Spittmann-Rühle*, Cologne 1995, 120–31, here 129f.

21. Ralph Jessen: "Partei, Staat und ‚Bündnispartner': Die Herrschaftsmechanismen der SED-Diktatur," in Matthias Judt, ed.: *DDR-Geschichte in Dokumenten. Beschlüsse, Berichte, interne Materialien und Alltagszeugnisse*, Bonn 1998, 27–86, here 42.

22. M. Rainer Lepsius: "Die Institutionenordnung als Rahmenbedingung der Sozialgeschichte der DDR," in Hartmut Kaelble, Jürgen Kocka, Hartmut Zwar, ed.: *Sozialgeschichte der DDR*, Stuttgart 1994, 17–30.

23. Walter Schilling: "Die Bearbeitung der Landeskirche Thüringen durch das MfS," in Clemens Vollnhals, ed.: *Die Kirchenpolitik von SED und Staatssicherheit. Eine Zwischenbilanz*, Berlin 1996, 211–66, here 263.

24. Ibid.

25. Clemens Vollnhals: "Die kirchenpolitische Abteilung des Ministeriums für Staatssicherheit," in Vollnhals: *Die Kirchenpolitik von SED und Staatssicherheit. Eine Zwischenbilanz*, 79–119, here 119.

26. This was how writer Bert Papenfuss characterized the situation in retrospect. See Birgit Dahlke: "‚Temporäre autonome Zone.' Mythos und Alltag der inoffiziell publizierenden Literaturszene im letzten Jahrzehnt der DDR," in Günter Rüther, ed.: *Literatur in der Diktatur. Schreiben in Nationalsozialismus und DDR-Sozialismus*, Paderborn 1997, 463–78.

27. The term *informal rule* is taken from the indirect forms of rule practiced by colonial powers before the actual imperialism of the nineteenth century, i.e., the exploitation of territories under colonial rule without setting up state structures.

28. Gerhard Bergt: *Die Erarbeitung von Informationen an leitende Kader der Partei sowie staatlicher und wirtschaftsleitender Organe in Realisierung problem- und aufgabenbezogener Lageeinschätzungen als Bestandteil der politisch-operativen Arbeit und ihrer Leitung*, thesis paper, JHS Potsdam-Eiche 1988, BStU, MfS, ZA, JHS 21265, 14f.

29. Uta Stolle: "Traumhafte Quellen. Vom Nutzen der Stasi-Geschichtsschreibung," in *DA* 30 (1997) 1/2, 209–21, here 211.

30. Cited in Engelmann, Schumann: *Kurs auf die entwickelte Diktatur*, 37.
31. "Befehl Nr. 299/65 über die Organisierung eines einheitlichen Systems der politisch-operativen Auswertungs- und Informationstätigkeit im Ministerium für Staatssicherheit, 24. Juli 1965," in Roger Engelmann, Frank Joestel, ed.: *Grundsatzdokumente des MfS*, (MfS-Handbuch Teil V/5), Berlin 2004, 141–49.
32. See Jens Gieseke: "Bevölkerungsstimmungen in der geschlossenen Gesellschaft. MfS-Berichte an die DDR-Führung in den 60er und 70er Jahren," in *Zeithistorische Forschungen* 5, 2 (2008), 236–57; Siegfried Suckut: "Willy Brandt in der DDR. Oder: Die Schwierigkeiten des MfS mit der 'Autoritätsperson im Weltmaßstab,'" in *Jahrbuch für Historische Kommunismusforschung* 2008, 170–82.
33. The reports can be found in Armin Mitter and Stefan Wolle, eds.: *Ich liebe Euch doch alle! Befehle und Lageberichte des MfS Januar—November 1989*, Berlin 1990, 141–50, 204–7; see also Jens Gieseke: "'Seit langem angestaute Unzufriedenheit breitester Bevölkerungskreise'—Das Volk in den Stimmungsberichten des MfS," in Klaus-Dietmar Henke, ed.: *Revolution und Vereinigung 1989/90. Als in Deutschland die Realität die Phantasie überholte*, Munich 2009, 130–48
34. Cited in Daniela Münkel: *Staatssicherheit in der Region. Die geheimen Berichte der MfS-Kreisdienststelle Halberstadt an die SED, DA* 43, 1 (2010), 31–38.
35. Volker Wünderich: "Die 'Kaffeekrise' von 1977. Genußmittel und Verbraucherprotest in der DDR," in *Historische Anthropologie* 11 (2003), 240–61; Mark Allinson: "1977: 'The Most Normal Year of the GDR?'" in Mary Fulbrook, ed.: *Power and Society in the GDR, 1961–79*, New York/Oxford 2009, 253–77; [ZAIG] "Hinweise auf Tendenzen der Unzufriedenheit in der Reaktion der Bevölkerung der DDR, 12. 9. 1977," BStU, ZA, ZAIG 4119.
36. "Hinweise über einige beachtenswerte Entwicklungstendenzen in der Reaktion der Bevölkerung auf innenpolitische Fragen, 24. 11. 1988," in BStU, ZA, ZAIG 4158, 107–13, here 111.
37. ZAIG: "Erste Hinweise zur Reaktion der Bevölkerung auf die 4. Tagung des ZK der SED vom 18. bis 19. Juni 1987 in Berlin, 29. 6. 1987," in BStU, ZA, ZAIG 4226, 2–8, here 6.
38. ZAIG: "Hinweise über einige aktuelle Gesichtspunkte der Reaktion der Bevölkerung, 8. 8. 1985," in BStU, ZA, ZAIG 4158, 59–63, here 59f.; ZAIG: "Erste Hinweise über Reaktionen der Bevölkerung der DDR zum Inhalt und Verlauf des XI. Parteitages der SED, 18. 4. 1986," BStU, ZA, ZAIG 4199, 56–58.
39. Götz Aly, ed.: *Volkes Stimme. Skepsis und Führervertrauen im Nationalsozialismus*, Frankfurt/Main 2006, 9f.
40. Stefan Wolle: *Die heile Welt der Diktatur. Alltag und Herrschaft in der DDR 1971–1989*, Bonn/Berlin 1998, 152; the Auschwitz metaphor is from Jürgen Fuchs, see below, chapter 8.
41. Jan Palmowski: *Inventing the Socialist Nation: Heimat and the Politics of Everyday Life in the GDR, 1945–90*, Cambridge 2009, 285–89.
42. *10. Tätigkeitsbericht der Bundesbeauftragten für die Unterlagen des Staatssicherheitsdienstes der ehemaligen DDR*, Berlin 2011, 52.
43. On contact persons see Gary Bruce: *The Firm: The Inside Story of the Stasi*, Oxford 2010.
44. Andrew Port: *Die rätselhafte Stabilität der DDR. Arbeit und Alltag im sozialistischen Deutschland*, Berlin 2007.
45. See Bettina Greiner: *Verdrängter Terror. Geschichte und Wahrnehmung sowjetischer Speziallager in Deutschland*, Hamburg 2010, 31–458.

46. Jens Reich: "Sicherheit und Feigheit—der Käfer im Brennglas," in Walter Süß, Siegfried Suckut, ed.: *Staatspartei und Staatssicherheit. Zum Verhältnis von SED und MfS*, Berlin 1997, 25–37, first published in 1989 under the pseudonym Thomas Asperger in *Lettre international*.
47. Palmowski, *Inventing the Socialist Nation*, 252.
48. Joachim Gauck: "Der sozialistische Gang," in *Der Spiegel*, 25/2006, 38f., here 39. See also the much earlier work of Hans-Joachim Maaz: *Der Gefühlsstau. Ein Psychogramm der DDR*, Berlin 1990.
49. Dietrich Staritz: "Untertänigkeit. Heritage and Tradition," in *Studies in GDR Culture and Society* 6, London/New York 1986, 37–48; see also Sigrid Meuschel: *Legitimation und Parteiherrschaft in der DDR. Zum Paradox von Stabilität und Revolution in der DDR 1945–1989*, Frankfurt/ Main 1992.
50. Thomas Lindenberger: "Die Diktatur der Grenzen," in idem., ed.: *Herrschaft und Eigen-Sinn in der Diktatur. Studien zur Gesellschaftsgeschichte der DDR*, Cologne et al. 1999, 13–44, here 32.
51. See Sybille Plogstedt: *Knastmauke. Das Schicksal von politischen Häftlingen der DDR nach der deutschen Wiedervereinigung*, Giessen 2010.

Chapter 5. Resistance—Opposition—Persecution

1. The term apparently included nonmanagerial salaried employees.
2. Cited in Monika Tantzscher: *"Maßnahme Donau und Einsatz Genesung." Die Niederschlagung des Prager Frühlings 1968/69 im Spiegel der MfS-Akten*, Berlin 1994, 35f.
3. An English translation was published one year later in the United States under the title *The Alternative in Eastern Europe* by Verso, London 1988.
4. Hans Kremendahl, Thomas Meyer, eds.: *Menschliche Emanzipation. Rudolf Bahro und der Demokratische Sozialismus (Studientexte der Hochschulinitiative Demokratischer Sozialismus)*, Frankfurt/Main 1981.
5. "ZAIG-Information über beachtenswerte Aspekte des aktuellen Wirksamwerdens innerer feindlicher, oppositioneller und anderer negativer Kräfte in personellen Zusammenschlüssen, 1. 6. 1989," in Armin Mitter, Stefan Wolle, ed.: *Ich liebe euch doch alle! Befehle und Lageberichte des MfS Januar—November 1989*, Berlin 1990, 46–71.
6. Johannes Raschka: "Die Ausreisebewegung—eine Form von Widerstand gegen das SED-Regime," in Ulrich Baumann, Helmut Kury, ed.: *Politisch-motivierte Verfolgung. Opfer von SED-Unrecht*, Freiburg 1998, 257–74, here 273.
7. Added to this were the less serious cases or nonpolitical offenses handled by the People's Police but likewise sentenced under to the political paragraphs of the criminal code.
8. Ulrich Herbert: "Das 'Jahrhundert der Lage': Ursachen, Erscheinungsformen, Auswirkungen," in Peter Reif-Spirek, Bodo Ritscher, ed.: *Speziallager in der SBZ. Gedenkstätten mit "doppelter Vergangenheit,"* Berlin 1999, 11–27.
9. Nazi crimes are not included here. A total of 208 executions in the Soviet Occupation Zone and GDR have been documented; convictions by Soviet courts are not included in this figure. In eight additional cases (all from the years up to 1956) it is not clear if the death sentence was carried out.

10. In its own publications (as of December 2004), the "Arbeitsgemeinschaft 13. August" (August 13th Working Group) counts an additional 300 deaths at the border not included here, most of which involved shooting accidents among East German border soldiers. All of these figures are to be handled with caution, as the working group refuses to publish the sources of its information for scholarly verification.

11. See Walter Süß: "'Lieber einen Menschen abhauen lassen. . .' Wie es vor zehn Jahren zur Aufhebung des Schießbefehls kam," in *Frankfurter Allgemeine Zeitung*, 2 February 1999, 14.

12. "Richtlinie 1/76 zur Entwicklung und Bearbeitung Operativer Vorgänge," in David Gill, Ulrich Schröter: *Das Ministerium für Staatssicherheit. Anatomie des Mielke-Imperiums*, 346–402, here 390.

13. *Lehrmaterial der Hochschule des MfS zum Thema: Anforderungen und Wege für eine konzentrierte, rationelle und gesellschaftlich wirksame Vorgangsbearbeitung.* "11. Kapitel: Die Anwendung von Maßnahmen der Zersetzung in der Bearbeitung Operativer Vorgänge," December 1977, BStU, ZA, JHS 24 503, 11, cited in Süß: Repressive Strukturen, 205.

14. Ibid.

15. "Maßnahmeplan zur weiteren politisch-operativen Kontrolle und Bearbeitung des OV 'Verräter,' 17. 2. 1987," in *Auszügen dokumentiert in: Stasi-Akte "Verräter." Bürgerrechtler Templin: Dokumente einer Verfolgung, Spiegel Special* 1/1993, 29.

16. Ibid., 30.

17. Sonja Süß: "Repressive Strukturen in der SBZ/DDR—Analyse von Strategien der Zersetzung durch Staatsorgane der DDR gegenüber Bürgern der DDR," in *Materialien der Enquete-Kommission "Überwindung der Folgen der SED-Diktatur im Prozeß der deutschen Einheit"* (*13. Wahlperiode des Deutschen Bundestages*), Baden-Baden/Frankfurt am Main 1999, vol. II, 193–250, here 217.

18. Ibid., 227.

19. "Plan zum abgestimmten IM-Einsatz bei der inoffiziellen Bearbeitung des maßgeblichen Mitinitiators der sogenannten Arbeitsgruppe Menschenrechte Wolfgang Templin, 5. 2. 1986"; excerpts documented in *Stasi-Akte "Verräter,"* 27.

20. Jürgen Fuchs: *Unter Nutzung der Angst. Die "leise Form" des Terrors—Zersetzungsmaßnahmen des MfS*, BF informiert 2, Berlin 1994.

21. Clemens Vollnhals: "Das Ministerium für Staatssicherheit. Ein Instrument totalitärer Herrschaftsausübung," in Hartmut Kaelble, Jürgen Kocka, Hartmut Zwahr, eds.: *Sozialgeschichte der DDR*, Stuttgart 1994, 498–518, here 514.

Chapter 6. Wolf and Co.—MfS Operations Abroad

1. "Die zehn besten Geheimdienste der Welt," in *Die Welt der Agenten, Spiegel Special* 1/1996, 14.

2. Karl Wilhelm Fricke: "Ordinäre Abwehr—elitäre Aufklärung? Zur Rolle der Hauptverwaltung A im Ministerium für Staatssicherheit," in *Aus Politik und Zeitgeschichte* B 50/97, 17–26.

3. "Die Informationsschwerpunkte der HV A. Anlage 1 zum 1. Kommentar zur Richtlinie 2/79 für die Arbeit mit Inoffiziellen Mitarbeitern im Operationsgebiet, Mai 1980," in Helmut Müller-Enbergs, ed.: *Inoffizielle Mitarbeiter des Ministeriums für Staatssicherheit. Teil 2: Anleitungen für die Arbeit mit Agenten, Kundschaf-*

tern und Spionen in der Bundesrepublik Deutschland, Berlin 1998, 542–52, here 546.

4. Hubertus Knabe: "Die Stasi war immer mit dabei," in *Frankfurter Allgemeine Zeitung*, 8 December 1997, 10f.; idem.: *Die unterwanderte Republik. Stasi im Westen*, Berlin 1999; idem.: *Der diskrete Charme der DDR. Stasi und Westmedien*, Berlin, Munich 2001.

5. Hubertus Knabe et al.: *Westarbeit des MfS*, 303.

6. Großmann: *Bonn im Blick*.

7. Christopher Andrew: "Nachrichtendienste im Kalten Krieg: Probleme und Perspektiven," in Wolfgang Krieger, Jürgen Weber: *Spionage für den Frieden? Nachrichtendienste in Deutschland während des Kalten Krieges*, Munich 1997, 23–48, here 23.

8. Joachim Lampe: *Juristische Aufarbeitung der Westspionage des MfS. Eine vorläufige Bilanz. Festvortrag gehalten am 18. Juni 1999 in der Akademie für politische Bildung Tutzing*, BF informiert 24, Berlin 1999, 16.

9. All figures are taken from the personnel statistics of the Main Department for Cadre and Training (Hauptabteilung Kader und Schulung); see Gieseke: *Die Hauptamtlichen Mitarbeiter*.

10. "Kaderbestandsmeldungen," BStU, ZA, HA KuSch, Bündel Abt. Planung 10 III. All figures include the respective Department XV of the regional administrations of State Security.

11. Gieseke: *Die hauptamtlichen Mitarbeiter*, supplement.

12. See for example, "Redebeitrag der Delegation des MfS der DDR für die Beratung der Aufklärungsorgane in Budapest, Dezember 1970," in Hubertus Knabe et al.: *Die Westarbeit des MfS. Das Zusammenspiel von "Aufklärung" und "Abwehr,"* Berlin 1999, 316.

13. Müller-Enbergs: *Inoffizielle Mitarbeiter II*, 40.

14. Wolfgang Hartmann: "Kaleidoskop: Vorzeichen für ein Scheitern der DDR," in *Spurensicherung IV. Niedergang der DDR. Ehrlich gekämpft und verloren*, published by the Unabhängige Autorengemeinschaft "So habe ich das erlebt," Schkeuditz 2002, 178–87, here 183f. Hartmann was deployed as an illegal resident in the Federal Republic.

15. "Redebeitrag von Oberstleutnant Werner Groth, Delegiertenkonferenz der SED-Parteiorganisation der HVA, 16. 1. 1986"; BStU, MfS ZAIG/ Tb/5, cited in Georg Herbstritt, "Erkenntnisse über die Westarbeit des MfS aus den Spionageverfahren der neunziger Jahre," in Änne Bäumer-Schleinkofer,ed.: *Die Westlinke und die DDR: Journalismus, Rechtsprechung und der Einfluß der Stasi in der DDR und der BRD*. Frankfurt am Main 2005, 109–33.

16. "Richtlinie für die Arbeit mit inoffiziellen Mitarbeitern außerhalb des Gebietes der DDR, 3. Entwurf, 17. Juni 1959," in: Müller-Enbergs: *Inoffizielle Mitarbeiter, Teil 2*, 290–340, here 291; "Richtlinie 2/68 über die Arbeit mit Inoffiziellen Mitarbeitern im Operationsgebiet, Januar 1968"; in: Müller-Enbergs: *Inoffizielle Mitarbeiter, Teil 2*, 352–88, here 353.

17. "Richtlinie 2/79 für die Arbeit mit Inoffiziellen Mitarbeitern im Operationsgebiet," in: Müller-Enbergs: *Inoffizielle Mitarbeiter, Teil 2*, 471–513, here p. 472; 1. "Kommentar zur Richtlinie 2/79"; in: Müller-Enbergs: *Inoffizielle Mitarbeiter, Teil 2*, 514–52, here pp. 542–46.

18. "Die Informationsschwerpunkte der HV A. Anlage 1 zum 1. Kommentar zur Richtlinie 2/79 für die Arbeit mit Inoffiziellen Mitarbeitern im Operationsgebiet, Mai 1980," in: Müller-Enbergs: *Inoffizielle Mitarbeiter, Teil 2*, pp. 542–552, here 549f.

19. Werner Stiller: *Im Zentrum der Spionage*, Mainz 1986, 200.
20. Kristie Macrakis : "Espionage and Technology Transfer in the Quest for Scientific-technical Prowess," in Dieter Hoffmann, Kristie Macrakis, ed.: *Science under Socialism: East Germany in Comparative Perspective*, Cambridge, MA, 1999, 82–121, here 116.
21. Großmann: *Bonn im Blick*, 99.
22. Cited in Reinhard Borgmann, *Jochen Staadt: Deckname Markus. Zwei Top-Agentinnen im Herzen der Macht*, Berlin 1998, 154; see also Jochen Staadt: "Spione im ZK—Der Fall Arno Heine. Die westlichen Dienste waren gut informiert und hüten bis heute ihre Geheimnisse," in *Zeitschrift des Forschungsverbundes SED-Staat* 14 (2003), 22–38.
23. Cited in Erich Schmidt-Eenboom: *Der BND—die unheimliche Macht im Staate*, Düsseldorf 1993, 100.
24. Hans-Georg Wieck: "Die DDR aus der Sicht des BND 1985–1990," in Heinz Timmermann, ed.: *Die DDR in Europa—zwischen Isolation und Öffnung*, Münster 2005, 190–207, here 196f. On the interception of SED directional radio see Peter F. Müller, Michael Mueller: *Gegen Freund und Feind. Der BND: Geheime Politik und schmutzige Geschäfte*, Reinbek 2002, 549.
25. Apparently no one in State Security was overly concerned about the obvious associations with the Nazi mass-execution squads by the same name, the *Einsatzgruppen der* SS *und des* SD.
26. "Bericht über die Ergebnisse der Konsultationen, die mit Vertretern des Komitees für Staatssicherheit der UdSSR zu Fragen der Arbeit der Linie IV des MfS geführt wurden, 16. 12. 1969," in Thomas Auerbach: *Einsatzkommandos an der unsichtbaren Front. Terror- und Sabotagevorbereitungen des MfS gegen die Bundesrepublik Deutschland*, Berlin 1999, 114–31, here 116–18.
27. Cited in ibid., 22f.
28. "Die Einsatz- und Kampfgrundsätze tschekistischer Einsatzkader bei der Durchführung offensiver tschekistischer Kampfmaßnahmen im Operationsgebiet," in "Bericht über die Ergebnisse der Konsultationen," 132–141, here 141.
29. This task belonged to Main Administration A, Department III (Hauptverwaltung A, Abteilung III) until 1959, before being transferred to the AGM in Department IV. In 1989 the AGM/S was absorbed by Main Department XXII for terror defense (Hauptabteilung XXII, *Terrorabwehr*) ein.
30. Markus Wolf: *Spionagechef im geheimen Krieg. Erinnerungen*, Munich 1997, 367.
31. Ronnie Kasrils: *Steckbrieflich gesucht. Undercover gegen Apartheid*, Essen 1997, 130.
32. See Voitech Mastny, "Superpower Détente: US-Soviet Relations, 1969–1972," in *GHI Bulletin*, Supplement 1 (2003), 24.
33. On the considerable attention the HVA gave to finding out the West's intentions behind the policy of détente see "Redebeitrag der Delegation des MfS der DDR für die Beratung der Aufklärungsorgane in Budapest, Dezember 1970," in Knabe, *Westarbeit*, 316–32; "Schlußfolgerungen aus der Unterzeichnung des Schlußdokuments der Konferenz über Sicherheit und Zusammenarbeit in Europa (KSZE) in Helsinki; 6. 8. 1975" in: Knabe, *Westarbeit*, 373–78.
34. "Axen bei einem Geheimtreffen von SED- und KPdSU-Führung am 17. 8.1984," in Detlef Nakath, Gerd-Rüdiger Stephan, ed.: *Die Häber-Protokolle. Schlaglichter der SED-Westpolitik 1973–1985*, Berlin 1999, 417.
35. Hubertus Knabe: *Die unterwanderte Republik*, Berlin 1999.
36. John Lewis Gaddis: "Intelligence, Espionage and Cold War," in *Diplomatic History*, 13, 2 (1989), 191–212, here 209.

37. See Donald P. Steury, ed.: *Intentions and Capabilities: Estimates on Soviet Strategic Forces, 1950–1983*, Washington, D.C. 1996, especially "Part III: Arms Control, Soviet Objectives, and Force Planning, 1968–1983," 286–500.

Chapter 7. Final Crisis and Collapse, 1989–90

1. Jessen: "Partei, Staat und 'Bündnispartner,'" in Judt: *DDR-Geschichte in Dokumenten*, 31f.
2. Uwe Hasenbein: *Zum tschekistischen Feindbild und damit verbundenen Problemen bei der Herausbildung des Berufsethos bei Offiziersschülern der Hochschule des MfS*, thesis paper, JHS Potsdam-Eiche 1989; BStU, ZA, JHS 21431, 31.
3. Ehrhart Neubert: *Geschichte der Opposition in der DDR 1949–1989*, second edition, Bonn 1998, 695.
4. Wolfgang Rüddenklau: *Störenfried. ddr-opposition 1986–1989*, Berlin 1992, 221.
5. "Referat des Mitglieds des Politbüros des ZK der SED und Minister für Staatssicherheit, Armeegeneral Erich Mielke, auf der Tagung der Aufklärungsorgane der sozialistischen Länder, Berlin 17. Oktober 1988"; BStU, ZA, ZAIG 5121, 3–44, here 12; cited in Walter Süß: "Selbstblockierung der Macht. Wachstum und Lähmung der Staatssicherheit in den siebziger und achtziger Jahren," in Konrad Jarausch, Martin Sabrow, ed.: *Weg in den Untergang. Der innere Zerfall der DDR*, Göttingen 1999, 239–57, here 244.
6. Vladimir Il'ich Lenin: *Selected Works in Three Volumes. July 1918 to March 1923*, New York 1967, 392.
7. Detlef Pollack: *Politischer Protest. Politisch alternative Gruppen in der DDR*. Opladen 2000, 258.
8. "'Aufbruch 89—Neues Forum.' Gründungsaufruf des Neuen Forums vom 10. 9. 1989," in Charles Schüddekopf , ed.: *"Wir sind das Volk!" Flugschriften, Aufrufe und Texte einer deutschen Revolution*, Reinbek 1990, 29–31.
9. "Oberstleutnant Stark, Leiter der Abteilung XX der Bezirksverwaltung Erfurt: 'Die Anwendung von Maßnahmen der Zersetzung im Rahmen der operativen Bearbeitung feindlich-negativer Personenzusammenschlüsse,' 18. 1. 1989"; VVS Eft o024 30/89; BStU, ASt Erfurt; cited in Süß: *Staatssicherheit am Ende*, 245.
10. Süß: "Selbstblockierung der Macht," 247.
11. "Protokoll der Dienstversammlung des BV-Leiters am 16. 11. 1989"; BStU, ASt Chemnitz, AKG 441, 13; cited in Holger Horsch: *"Hat nicht wenigstens die Stasi die Stimmmung im Lande gekannt?" MfS und SED im Bezirk Karl-Marx-Stadt*, BF informiert 19, Berlin 1997, 42.

Chapter 8. Legacy—*Aufarbeitung*—Culture of Memory: The Second Life of the Stasi

1. "Erklärung der Kontrollkommission zur Auflösung des MfS/AfNS Bezirk Schwerin vom 12. 2. 1990, vorgetragen auf der 12. Sitzung des Zentralen Runden Tisches am 12. 2. 1990," in Thaysen: *Der Zentrale Runde Tisch, Band III*, 752f.
2. Letter from Werthebach to the director of the Legal Department of the East German Ministry of the Interior, 21 August 1990, in Jens Gieseke, Doris Hubert: *Die DDR-Staatssicherheit. Schild und Schwert der Partei*, Bonn 2000, 101.

3. Lothar de Maizière: "Rede vor der Volkskammer am 15. 9. 1990," in Silke Schumann: *Vernichten oder Offenlegen? Zur Entstehung des Stasi-Unterlagen-Gesetzes. Eine Dokumentation der öffentlichen Debatte 1990/1991*, published by the BStU, Berlin 1995, document 13.

4. Hans Schwenke: "Mielkes Befehl 6/86 und die Überlebensordnung des MfS," in *Neues Deutschland*, 9–10 June 1990; see also Michael Richter, *Die Staatssicherheit im letzten Jahr der DDR*, Weimar, Cologne, Vienna 1996.

5. Cited in Andreas Niemann, Walter Süß: *"Gegen das Volk kann nichts mehr entschieden werden." MfS und SED im Bezirk Neubrandenburg*, Berlin 1996, 31.

6. See Andreas Förster: "Neue Erkenntnisse zur Hinterbühne der Stasi-Auflösung 1990," in *Horch und Guck* 21 (1997), 28–37.

7. "EDV-Auswertungen 16, 15. 2. 1983 und 22. 2. 1988"; BStU, ZA, HA KuSch Abt. Plg. 18 III.

8. There is no separate data for full-time employees in Mecklenburg, Western Pomerania, only mixed data, including IMs; for details see: Gieseke: *Die hauptamtlichen Mitarbeiter*, 528.

9. As indicated by ISOR chairman Horst Parton in a hearing before the Petition Committee of the German Bundestag, 8 November 2010.

10. See Constanze von Bullion: "Stasi-Forscher mit Neigung zu Alleingängen," in *Süddeutsche Zeitung*, 28 May 2009; Einar Koch: "Schnüffel-Vorwürfe in der Stasi-Behörde," in *Bild-Zeitung*, 14 March 2011; Julia Emmrich: "Bei Gauck stimmte die Chemie," in *Der Westen*, 25 June 2010; http://www.derwesten. de/staedte/dor sten/Bei-Gauck-stimmte-die-Chemie-id3349123.html.

11. On the following, see my essay "'Different Shades of Gray.' Denunziations- und Informantenberichte als Quellen der Alltagsgeschichte des Kommunismus," in *Zeithistorische Forschungen* 7, 2 (2010), 287–95.

12. See Ralph Jessen, "Diktatorische Herrschaft als kommunikative Praxis. Überlegungen zum Zusammenhang von 'Bürokratie' und Sprachnormierung in der DDR-Geschichte," in Alf Lüdtke, Peter Becker, ed.: *Akten. Eingaben. Schaufenster. Die DDR und ihre Texte. Erkundungen zu Herrschaft und Alltag*, Berlin 1997, 57–75.

13. 10. Tätigkeitsbericht der BStU, Berlin 2011, 52.

14. Palmowski: *Inventing the Socialist Nation*, 311.

15. Johannes Gross: "Notizbuch," in *Frankfurter Allgemeine Zeitung*, 1 December 1984.

16. "Auf mir bestehen. Christa Wolf im Gespräch mit Günter Gaus," reprinted in Hermann Vinke: *Akteneinsicht Christa Wolf. Zerrspiegel und Dialog*, Hamburg 1993, 242–63, here 253.

17. See the various declarations and letters in Vinke: *Akteneinsicht Christa Wolf*.

18. The charismatic Gysi (PDS) was accused of having worked as an IM in the 1970s and 1980s. The Bundestag's Immunity Committee reached a majority decision that this was indeed the case, yet Gysi successfully defended himself in court.

19. Allgemeine Bevölkerungsumfrage der Sozialwissenschaften (ALLBUS), *Datenhandbuch 1980–2006*, ZA-Nr. 4241, published by GESIS/ZUMA, Cologne/ Mannheim 2007, 114.

20. See also the Forsa Institute surveys (with different survey questions) from 2000 and 2003; *Die Welt*, 4 May 2000, 4; http://www.focus.de/politik/deutschland/ stasi-akten_aid_191058.html.

21. Timothy Garton Ash: "The Stasi on Our Minds," in *The New York Review of Books*, 54, 31. May 2007.

22. Susanne Sturm: "Hart, aber herzlich. Interview mit Henry Hübchen," in *Stern TV Magazin*, 23 (2006), 1 June 2006.

23. Claus Leggewie: "Schlachtfeld Europa. Transnationale Erinnerung und europäische Identität," in http://www.eurozine.com/pdf/2009-02-04-leggewie-de.pdf.

24. Sandra Kalniete: "Altes Europa, neues Europa." Speech at the opening of the Leipzig Book Fair, 24 March 2004, http://www.die-union.de/reden/altes_neues_europa.htm.

25. Horst Möller, ed.: *Der rote Holocaust und die Deutschen. Die Debatte um das "Schwarzbuch des Kommunismus,"* Munich 1999.

26. Ehrhart Neubert: "Politische Verbrechen in der DDR," in Stéphane Courtois et al.: *Das Schwarzbuch des Kommunismus. Unterdrückung, Verbrechen und Terror,* Munich, Zurich 1997, 829–84, here 837.

27. *Die Welt,* 4 November 1991.

28. "It is, if you can compare it at all, the Dachau of Communism. . . . I think that, in the future, we will equate the two big dictatorships of the twentieth century much more than we are used to doing. In fifty years we will look at both systems equally perplexed."; "'Das Dachau des Kommunismus.' Der neue Leiter über die Gedenkstätte Hohenschönhausen," Interview in *Berliner Zeitung,* 1 December 2000; "Die deutsche Lubjanka," in *Frankfurter Allgemeine Zeitung,* 11 January 2002, 6.

29. Ilko-Sascha Kowalzuk: *Endspiel. Die Revolution von 1989 in der DDR,* Bonn 2009.

30. Bernd Eisenfeld, Ilko-Sascha Kowalczuk, Ehrhart Neubert: *Die verdrängte Revolution, Der Platz des 17. Juni in der deutschen Geschichte,* Bremen 2003, 64f.

31. "Verantwortung wahrnehmen, Aufarbeitung verstärken, Gedenken vertiefen. Fortschreibung der Gedenkstättenkonzeption des Bundes," 18 June 2008; http://www.bundesregierung.de/nsc_true/Content/DE/ Anlagen/BKM/2008-06-18-fortschreibung-gedenkstaettenkonzepion-barrierefrei,property=publicationFile.pdf/2008-06-18-fortschreibung-gedenkstaettenkonzepion-barrierefrei.

32. Joachim Gauck: *Die Stasi-Akten,* Reinbek 1991, 93f.

33. Jan T. Gross: *Neighbors: The Destruction of the Jewish Community in Jedwabne, Poland,* Princeton, N.J. 2001.

34. "Podiumsgespräch der Enquetekommission, 4. 5. 1994, 76. Sitzung, 'Zur Auseinandersetzung mit den beiden Diktaturen in Deutschland in Vergangenheit und Gegenwart,'" in *Materialien der Enquete-Kommission "Aufarbeitung von Geschichte und Folgen der SED-Diktatur in Deutschland" (12. Wahlperiode des Deutschen Bundestages).* Published by the German Bundestag, Baden-Baden, Frankfurt am Main 1995, vol. IX, 676–749, here 690.

SELECTED BIBLIOGRAPHY

The facts and interpretation presented in this book are based on a broad range of literature, mostly in German. A general overview of these scholarly works can be found in the annotated bibliography of the German edition of this volume. The following is a select list of relevant books and articles in English.

General

Childs, David, and Richard Popplewell. *The Stasi: The East German Intelligence and Security Service*. London: New York University Press, 1996.

Dennis, Mike. *The Stasi: Myth and Reality*. Harlow: Pearson/Longman, 2003.

Gieseke, Jens. *The GDR State Security: Shield and Sword of the Party*. Berlin: BStU, 2002.

Kaminski, Łukasz, and Krzysztof Persak, eds. *Handbook of the Communist Security Apparatus in East Central Europe, 1944–1989*. Warsaw: Instytut Pamięci Narodowej, 2005.

Early Period

Applebaum, Anne. *Iron Curtain: The Crushing of Eastern Europe, 1944–1956*. New York: Doubleday, 2012.

Bruce, Gary. *Resistance with the People: Repression and Resistance in Eastern Germany, 1945–1955*. Lanham u.a.: Rowman and Littlefield, 2003.

Gieseke, Jens. "Ulbricht's Secret Police: The Ministry of State Security." In *The Workers' and Peasants' State: Communism and Society in East Germany, 1945–71*, edited by Patrick Major and Jonathan Osmond, 41–58. Manchester, New York: Manchester University Press, 2002.

Grift, Liesbeth van de. *Securing the Communist State: The Reconstruction of Coercive Institutions in the Soviet Zone of Germany and Romania*. Lanham, Md.: Lexington Books, 2011.

Murphy, David E., Sergei A. Kondraschow, and George Bailey. *Battleground Berlin: CIA vs. KGB in the Cold War*. New Haven: Yale University Press, 1997.

Naimark, Norman M. *The Russians in Germany: A History of the Soviet Zone of Occupation, 1945–1949*. Cambridge: Harvard University Press, 1995.

Ostermann, Christian. *Uprising in East Germany, 1953: The Cold War, the German Question, and the First Major Upheaval Behind the Iron Curtain*. New York: Central European University Press, 2001.

Tismaneanu Vladimir, ed. *Stalinism Revisited: The Establishment of Communist Regimes in East-Central Europe*. Budapest: Central European University Press, 2009.

Apparatus and Staff

Bruce, Gary. *The Firm: The Inside Story of the Stasi*. Oxford, New York: Oxford University Press, 2010.

Glaeser, Andreas. *Political Epistemics: The Secret Police, the Opposition, and the End of East German Socialism*. Chicago, London: Chicago University Press, 2011.

Sarotte, Mary E. *Dealing with the Devil: East Germany, Détente, and Ostpolitik, 1969–1973*. Chapel Hill u.a.: University of North Carolina Press, 2001.

Informers

Fitzpatrick, Sheila, and Robert Gellately, eds. *Accusatory Practices: Denunciations in Modern European History, 1789–1989*. Chicago, London: Chicago University Press, 1997.

Fulbrook, Mary. *The People's State: East German Society from Hitler to Honecker*. New Haven: Yale University Press, 2005.

Miller, Barbara. *Narratives of Guilt and Compliance in Unified Germany: Stasi Informers and Their Impact on Society*. London, New York: Routledge, 1999.

Surveillance

Augustine, Dolores. *Red Prometheus: Engineering and Dictatorship in East Germany, 1945–1990*. Cambridge: MIT Press, 2007.

Betts, Paul. *Within Walls: Private Life in the German Democratic Republic*. Oxford, New York: Oxford University Press, 2010.

Major, Patrick. *Behind the Berlin Wall: East Germany and the Frontiers of Power*. Oxford, New York: Oxford University Press, 2010.

Palmowski, Jan. *Inventing the Socialist Nation: Heimat and the Politics of Everyday Life in the GDR, 1945–90*. Cambridge: Cambridge University Press, 2009.

Pfaff, Steven. "The Limits of Coercive Surveillance: Social and Penal Control in the German Democratic Republic." *Punishment and Society* 3, no. 3 (2001): 381–407.

Port, Andrew. *Conflict and Stability in the German Democratic Republic.* Cambridge, New York: Cambridge University Press, 2007.

Spiekermann, Uwe, and Christian Ostermann, eds. "The Stasi and Its Foreign Intelligence Service." *German Historical Institute Bulletin,* Supplement 9 (2013).

Zatlin, Jonathan R. "Out of Sight: Industrial Espionage, Ocular Authority, and East German Communism, 1965–1989." *Contemporary European History* 17, no. 1 (2008): 45–71.

Opposition and Persecution

Dale, Gareth. *Popular Protest in East Germany, 1945–1989.* London, New York: Routledge, 2005.

Erler, Peter, and Hubertus Knabe. *The Prohibited District: The Stasi Restricted Area, Berlin-Hohenschönhausen.* Berlin: Jaron, 2008.

Evans, Richard J. *Rituals of Retribution: Capital Punishment in Germany, 1600–1987.* London: Penguin Books, 1997.

Horster, Maximilian. "The Trade in Political Prisoners Between the Two German States, 1962–89." *Journal of Contemporary History* 39, no. 3 (2004): 403–24.

Pfaff, Steven. *Exit-Voice Dynamics and the Collapse of East Germany: The Crisis of Leninism and the Revolution of 1989.* Durham N.C.: Duke University Press, 2006.

Woods, Roger. *Opposition in the GDR under Honecker, 1971–1985.* Basingstoke, Hampshire: Macmillan, 1986.

Foreign Espionage and Counterespionage

Adams, Jefferson, ed. *Historical Dictionary of German Intelligence.* Lanham, Md.: Scarecrow Press, 2009.

Gaddis, John Lewis. "Intelligence, Espionage, and Cold War." *Diplomatic History* 13, no. 2 (1989): 191–212.

Garthoff, Raymond. "Foreign Intelligence and the Historiography of the Cold War." *Journal of Cold War Studies* 6, no. 2 (2004): 21–56.

Gieseke, Jens. "East German Espionage in the Era of Détente." *Journal of Strategic Studies* 31, no. 3 (2008): 395–424.

Macrakis, Kristie. *Seduced by Secrets: Inside the Stasi's Spy-Tech World.* Cambridge, New York: Cambridge University Press, 2008.

Schäfer, Bernd. *The Warsaw Pact's Intelligence on NATO: East German Military Espionage Against the West.* Online: <http://www.isn.ethz.ch/php/research/MutualReceptions/ifs2_02_schaefer.pdf>.

Stiller, Werner, and Jefferson Adams. *Beyond the Wall: Memoirs of an East and West German Spy.* Washington: Brassey's (US), 1992.

Vodopyanov, Anya. *A Watchful Eye Behind the Iron Curtain: The U.S. Military Liaison Mission in East Germany, 1953–61.* Online: PHP-website http://www.isn.ethz.ch/php/collections/coll_mlm.htm.

Wegener Friis, Thomas, Kristie Macrakis, and Helmut Müller-Enbergs. *East German Foreign Intelligence: Myth, Reality, and Controversy.* London, New York: Routledge, 2010.

Wolf, Markus, Anne McElvoy. *Man Without a Face: The Autobiography of Communism's Greatest Spymaster.* New York: Random House, 1997.

Wende Period

Jarausch, Konrad. *The Rush to German Unity.* New York, Oxford: Oxford University Press, 1994.

Maier, Charles. *Dissolution: The Crisis of Communism and the End of East Germany.* Princeton: Princeton University Press, 1997.

Memory

Cooke, Paul, and Andrew Plowman, eds. *German Writers and the Politics of Culture: Dealing with the Stasi.* Houndmills, New York: Palgrave Macmillan, 2003.

Dealing with the GDR Past in Today's Germany: The Lives of Others, in *German Studies Review* 31, no. 3 (2008), 557–609.

Fulbrook, Mary, ed. *Power and Society in the GDR, 1961–1979: The "Normalisation of Rule"?* New York: Berghahn Books, 2009.

Funder, Anna. *Stasiland.* London: Granta Books, 2003.

Garton Ash, Timothy. *The File: Personal History.* New York: Random House, 1997.

Hodgin, Nick, and Caroline Pearce, eds. *The GDR Remembered: Representations of the East German State since 1989.* Rochester, N.Y.: Camden House, 2011. (Studies in German Literature, Linguistics, and Culture Studies series)

Maier, Charles S. "Hot Memory, Cold Memory: On the Political Half-life of Fascist and Communist Memory." *Transit* 22 (winter 2001/2002): 153–65.

McAdams, A. James. *Judging the Past in Unified Germany.* New York: Cambridge University Press, 2001.

Snyder, Timothy. *Bloodlands.* New York: Basic Books, 2010.

INDEX

Printed in February 2021
by Rotomail Italia S.p.A., Vignate (MI) - Italy